LUDWIG
WITTGENSTEIN

LUDWIG WITTGENSTEIN

A COMPREHENSIVE BIBLIOGRAPHY

COMPILED BY
FRANÇOIS H. LAPOINTE

GREENWOOD PRESS
WESTPORT, CONNECTICUT • LONDON, ENGLAND

Library of Congress Cataloging in Publication Data

Lapointe, François.
  Ludwig Wittgenstein : a comprehensive bibliography.

  Includes index.
  1. Wittgenstein, Ludwig, 1889-1951—Bibliography.
I. Title.
Z8979.4.L36   [B3376.W564]   016.192   79-6565
ISBN 0-313-22127-8

Library of Congress Catalog Card Number: 79-6565
ISBN: 0-313-22127-8

First published in 1980

Greenwood Press
A division of Congressional Information Service, Inc.
51 Riverside Avenue, Westport, Connecticut 06880

Printed in the United States of America

10 9 8 7 6 5 4 3 2 1

Contents

Introduction

When Ludwig Wittgenstein died on 29 April 1951 his only published work, apart from a short address to the Aristotelian Society in 1929, was his celebrated *Tractatus Logico-Philosophicus,* the English version of which appeared in 1922. But in the last twenty or so years of his life Wittgenstein turned his back on the *Tractatus* and went on to produce and to teach at Cambridge University a whole new way of philosophizing. Although none of this later work had been published by his death, he had still become one of the most influential thinkers.

Ludwig Wittgenstein has been described by many as one of the greatest philosophers of our time, and as K. T. Fann says, "numerous philosophers in English-speaking countries would be quite prepared to describe him as *the* greatest."[1] G. J. Warnock wrote that "there can be no serious doubt that the most powerful and pervasive influence upon the practice of philosophy in this country [Great Britain] today has been that of Ludwig Wittgenstein."[2] Judging by the number of books, articles, and dissertations to be found in this bibliography, it is clear that his influence has now extended to many other countries. In France, Wittgenstein is seen by some as not so very far removed from Existentialism. In an interview with Pierre Vicary, Simone de Beauvoir stresses that the whole way of conceiving of the philosopher's task in Existentialism is so different from that of "the mainstream of contemporary British philosophy that there has been very little communication between the two. English philosophy has over the last thirty years been dominated by the movement of Linguistic Analysis, and at first sight it would be hard to imagine any two more radically different views of philosophy, and of the task of the philosopher, than that of Existentialism and Linguistic Analysis."[3] But, on the other hand, de Beauvoir says,

the later work of Wittgenstein emphasizes that language is always part of what he calls "forms of life" and that we can only determine the meaning of any piece of language by resituating it within the tissue of activities, practices, and relationships that constitute a "form of life." . . . Wittgenstein seems to suggest that it is the task of the philosopher to describe these primordial forms of life or contexts which underlie our language. Clearly this form of Analysis is not very far removed from the Existentialism of a Merleau-Ponty or a Heidegger.[4]

Another important development ought to be mentioned. In the past decade a great deal of Wittgenstein's *Nachlass,* and several of his lectures and letters, have been made available to the public for the first time. The result has been that Wittgensteinian scholarship has become more complex than ever before. As C. G. Luckhardt recently pointed out, "it is no longer possible to speak only of Wittgenstein's 'earlier' and 'later' periods of philosophy, and to mean by those terms simply the *Tractatus* and the *Investigations.*"

Although Wittgenstein's work has now come to be widely read and reviewed, and has exerted a significant influence on contemporary thought, until now no comprehensive and up-to-date bibliography of the wide range of critical response to his writings has appeared. It is true that we have had a bibliography provided by K. T. Fann in his book, *Wittgenstein's Conception of Philosophy,* and a supplement that appeared in the *Revue Internationale de Philosophie,* but these bibliographic surveys do not extend beyond 1969.

A bibliography has only one conceivable justification: its usefulness. To serve its utilitarian purpose a bibliography must be well organized. Naturally, the decisions a bibliographer makes regarding the organization and character of his work can never satisfy the demands of all users. Nevertheless, flexibility, accuracy, and comprehensiveness are basic requirements.

Following the example of the *Repertoire Bibliographique de la Philosophie,* I have numbered every entry, even when the same entry appears twice.

The bibliography is divided into two parts. Part one lists the works by Wittgenstein arranged in order of composition, for the most part. All available translations into the major European languages have been included. After long deliberation, I have decided to distribute the material of part two into six chapters. Chapter 1 contains books devoted to Wittgenstein (or almost exclusively so), as well as all available reviews; the books are classified by language. Chapter 2 lists dissertations and theses, also indicating the entries, when available, in *Dissertation Abstracts International.* In chapter 3 are to be found critical studies (and reviews) of individual works by Wittgenstein, and the works are listed in the same order as they appear in part one. In chapter 4 works dealing with a general discussion and presentation of Wittgenstein's contributions are included. Chapter 5 contains a list of items arranged by proper names. This chapter includes material in which Wittgenstein is being compared, or contrasted, with major figures in philosophy and science. Chapter 6 lists items arranged by subjects.

Although much will have escaped me, the present bibliography is intended to be as complete as is technically feasible. My purpose is to provide an accurate, reasonably complete, and useful arrangement of materials for those interested in Wittgenstein's work and life. Although no bibliography can claim to be exhaustive, every attempt at completeness and accuracy has been made. All of the standard reference works known to me were consulted, and many periodicals and books were searched individually. Items through 1979 are included. An addendum contains entries that arrived too late to be included in the body of the manuscript.

The problem for any bibliographer of a major intellectual figure is that comprehensiveness can never be absolute. In part, this is because of the utter impossibility of discovering every title that contains major sections on the intellectual, and, in part, because errors of transcription do occasionally slip in. Although I have made every effort to compile an accurate, up-to-date, and reasonably complete bibliography, I am fully aware of the provisional nature of my work and feel no obligation to apologize for this. As is well known to bibliographers, publication constitutes a stage in the movement toward completeness, a more or less "complete" starting point for further work. My hope is that eventually I can come closer to the ideal of completeness in a second edition, which will not only continue beyond 1979 and will include earlier items I was regrettably unable to include, but, above all, to provide annotations for most of the items.

François H. Lapointe

NOTES

1. K. T. Fann, ed., *Ludwig Wittgenstein: The Man and His Philosophy: An Anthology* (New York: Dell Publishing Co., 1967), p. 11.

2. G. J. Warnock, *English Philosophy Since 1900* (London: Oxford University Press, 1958), p. 64.

3. Simone de Beauvoir in *The Existentialists and Jean-Paul Sartre,* ed. by Max Cherlesworth (New York: St. Martin's Press, 1975), p. 27.

4. Ibid., p. 27.

PART 1:
**Bibliography
of Wittgenstein's Writings**

WORKS BY WITTGENSTEIN (1889-1951)

Nachlass. The originals of the Wittgenstein papers are kept in the Wren Library, Trinity College, Cambridge, England. The total material microfilmed in twenty reels is available from Cornell University Library, Ithaca, New York. An account of the scope and character of the *Nachlass* is given by Georg Henrik von Wright in "Special supplement: the Wittgenstein Papers," *Philosophical Review* 78 (1969):483-503. [As indicated in the Introduction, in the past decade, a large amount of Wittgenstein's *Nachlass* and several of his lectures and letters have been made available to the public. This includes the *Prototractatus*, *Remarks on the Foundations of Mathematics*, *Zettel*, *On Certainty*, and *On Colour*.]

"Notes on Logic" (September 1913). H. T. Costello, ed. *Journal of Philosophy* 54 (1957):230-244. Reprinted in *Notebooks 1914-1916*. "Notas sobre lógica" (Versión castellana de Josep L. Blasco y Alfonso García Suárez). *Teorema*, número monográfico *Sobre el* Tractatus, 1972, 6-47.

"Notes dictated to G. E. Moore in Norway" (April 1914). Reprinted in *Notebooks 1914-1916*, 107-118.

Notebooks 1914-1916. G. E. M. Anscombe and G. H. von Wright, eds. With an English trans. by G. E. M. Anscombe. Oxford: Basil Blackwell, 1961; New York: Barnes and Noble, 1961; New York: Harper & Row, 1968. *Carnets 1914-1916*. Traduction, introduction et notes de Gilles-Gaston Granger. (Les essais, 158). Paris: Gallimard, 1971.

Letters to B. Russell, 1912-1921. Some extracts contained
in *Notebooks 1914-1916*. In *Letters to Russell, Keynes and
Moore*. Ed. with an introduction by G. H. von Wright.
Assisted by B. F. McGuinness. Ithaca (New York): Cornell
Univ. Press, 1974, 190p; Oxford: Basil Blackwell & Mott,
1974. Also in *The Autobiography of Bertrand Russell*,
Vol. 2, 1914-1944. New York: Simon & Schuster, 161-170.

Logisch-philosophische Abhandlung (finished in 1918). First
published in *Annalen der Naturphilosophie*, M. Ostwald, ed.,
14 (1921):185-262. *Tractatus Logico-Philosophicus*, German-
English, English trans. by C. K. Ogden and F. P. Ramsey,
introduction by Bertrand Russell. London: Routledge &
Kegan Paul, 1922; corrected reprint, 1933; reprint (with
index) by Max Black, 1955; English trans. by D. F. Pears
and B. F. McGuinness. London: Routledge & Kegan Paul;
New York: Humanities Press, 1961. Many translations available: <u>French</u>: *Tractatus Logico-Philosophicus*. Traduit de
l'allemand par Pierre Klossowski. Introd. de B. Russell.
Notes d'Aimé Patri (Idées, 264). Paris: Gallimard, 1972.
189p. <u>German</u>: (Edition Suhrkamp, 12). 4 Aufl. Frankfurt
am Main: Suhrkamp, 1966. 114p. 6 Aufl. 1969. <u>Italian</u>:
Trans. by G. C. Colombo. Milan-Rome: Fratelli Bocca, 1954.
A new trans. with *Notebooks* by Amando G. Conte. Torino:
Einaudi, 1964. <u>Portuguese</u>: Trad. de José Arthur Giannotti.
São Paulo: Cia Editôra Nacional, 1968. 152p. <u>Spanish</u>:
Trad. por Enrique Tierno Galván. Madrid: Alianza Editorial,
1973. 232p. <u>Dutch</u>: Trans. by Willem Frederik Hermans.
Amsterdam: Atheneum; Amsterdam: Polak & Van Gennep, 1975.
188p.

Wörterbuch für Volksschulen. Vienna: Hölder-Pichler-
Tempsky A. G., 1926. New edition: With Wittgenstein's
unpublished "Geleitwort" and an introduction by Adolf Hübner.
Adolf Hübner and Werner and Elisabeth Leinfellner, eds.
Author's Preface and Introduction in both German and English.
Vienna: Verlag Hölder-Pichler-Tempsky, 1977, xxxiv-44p.
[A spelling book for elementary schools, containing more
than 6000 words]

"Some Remarks on Logical Forms." *Proceedings of the
Aristotelian Society*, Suppl. 9 (192):162-171. Reprinted
with note by Anscombe in Copi and Beard, eds. *Essays on
Wittgenstein's* Tractatus.

"A Lecture on Ethics." *Philosophical Review* 74 (1965):3-12.
Reprinted in *Philosophy Today*, Vol. 1, Jerry H. Gill, ed.
New York: Macmillan, 1968, 4-14. [See below, *Conférence
sur l'Éthique, Lectures et Conversations*. French trans.]

Philosophische Bemerkungen (1930). Rush Rhees, ed.
Oxford: Basil Blackwell, 1965. English trans.: *Philo-
sophical Remarks*. Trans. by G. E. M. Anscombe. New York:
Barnes and Noble, 1968. French trans.: *Remarques Philo-
sophiques*. Trad. de l'allemand par Jacques Fauve
(Bibliothèque des idées). Paris: Gallimard, 1975. 335p.
German ed.: Frankfurt am Main: Suhrkamp Verlag, 1965.
Italian trans.: Turin: Einaudi, 1972.

"Bemerkungen Über Frazers *The Golden Bough*." (One set in
1931, the other later.) Ed. with a note by Rush Rhees,
Synthese 17 (1967):233-253. "Remarks on Frazer's *Golden
Bough*," (trans. by John Beversluis) in *Wittgenstein:
Sources and Perspectives*. C. G. Luckhardt, ed. Ithaca
(New York): Cornell Univ. Press, 1979, 61-81. Wittgen-
stein, Ludwig. *Remarks on Fraser's* Golden Bough.
Atlantic Highlands (New Jersey): Humanities Press, 1979.
Note sul Ramo d'oro di Frazer. Con un saggio di Jacques
Bouveresse. Trad. Sabina De Waal (Piccola Biblioteca
Adelphi, 31). Milano: Adelphi, 1975. 92p.

Philosophische Grammatik. Rush Rhees, ed. Oxford: Basil
Blackwell, 1969. 491p. *Philosophical Grammar*. Part 1:
The Proposition and its Sense. Part 2: On Logic.
Rush Rhees, ed. Trans. by Anthony Kenny. Oxford: Basil
Blackwell; Berkeley: Univ. of California Press, 1974. 495p.
German ed.: Frankfurt am Main: Suhrkamp, 1973.

"Letter to the Editor of *Mind*." *Mind* 42 (1933):415-416.

Preliminary Studies for the Philosophical Investigations.
Generally known as the Blue and Brown Books. Preface by
R. Rhees. Oxford: Basil Blackwell; New York: Harper & Row,
1958; corrected reprint, Oxford: Basil Blackwell, 1960;
2d ed. (with index), 1969. French: *Le cahier bleu et le
cahier brun, Études préliminaires aux* Investigations
Philosophiques, *suivi de Ludwig Wittgenstein*. Par Norman
Malcolm. Avec une notice biographique de Georg Henrik von
Wright. Préface de Jean Wahl (Les essais, 116). Paris:
Gallimard, 1965, xx-433p. Spanish: *Los cuadernos azul
marrón*. Prefacio de R. Rhees. Trad. del ingles por

Francisco Garcia (Col. Estructura y Función, 25). Madrid:
Estructura y Función, 1968. 230p.

"Notes for Lectures on 'Private Experience' and 'Sense
Data'." (1934-1936). *Philosophical Review* 77 (1968):271-
320. Ed. with a note by Rush Rhees. Reprinted in
Introduction to the Philosophy of Mind. Harold Morick, ed.
Glenview (Illinois): Scott, Foresman, 1970, 155-194.

Bemerkungen über die Grundlagen der Mathematik (*Remarks on
the Foundations of Mathematics*). [German and English on
opposite pages] G. H. von Wright, R. Rhees, and G. E. M.
Anscombe, eds. Trans. by G. E. M. Anscombe. Oxford:
Basil Blackwell; New York: Macmillan, 1956, 1st ed.;
2d ed. 1967. Hardback ed., New York: Barnes and Noble,
1962. Paper ed., Cambridge (Massachusetts): M.I.T. Press,
1967. A long excerpt is included in P. Benacerraf and
H. Putnam, eds., *Philosophy of Mathematics*. Englewood
Cliffs (New Jersey): Prentice-Hall, 1964. Another selection entitled, "Remarks on Mechanical Mathematics," is
included in K. M. Sayre and F. J. Crosson, eds., *The
Modelling of Mind: Computers and Intelligence*. New York:
Simon & Schuster, 1968, 121-140. A selection in German
in *Kursbuch* 8 (1967):93-105. *Remarks on the Foundations
of Mathematics*. Revised ed. G. H. von Wright, R. Rhees,
and G. E. M. Anscombe, eds. Trans. by G. E. M. Anscombe.
Cambridge (Massachusetts): M.I.T. Press, 1978. 444p.
German text in *Schriften, VI*. Suhrkamp, 1974. 445p.
Italian trans.: *Osservazioni sopra i fondamenti della
matematico*. Trad. di Mario Trinchero. Torino: G. Einaudi,
1971, xxxvii-263p.

*Lectures and Conversations on Aesthetics, Psychology and
Religious Belief*. Compiled from notes taken by Y. Smythies,
R. Rhees and J. Taylor. Cyril Barrett, ed. Oxford: Basil
Blackwell, 1966; Berkeley: Univ. of California Press, 1966.
French trans.: *Leçons et conversations sur l'esthétique,
la psychologie et la croyance religieuse*. Textes établis
par Cyril Barrett. D'après les notes prises par Yorick
Smythies, Rush Rhees et James Taylor. Suivies de *Conférence
sur L'Éthique*. Editée et commentée par Rush Rhees. Avec
des extraits de notes prises par Friedrich Waismann. Trad.
de l'anglais par Jacques Fauve (Les Essais, 160). Paris:
Gallimard, 1971. 189p. German trans.: *Vorlesungen und
Gespräche über Ästhetik, Psychologie und Religion*. Übers.
u. eingel. von Eberhard Bubser. Hrsg. von Cyril Barrett
(Kleine Vandenhoeck-Reihe, 267/268/269). Göttingen:
Vandenhoeck und Ruprecht, 1968. 111p. Italian trans.:
Lezioni e conversazioni sull'etica, l'estetica, la psicologia

e la credenza religiosa. A cura di Michele Ranchetti
(Biblioteca Adelphi, 14). Milano: Adelphi (E. Sormani),
1967. 172p. Spanish trans.: *Estética, psicoanálisis y
religión* (Col. Biblioteca de Filosofía). Buenos Aires:
Sudamericana, 1976. 180p. Portuguese trans.: *Estética,
psicologia e religião. Palestras e conversações.* Trad.
de José Paulo Paes. São Paulo: Ed. Cultrix, 1970. 115p.

Philosophische Untersuchungen (Philosophical Investigations).
[Part 1 finished in 1945; Part 2 written between 1947 and
1949]. Trans. by G. E. M. Anscombe. Oxford: Basil Black-
well; New York: Macmillan, 1953; 2d ed., 1958; 3d ed.
(with index), 1967. [German text facing English transla-
tion] *Philosophical Investigations* (English text only),
3d ed. (with index), reprinted. Oxford: Basil Blackwell &
Mott, 1969. 250p. George Pitcher, ed. Univ. of Notre
Dame Press, 1968. 510p; New York: Doubleday, 1966. 510p.
French trans.: *Recherches philosophiques.* Trad. par
P. Klossowski. Paris: Gallimard, 1961. German ed.:
Philosophische Untersuchungen (Suhrkamp-Taschenbücher, 14).
Frankfurt am Main: Suhrkamp, 1971. 268p. Diese Ausg. ist
erw. um e. umfangreiches Begriffsreg. d. Wolfgang Breidert
zostellte (Suhrkamp-Taschenbücher Wissenschaft, 203).
Suhrkamp, 1977. 412p. Italian trans.: *Ricerche filoso-
fiche.* Trad. R. Piovresan. Torino: Einaudi 1967, xx-298p.

Zettel. G. E. Anscombe and G. H. von Wright, eds. Trans.
by G. E. M. Anscombe. Oxford: Basil Blackwell; Berkeley:
Univ. of California Press, 1967, xix-248p. [German text
facing English translation] French trans.: Paris:
Gallimard. German ed.: Frankfurt am Main: Suhrkamp.
Italian trans.: Turin: Einaudi. Spanish trans.: México:
Centro de Estudios Filosóficos.

On Certainty. G. E. M. Anscombe and G. H. von Wright, eds.
Trans. by Denis Paul and G. E. M. Anscombe. Oxford:
Basil Blackwell & Mott, 1969. [Parallel German and English
texts] New York: Harper & Row, 1969. Reprinted with
corrections (Open university set book). Oxford: Blackwell,
1977. 105p. French trans.: *De la certitude.* Trad. de
l'allemand par Jacques Fauve. (Collection Idées, 344).
Paris: Gallimard, 1976. 151p. German ed.: *Über Gewissheit.*
Frankfurt am Main: Suhrkamp, 1970. 179p.

Schriften, I. Includes *Tractatus Logico-Philosophicus,
Tagebücher 1914-1916, Philosophische Untersuchungen.*
Frankfurt am Main: Suhrkamp, 1960.

Schriften, II. Philosophische Bemerkungen. 1964.

*Schriften, III. Wittgenstein und der Wiener Kreis von
Friedrich Waismann.* 1967.

Schriften, IV. Philosophische Grammatik. T. 1: *Satz.
Sinn des Satzes.* T. 2: *Über Logik und Mathematik.* 1969.

*Schriften, V. Das Blaue Buch. Eine philosophische
Betrachtung. Zettel.* 1970.

Prototractus. An early version of *Tractatus Logico-Philo-
sophicus.* B. F. McGuinness, T. Byberg and G. H. von
Wright, eds. With a trans. by D. F. Pears and B. F.
McGuinness, an historical introduction by G. H. von Wright,
and a facsimile of the author's manuscript. London:
Routledge & Kegan Paul, 1971; Ithaca (New York): Cornell
Univ. Press, 1971. 256p.

Philosophical Remarks. Ed. from his posthumous writings
by Rush Rhees and trans. into English by Raymond Hargreaves
and Roger White. Oxford: Basil Blackwell & Mott, 1975.
357p. <u>Italian trans</u>.: *Osservazioni filosofiche.* Introduzione e traduzione di Marino Rosso (Biblioteca di
Cultura Filosofica, 44). Torino: G. Einaudi, 1976, lxxvi-
313p.

*Wittgenstein's Lectures on the Foundations of Mathematics,
Cambridge, 1939.* From the notes of R. G. Bosanquet and
others. Cora Diamond, ed. Ithaca (New York): Cornell
Univ. Press, 1976, 300p; Hassocks (Sussex): The Harvester
Press.

Ursache und Wirkung. Intuitives Erfassen. Editor's note
by Rush Rhees. English trans. by Peter Winch. Appendices
A, B, C: Notes by L. Wittgenstein and notes by R. Rhees,
I, II, III. *Philosophia* (Israel) 6 (1976):427-445.

Vermischte Bemerkungen: e. *Ausw. aus* d. Nachlass.
Georg Henrik von Wright, hrsg. Unter Mitarb. von Heikki
Nyman (Bibliothek Suhrkamp, 535). Frankfurt am Main:
Suhrkamp, 1977. 167p.

Remarks on Colour. G. E. M. Anscombe, ed. Trans. by
Linda L. McAlister and Margarete Schättle. Bemerkungen
über die Farben. Herausgegeben von G. E. M. Anscombe.
Berkeley: Univ. of California Press, 1977, 63p and 63ep;
Oxford: Basil Blackwell, 1978.

"On Heidegger on Being and dread." In *Heidegger and Modern
Philosophy. Critical Essays.* Michael Murray, ed.
New Haven-London: Yale Univ. Press, 1977.

La filosofia del linguaggio. Antologia dal Tractatus e
dalle Ricerche. A cura di Pietro Castagnoli (Collana
di letture critiche e filosofiche). Bologna: Calderini,
1970, ii-136p.

Scritti scelti. Introduzione e note a cura di Aldo G.
Gargani (Collana filosofica). Milano: Principato, 1970.
162p.

LETTERS

Eccles, W. "Some Letters of Wittgenstein, 1912-1939."
Hermathena (Dublin) (1963):57-65.

Letters from Ludwig Wittgenstein. With a memoir by Paul
Engelmann. Trans. by L. Furtmüller. B. F. McGuinness, ed.
Oxford: Basil Blackwell & Mott, 1967, 150p; New York:
Horizon Press, 1968. [Includes parallel German-English
text of 54 letters] *Letters.* With a memoir by Paul
Engelmann. Trans. by L. Furtmüller. B. F. McGuinness, ed.
New York: Horizon Press, 1974. 150p. [Includes parallel
German-English text of 54 letters] Engelmann, Paul,
Ludwig Wittgenstein. Briefe u. Begegnungen. Bernard
Francis MacGuiness, hrsg. Anm. u. Nachw. aus d. Engl. übers.
von Arvid Sjögren. Wien, München: Oldenburg, 1970. 127p.

Engelmann, Paul. *Lettere di Ludwig Wittgenstein con ricordi.*
Prefazione di Josef Schächter. Appendice di Brian F.
McGuinness. Trad. I. Roncaglia Cherubini (Dimensioni, 2).
Firenze: La Nuova Italia, 1970, ix-123p.

Briefe an Ludwig von Ficker. G. H. von Wright, hrsg.,
unter Mitarbeit von W. Methlag [im Rahmen der Brenner-
Studien]. Salzburg: Müller, 1969. 110p. *Lettere a
Ludwig von Ficker.* A cura di Georg Henrik von Wright,
con la collaborazione di Walter Methlagl. Prefazione
all'ed. italiana di Dario Antiseri. Trad. D. Antiseri
(Filosofia e problemi d'oggi, 35). Roma: A. Armando, 1974.
149p. "Letters to Ludwig von Ficker (trans. by Bruce
Gillette; ed. by Allan Janik)." In *Wittgenstein: Sources
and Perspectives.* C. G. Luckhardt, ed. Ithaca (New York):
Cornell Univ. Press, 1979, 82-98.

Letters to C. K. Ogden. With comments on the English trans.
of the *Tractatus Logico-Philosophicus.* Ed. and introduction by G. H. von Wright. With an appendix of Letters
by Frank Plumpton Ramsey. Oxford: Basil Blackwell;
London-Boston: Routledge & Kegan Paul, 1973, x-90p.

Letters to Russell, Keynes and Moore. Ed. with an introduction by G. H. von Wright. Assisted by B. F. McGuinness.
Ithaca (New York): Cornell Univ. Press, 1974. 190p.

LECTURES

Ambrose, Alice, and Masterman, Margaret. *The Yellow Book*
(1933-34). Notes taken by Ambrose and Masterman in the
intervals between dictation of *The Blue Book.* See
Bouwsma's *The Blue Book.* Some quotations from it appeared
in Alice Ambrose and Morris Lazerowitz's writings on
Wittgenstein.

Geach, Peter. *Wittgenstein's Lectures on Philosophical
Psychology.* Notes taken by Geach of Wittgenstein's lectures
in 1946-47. There exist two other sets of notes from the
same course of lectures: one by K. Shah, the other by
A. G. Jackson. In private circulation.

Macdonald, Margaret. *Notes of Wittgenstein's Lectures in 1934-35.* Unpublished. A typed copy of Lectures 8-15 (May 20, 1935-June 12, 1935) is appended to a typewritten copy of *The Blue Book* on deposit at the Univ. of Southern California Library.

Malcolm, Norman. *Wittgenstein's Lectures on the Foundations of Mathematics.* Notes by Malcolm of Wittgenstein's lectures given in the spring of 1939. In private circulation.

Moore, G. E. "Wittgenstein's Lectures in 1930-33." Part 1, *Mind* 63 (1954):1-15; Part 2, *Mind* 63 (1954):289-315; Part 3, *Mind* 64 (1955):1-27; "Two Corrections," *Mind* 64 (1955):264. Reprinted in his *Philosophical Papers* (London: George Allen & Unwin, 1959, 252-324), and in *Classics in Analytic Philosophy*, R. Ammerman, ed. (New York: McGraw-Hill, 1965).

PART 2:
**Bibliography
on Wittgenstein**

CHAPTER 1:
Books and Reviews on Wittgenstein

BOOKS IN ENGLISH

1. Ambrose, Alice, and Lazerowitz, Morris, eds. *Ludwig Wittgenstein. Philosophy and Language*. Muirhead Library of Philosophy. London: George Allen & Unwin; New York: Humanities Press, 1972. 326p.

CONTENTS:
Ambrose, Alice. "Ludwig Wittgenstein: A portrait."
    13-25;
Wisdom, John. "Wittgenstein on *private language*."
    26-36;
Cook, John W. "Solipsism and language." 37-72;
Hanly, Charles. "Wittgenstein on psychoanalysis."
    73-94;
Redpath, Theodore. "Wittgenstein and ethics." 95-119;
Pitcher, George. "About the same." 120-139;
Kennick, W. E. "Philosophy as grammar and the reality
    of universals." 140-185;
Ebersole, Frank. "Saying and meaning." 186-221;
Fujimoto, Takashi. "The notion of *Erklärung*." 222-232;
Lazerowitz, Morris. "Necessity and language " 233-270;
Goodstein, R. L. "Wittgenstein's philosophy of mathe-
    matics." 271-286;
Ambrose, Alice. "Mathematical generality." 287-318.

book reviews:
R. Butterworth, *The Heythrop Journal* 15 (1974):81-84;
C. Lyas, *Philosophical Books* 13 (1972):1-3;
M. Proudfoot, *Philosophical Quarterly* 23 (1973):263-
    265;
C. Radford, *Mind* 84 (1975):295-297.

2. Ambrose, Alice. *Essays in Analysis*. London: George Allen & Unwin; New York: Humanities Press, 1966.

3.   Anscombe, Gertrude Elizabeth Margaret. *An Introduction to Wittgenstein's* Tractatus.   London: Hutchinson, 1959; 2d ed., revised, New York: Harper Torchbooks, 1963; 3d ed., 1967.   179p.

> book reviews:
> Anonymous, *The Month* 22 (1959):181-182;
> D. Campanale, *Rivista Critica di Storia della Filosofia* 13 (1960):378-379;
> J. D. Carney, *Philosophy of Science* 27 (1960):408;
> E. Cassirer, *British Journal for the Philosophy of Science* 14 (1963-64):359-365;
> J. H. Gill, *Philosophy and Phenomenological Research* 27 (1966-67):137-138 (2d ed., 1963);
> W. W. Gustason, "Miss Anscombe on the 'general propositional form'." *Analysis* 32 (1971-72):195-196;
> J. Jarvis & F. Sommers, *Philosophy* 36 (1961):374-376;
> G. K. Plochman, *Modern Schoolman* 39 (1959-60):242-246 (1st ed.);
> R. Rhees, *Philosophical Quarterly* 16 (1961):21-31;
> E. Riverso, *Asprenas* 8 (1961):383;
> A. Shalom, *Etudes Philosophiques* 16 (1961):239;
> C. A. V., *Rivista di Filosofia* 51 (1960):99.

4.   Barrett, William. *The Illusion of Technique: A Search for Meaning in a Technological Civilization.*   Garden City (New York): Anchor Books, 1978, 1-15, 27-100.

5.   Bartley, William W., III. *Wittgenstein.*   Philadelphia: J. B. Lippincott, 1973, 192p; London: Quartet Books, 1974, 145p.

> book reviews:
> J. Bouveresse, *Critique* 31 (1975):796-804;
> W. De Angelis, *Philosophy and Phenomenological Research* 35 (1974-75):289-290;
> W. A. Frank, *Review of Metaphysics* 27 (1973-74):601-602;
> R. L. Goodstein, *Philosophy* 48 (1974):403-404;
> I. C. Jarvie, *British Journal for the Philosophy of Science* 25 (1974):195-198;
> I. C. Jarvie, *The Heythrop Journal* 15 (1974):195-198;
> J. T. Price, *Man and World* 7 (1974):423-434;
> C. H. Soto, *Diálagos* 11 (1978):163-165.

6.   Bell, Richard H., and Hustwit, Ronald E., eds. *Essays on Kierkegaard and Wittgenstein: On Understanding the Self.*   College of Wooster, 1978.

7.   Binkley, Timothy. *Wittgenstein's Language*.   The Hague:
Martinus Nijhoff, 1973.   227p.

     book reviews:
     R. Goff, *Man and World* 8 (1975):227-232;
     A. Lichtigfeld, *Tijdschrift voor Filosofie* 37 (1975):
       147-149;
     D. D. Todd, *Philosophy and Rhetoric* 8(1975):187-189;
     C. H. Soto, *Diálagos* 11 (1978):163-165.

8.   Black, Max. A *Companion to Wittgenstein's* Tractatus.
Ithaca (New York): Cornell Univ. Press, 1964, xv-452p.

     book reviews:
     R. J. B., *Review of Metaphysics* 19 (1965-66):149;
     J. D. Bastable, *Philosophical Studies* 17 (1968):320-
       323;
     J. Bogen, *Philosophical Review* 78 (1969):374-382;
     F. C. Copleston, *The Heythrop Journal* 6 (1965):321-327;
     A. Flew, *Spectator* 213 (November 13, 1964):640;
     J. Griffin, *Philosophical Books* 6 (1965):2-4;
     J. B. Grize, *Revue de Théologie et de Philosophie*
       99 (1966):224;
     P. Hinst, *Philosophische Rundschau* 15 (1968):149-150;
     A. Kenny, *Mind* 75 (1966):452-453;
     G. Küng, *New Scholasticism* 40 (1966):403-406;
     A. MacIntyre, *Guardian* (October 23, 1964):13;
     A. Narveson, *Philosophy of Science* 34 (1967):69-73;
     D. S. Shwayder, *Foundations of Language* 5 (1969):289-
       296;
     R. Sternfeld, *Philosophy and Phenomenological Research*
       26 (1965-66):287-290.
     B. Wolniewicz, "A note on Black's *Companion*." *Mind*
       78 (1969):141.

9.   Bogen, James. *Wittgenstein's Philosophy of Language*.
Some Aspects of its Development. London: Routledge & Kegan
Paul, 1972, xii-244p; New York: Humanities Press, 1972.

     book reviews:
     G. Hallet, *The Heythrop Journal* 14 (1973):445-447;
     J. E. Llewelyn, *Inquiry* 16 (1973):431-439;
     G. Lyas, *Philosophical Books* 14 (1973):3-5;
     G. H. Merrill, *Modern Schoolman* 52 (1974-75):207-211;
     R. A. Shiner, *Dialogue* 12 (1973):683-699;
     D. Sievert, *Philosophical Review* 84 (1974):117-122;
     G. Stock, *Mind* 83 (1974):300-303;
     M. Wolf, *Philosophical Studies* 21 (1971):285-287.

10.   Brown, Cecil H. *Wittgensteinian Linguistics*
(Approaches to semiotics, paperback series, 12). The Hague:
Mouton, 1974. 135p.

11.   Cavell, Stanley. *The Claim of Reason. Wittgenstein,
Skepticism, Morality, and Tragedy*. New York: Oxford Univ.
Press, 1979.

12.   Charlesworth, M. J. *Philosophy and Linguistic
Analysis*. Pittsburgh: Duquesne Univ. Press, 1959. [cf. esp.
ch. 3, 75-125]

> book reviews:
> S. A., *Razón y Fe* 162 (1963):386-387;
> L. A. Barth, *Modern Schoolman* 38 (1960-61):69-72;
> J. D. Bastable, *Philosophical Studies* 9 (1959):242-243;
> J. Collins, *Cross Currents* 9 (1959):170;
> J. Deledalle, *Etudes Philosophiques* 17 (1962):182-183;
> P. Durao, *Revista Portuguesa de Filosofia* 16 (1960):
>   495;
> J. Gerardo, *Pensamiento* 17 (1961):246-247;
> S. Issman, *Revue Internationale de Philosophie* 13
>   (1959):368-369;
> E. H. Madden, *Philosophy and Phenomenological Research*
>   20 (1959-60):561-562;
> A. R. Manser, *Mind* 69 (1960):274-275;
> A. J. Moreno, *Sapientia* 5 (1960):148-150;
> M. Nédoncelle, *Revue des Sciences Religieuses* 33 (1959):
>   313-314;
> H. A. Nielsen, *New Scholasticism* 34 (1960):262-265;
> H. Ogiermann, *Scholastik* 35 (1960):80-82;
> E. Riverso, *Rivista Critica di Storia della Filosofia*
>   14 (1961):227-228;
> H. Saint-Denis, *Revue de l'Université d'Ottawa* 29
>   (1959):169-172;
> R. Smith, *The Thomist* 23 (1960):306-308;
> M. de Tollenaere, *Revue des Questions Scientifiques*
>   21 (1960):311-312;
> C. Vansteenkeste, *Angelicum* 37 (1960):120-122;
> P. A. Verburg, *Bidjragen* 23 (1962):12-22;
> J. Wahl, *Revue de Métaphysique et de Morale* 74 (1969):
>   482;
> W. H. Werkmeister, *The Personalist* 41 (1960):72-73.

13.   Coope, Christopher, Geach, Peter, Potts, Timothy, and
White, Roger. *A Wittgenstein Workbook*. Berkeley (California): Univ. of California Press, 1970. 51p.

> book review:
> A. B. Wolter, *The Thomist* 35 (1971):551-552.

14. Copi, Irving M., and Beard, R. W., eds. *Essays on Wittgenstein's* Tractatus. New York: Macmillan, 1966; London: Routledge & Kegan Paul, 1966. 424p.

CONTENTS:
Introduction, viii;
Ryle, Gilbert. "Ludwig Wittgenstein." 1-9;
    (Italian trans. in *Rivista di Filosofia* 43 (1952):
    186-193)
Ramsey, Frank P. "Review of *Tractatus*." 9-24;
de Laguna, Theodore. "Review of *Tractatus*." 25-30;
Wittgenstein, Ludwig. "Some remarks on logical form."
    31-38;
Wisdom, John. "Logical constructions (1)." 39-66;
Bell, Julian. "An epistle." 67-74;
Weinberg, Julius R. "Are there ultimate simples?"
    75-86;
Moore, Willis. "Structure in sentence and in fact."
    87-94;
Black, Max. "Some problems connected with language."
    95-114;
O'Shaughnessy, Edna. "The picture theory of meaning."
    115-132;
Evans, Ellis. "*Tractatus* 3.1432." 133-136;
McGuinness, B. F. "Pictures and form in Wittgenstein's
    Tractatus." 137-156;
Hintikka, Jaakko. "On Wittgenstein's 'solipsism'."
    157-162;
Copi, Irving M. "*Tractatus* 5.542." 163-166;
Copi, Irving M. "Objects, properties, and relations
    in the *Tractatus*." 167-186;
Anscombe, G. E. M. "Mr. Copi on 'Objects, properties,
    and relations in the *Tractatus*'." 187-188;
Allaire, Edwin B. "*Tractatus* 6.3751." 189-194;
Evans, Ellis. "About 'aRb'." 195-200;
Proctor, George L. "Scientific laws and scientific
    objects in the *Tractatus*." 201-216;
Thomson, Judith Jarvis. "Professor Stenius on the
    Tractatus." 217-230;
Bernstein, Richard J. "Wittgenstein's three languages."
    231-248;
Sellars, Wilfrid. "Naming and saying." 249-270;
Schwyzer, H. R. G. "Wittgenstein's picture-theory of
    language." 271-288;
Keyt, David. "Wittgenstein's notion of an object."
    289-304.
Shwayder, D. S. "On the picture theory of language:
    Excerpts from a review." 305-312;
Stenius, Erik. "Wittgenstein's picture-theory." 313-
    324;
Allaire, Edwin B. "The *Tractatus*: Nominalistic or
    realistic?" 325-342;
Bergmann, Gustav. "The glory and the misery of Ludwig
    Wittgenstein." 343-358;
Zemach, Eddy. "Wittgenstein's philosophy of the
    mystical." 359-376;

Keyt, David.   "Wittgenstein's picture theory of
    language."   377-393.

book reviews:
F. C. Copleston, *The Heythrop Journal* 9 (1968):344-346;
R. M. Gale, *Philosophy and Phenomenological Research*
    29 (1968):146-147.

15.   Cornforth, Maurice. *Marxism and Linguistic Philosophy*.
London: Lawrence & Wishart, 1965; New York: International
Publishers, 1965.

    book reviews:
    E. Albrecht, *Deutsche Literaturzeitung* 87 (1966):585-
        587;
    T. J. Blakeley, *Justice dans le monde* (Louvain) 10
        (1968-69):378-379;
    F. C. Copleston, *The Heythrop Journal* 9 (1968):5-16;
    D. E. Cooper, "The 'Fallacies' of linguistic philosophy."
        Oxford Review (1968):79-89;
    J. Coulter, *The Human Context* 4 (1972):413-416;
    A. Holloway, *Philosophical Quarterly* 17 (1967):79-80;
    A. Lingis, *Foundations of Language* 7 (1971):131-133;
    E. F. Pomogajewa, *Deutsche Zeitschrift für Philosophie*
        16 (1968):267-271.

16.   de Mauro, Tullio. *Ludwig Wittgenstein. His Place in
the Development of Semantics* (Foundations of Language,
Suppl. series, 3).   New York: Humanities Press, 1967, 63p;
Dordrecht (Holland): D. Reidel, 1967.

    book reviews:
    J. D. Bastable, *Philosophical Studies* 18 (1969):258;
    P. T. Geach, *British Journal for the Philosophy of
        Science* 20 (1969):277-279;
    J.-P. Leyvras, *Revue de Théologie et de Philosophie*
        (1970):204-205.

17.   Danford, John W. *Wittgenstein and Political Philosophy.
A Reexamination of the Foundations of Social Science.*
Chicago: Univ. of Chicago Press, 1978.   280p.

18.   D'hert, Ignace. *Wittgenstein's Relevance for Theology*
(Europäische Hochschulschriften: Reihe 23, Theologie, 44).
Bern: Lang; Frankfurt am Main: Lang, 1975.   237p.

    book reviews:
    P. J. Sherry, *Philosophical Books* 18 (1977):32-34;

K. Wuchlech, *Philosophischer Literaturanzeiger* 30
(1977):358-362.

19. Dilman, Ilham. *Induction and Deduction. A Study in
Wittgenstein*. Oxford: Basil Blackwell & Mott, 1973, 225p;
New York: Harper & Row, 1973.

book reviews:
J. Bogen, *Dialogue* 13 (1974):198-201;
J. Burnham, *Australasian Journal of Philosophy* 51
(1973):265-267;
P. T. Mackenzie, *Canadian Journal of Philosophy* 5
(1975):309-321;
T. E. Wilkerson, *Mind* 84 (1975):297-299.

20. Engel, S. Morris. *Wittgenstein's Doctrine of the
Tyranny of Language. An Historical and Critical Examina-
tion of his* Blue Book. With an introduction by Stephen
Toulmin, 1971, xvii-145p. The Hague: Nijhoff, 1971.
Reprint of the original, ed. 1975.

book reviews:
W. L. Altzer, *The Modern Schoolman* 50 (1973):383-384.
M. A. Bertman, *Philosophy and Rhetoric* 8 (1975):131-
133;
J. Collins, *The Modern Schoolman* 50 (1972-73):383-384.
W. de Pater, *Tijdschrift voor Filosofie* 35 (1973):653-
655;
A. Flew, *Philosophical Books* 14 (1973):14-15;
J. W. Sterling, *Review of Metaphysics* 25 (1971-72):750;
M. Wolf, *Philosophical Studies* (Ireland) 22 (1974):274-
275.

21. Englemann, Paul. *Ludwig Wittgenstein: A Memoir and
Letters*. Trans. by L. Furtmüller. Oxford: Basil Blackwell,
1968.

book reviews:
J. K. Amrhein, *Library Journal* 93 (1968):2502f.
W. H. Gass, "Wittgenstein- A man and a half." *New
Republic* 158 (1968):29-30. [Includes a reminiscence
of Wittgenstein in a meeting of the Cornell Philo-
sophical Club]
Unsigned, *Times Literary Supplement* (September 12,
1968):1024.

22. *Essays on Wittgenstein in Honour of G. H. von Wright*
(Acta Philos. Fenn. 28 (1976)). Amsterdam: North-Holland,
1976. 516p.

CONTENTS:
Tranøy, K. E. "Wittgenstein in Cambridge, 1949-51.
  Some personal recollections." 11-21;
Drury, M. O'C. "Some notes on conversations with
  Wittgenstein." 22-40;
Kenny, Anthony. "From the big typescript to the
  Philosophical Grammar." 41-53;
Geach, P. T. "Saying and showing in Frege and Wittgen-
  stein." 54-70;
Stenius, Erik. "The sentence as a function of its
  constituents in Frege and in the *Tractatus*." 71-84;
Gale, Richard M. "Could logical space be empty?"
  85-104;
Hintikka, Jaakko. "Language-games." 105-125;
Hertzberg, Lars. "On the factual dependence of the
  language-game." 126-153;
Ginet, Carl. "Wittgenstein's claim that there could
  not be just one occasion of obeying a rule." 154-165;
Kreisel, G. "Der unheilvolle Einbruch der Logik in die
  Mathematik." 166-187;
Anscombe, G. E. M. "The question of linguistic
  idealism." 188-215;
Malcolm, Norman. "Moore and Wittgenstein on the sense
  of *I Know*." 216-240;
Hartnack, Justus. "Me and my body." 241-249;
Sachs, David. "Wittgenstein on emotion." 250-285;
Stoutland, Frederick. "The causation of behavior."
  286-325;
Martin, Rex. "The problem of the 'tie' in von Wright's
  schema of practical inference. A Wittgensteinian
  solution." 326-363;
Tuomela, Raimo. "Psychological concepts and function-
  alism." 364-393;
Wellman, Carl. "The meaning of 'good'." 394-416;
Cioffi, Frank. "Aesthetic explanation and aesthetic
  perplexity." 417-449;
Rhees, Rush. "Wittgenstein on language and ritual."
  450-484;
Rotenstreich, Nathan. "Between persuasion and deeds."
  485-502;
Nyiri, I. C. "Wittgenstein's new traditionalism."
  503-512.

23. Fann, Kuant Tih., ed. *Wittgenstein. The Man and His
Philosophy: An Anthology.* New York: Dell, 1967. 415p.

CONTENTS:
Preface, 11;
von Wright, Georg H. "A biographical sketch." 13-29;

Memoirs of Wittgenstein:
  I.   Russell, Bertrand. 30;
  II. Carnap, Rudolf. 31-33;
  III. Moore, G. E. 33-39;
  IV. Wisdom, John. 40-46;
Wittgenstein as a Teacher:
  Gasking, D. A. T., and Jackson, A. C. 49-56;
Portrait of a Philosopher:
  Britton, Karl. 56-63;
A Symposium: Assessments of the Man and the Philosopher:
  I.   Heller, Eric. 64-66;
  II. Drury, M. O'C. 67-70;
  III. Malcolm, Norman. 71-73;
  IV. Rhees, Rush. 74-78;
Recollections of Wittgenstein:
  Mays, Wolfe. 79-88;
Heller, Erich. "Wittgenstein: Unphilosophical notes."
  89-106;
Ferrater Mora, José. "Wittgenstein, a symbol of
  troubled times." 107-115;
Ryle, Gilbert. "Ludwig Wittgenstein." 116-124;
Paul, George A. "Ludwig Wittgenstein." 125-130;
Lazerowitz, Morris. "Wittgenstein on the nature of
  philosophy." 131-147;
Bouwsma, O. K. "*The Blue Book*." 148-170;
Linsky, Leonard. "Wittgenstein on language and some
  problems of philosophy. 171-180;
Malcolm, Norman. "Wittgenstein's *Philosophical
  Investigations*." 181-213;
Feyeraband, Paul. "Wittgenstein's *Philosophical
  Investigations*." 214-250;
Rhees, Rush. "Wittgenstein's builders." 251-264;
Ambrose, Alice. "Wittgenstein on some questions in
  foundations of mathematics." 265-283;
Cowan, Joseph L. "Wittgenstein's philosophy of logic."
  284-296;
Levison, Arnold. "Wittgenstein and logical laws."
  297-314;
Pitcher, George. "Wittgenstein, nonsense and Lewis
  Carroll." 315-335;
Ambrose, Alice. "Wittgenstein on universals." 336-352;
Wisdom, John. "A feature of Wittgenstein's technique."
  353-365;
Levi, Albert W. "Wittgenstein as dialectician." 366-
  379;
O'Brien, Dennis. "The unity of Wittgenstein's thought."
  380-404.

24. Fann, Kuant Tih. *Wittgenstein's Conception of
Philosophy*. Berkeley: Univ. of California Press, 1969,
178p; Oxford: Basil Blackwell & Mott, 1969.

  book reviews:
  R. Bambrough, *Philosophical Books* 11 (1970):8-9;

A. A. Derksen, *Bijdragen* 31 (1970):1162;
W. G. Lycan, *Metaphilosophy* 3 (1972):301-309;
W. M. Richards, *Philosophy and Phenomenological Research*
33 (1972-73):134-135.

25.   Favrholdt, David. *An Interpretation and Critique of
Wittgenstein's* Tractatus.   Copenhagen (Denmark): Munksgaard,
1964; New York: Humanities Press, 1966.   228p.

book reviews:
S. Brown, *Philosophical Quarterly* 16 (1966):78-79;
J. Collins, *Cross Currents* 17 (1967):218;
I. M. Copi, *Philosophical Review* 80 (1971):530-532;
J. Griffin, *Mind* 74 (1965):438-441;
A. E. Johanson, *Review of Metaphysics* 20 (1966):150;
G. Nuchelmans, *Foundations of Language* 2 (1966):271-
273;
G. K. Plochmann, *Modern Schoolman* 46 (1968-69):157-160;
A. Stroll, *Journal of the History of Philosophy* 5
(1967):190-193.

26.   Feibleman, James. *Inside the Great Mirror* (Examination
of the philosophy of Russell, Wittgenstein, and their
followers). The Hague: Martinus Nijhoff, 1958.

book reviews:
J. Agassi, *British Journal for the Philosophy of Science*
11 (1960-61):83-84;
G. Deledalle, *Etudes Philosophiques* 14 (1959):78;
R. Egidi, *Giornale Critico della Filosofia Italiana*
38 (1959):418-422;
E. H. Madden, *Philosophy and Phenomenological Research*
20 (1959-60):561-562;
M. Schiavone, *Giornale di Metafisica* 13 (1960):89-90;
C. F. Wallraff, *The Personalist* 41 (1960):73-75.

27.   Fenichel, Hannah (Pitkin). *Wittgenstein and Justice.
On the Significance of Ludwig Wittgenstein for Social and
Political Thought.* Berkeley: Univ. of California Press,
1972.   360p.

book reviews:
R. Beekler, *Canadian Journal of Philosophy* 6 (1976):
755-771;
J. T. Price, *Man and World* 7 (1974):78-87;
L. Reinhardt, *Mind* 85 (1976):151-154;
D. A. L. Thomas, *Philosophical Quarterly* 24 (1974):
76-77;
J. Whelan, Jr., *Philosophical Review* 83 (1974):540-544.

28. Finch, Henry Leroy. *Wittgenstein--the Early Philosophy.*
An Exposition of the Tractatus. New York: Humanities Press,
1971. 291p.

> book reviews:
> C. H. Soto, *Diálogos* 8 (1972):204-206;
> J. R. Teske, *Modern Schoolman* 51 (1972-73):241-242.

29. Finch, Henry Leroy. *Wittgenstein--the Later Philosophy.*
An Exposition of the Philosophical Investigations.
Atlantic Highlands (New Jersey): Humanities Press, 1977.
284p.

30. Fogelin, Robert John. *Wittgenstein. The Arguments of
the Philosophers.* London, Boston (Massachusetts): Routledge
& Kegan Paul, 1976. 223p.

> book reviews:
> Stewart Candlish, *Australasian Journal of Philosophy*
>   56 (1978):81-86;
> J. Largeault, *Archives de Philosophie* 41 (1978):684-687;
> H. O. Mounce, *Philosophical Quarterly* 27 (1977):366-370;
> Howard L. Ralston, *Philosophical Review* 87 (1978):296-
>   299;
> P. Winch, *Mind* 87 (1978):443-445.

31. Ganguly, Sachindranath. *Logical Positivism as a Theory
of Meaning.* Calcutta: Allied Publishers, 1967.

32. Ganguly, Sachindranath. *Wittgenstein's* Tractatus. A
Preliminary. Santiniketan (W. Bengal, India): Visva-
Bharati Univ., Centre of Advanced Study in Philosophy, 1968.
130p.

33. Gellner, Ernest. *Words and Things. A Critical Account
of Linguistic Philosophy and a Study in Ideology.* Boston:
Beacon Press, 1960; the Pelican ed., 1968.

> book reviews:
> J. M. Cameron, *Philosophical Studies* 9 (1959):138-151;
> J. Coulson, *Downside Review* 79 (1961):124-127;
> W. Doney, *Philosophical Review* 71 (1962):252-257;
> J. Gourlie, "Findlay on *Words and Things.*" *Indian
>   Journal of Philosophy* 4 (1964):56-61;
> P. L. Heath, *Philosophy* 37 (1962):176-177;
> A. Isenberg, *Journal of Philosophy* 58 (1961):110-112;

W. Kneale, *The Hibbert Journal* 58 (1959-60):196-198;
S. Korner, *Philosophical Quarterly* 11 (1961):376-379;
G. Nuchelmans, *Synthèse* 13 (1961):88-97;
A. Quinton, *British Journal for the Philosophy of Science*
    11 (1960-61):337-344;
J. W. N. Watkins, *Ratio* 3 (1960):93-97.

34. Griffin, James. *Wittgenstein's Logical Atomism*
(Oxford classical and philosophical monographs). Oxford:
Clarendon Press; New York: Oxford Univ. Press, 1964,x-166p.

book reviews:
M. Black, *Philosophical Quarterly* 16 (1966):374-376;
R. Blanché, *Revue Philosophique* (1967):420-421;
C. C., *De Homini* (Rome) (1963):259;
J. Hunter, *Dialogue* 3 (1965):461-462;
D. Keyt, *Philosophical Review* 74 (1965):229-239;
F. von Kutschera, *Philosophische Rundschau* 12 (1965):
    291-295;
K. W. Rankin, *Australasian Journal of Philosophy*
    42 (1964):439-444;
D. S. Shwayder, "Gegenstände and other matters: A
    review discussion of James Griffin, *Wittgenstein's
    Logical Atomism*." *Inquiry* 7 (1964):387-413;
A. Sloman, *Philosophical Books* 5 (1964):8-10;
M. Trinchero, *Rivista di Filosofia* 58 (1967):487-491.

35. Gudmunsen, Chris. *Wittgenstein and Buddhism*.
New York: Harper & Row; London: Macmillan, 1977. 128p.

36. Hacker, P. M. S. *Insight and Illusion. Wittgenstein
on Philosophy and the Metaphysics of Experience*. Oxford:
Clarendon Press; London: Oxford Univ. Press, 1975. 321p.

book reviews:
K. Ameriks, *New Scholasticism* 49 (1975):94-118;
S. A. M. Burns, *Dialogue* 13 (1974):384-388;
P.-P. Druet, *Revue Philosophique de Louvain* 71 (1973):
    628-629;
A. Garcia Suarez, *Teorema* 3 (1973):415-417;
G. Hallet, *Gregorianum* 54 (1973):590-591;
J. F. M. Hunter, *Canadian Journal of Philosophy* 4
    (1974):201-211;
J. F. M. Hunter, *International Philosophical Quarterly*
    13 (1973):295-298;
J. E. Llewelyn, *Inquiry* 16 (1973):431-445;
A. Lyon, *Mind* 84 (1975):293-295;
H. O. Mounce, *Philosophical Books* 14 (1973):18-21;
R. J. Richman, *Philosophical Review* 84 (1975):113-117;
M. Wolf, *Philosophical Studies* (Ireland) 22: 277-279.

37.   Hallett, Garth.   *Wittgenstein's Definition of Meaning as Use* (The Oreste Brownson series on contemporary thought and affairs, 6).   Bronx (New York): Fordham Univ. Press, 1967.   210p.

    book reviews:
T. Binkley, *Philosophy and Phenomenological Research*
   31 (1970-71):429-432;
W. A. Frank, *Review of Metaphysics* 26 (1972-73):160-161;
J. H. Gill, *Thought* 43 (1968):632-633;
G. Pitcher, *Philosophical Review* 78 (1969):555-557;
P. Roper, *The Heythrop Journal* 9 (1968):427-428;
D. Zaslawsky, *Revue de Théologie et de Philosophie*
   102 (1969):428-429.

38.   Hallett, Garth.   *A Companion to Wittgenstein's Philosophical Investigations*.   Ithaca (New York): Cornell Univ. Press, 1977.   801p.

    book reviews:
Stuart Brown, *Philosophical Quarterly* 28 (1978):354-355;
Carla Cordua, *Diálogos* 13 (1978):179-182;
Jerry H. Gill, *International Philosophical Quarterly*
   18 (1978):227-231;
John F. M. Hunter, "A scholar's Wittgenstein." *Philosophical Review* 87 (1978):259-274;
D. Z. Phillips, *Philosophical Books* 19 (1978):68-72.

39.   Hardwick, Charles S.   *Language Learning in Wittgenstein's Later Philosophy* (Janua linguarum series minor, 104).   The Hague: Mouton, 1971.   152p.

40.   Hartnack, Justus.   *Wittgenstein and Modern Philosophy*.   Trans. by Maurice Cranston.   (Originally published in Danish, 1960; German trans., Stuttgart, 1962.)   New York: New York Univ. Press, 1965, 142p; London: Methuen; New York: Doubleday, Anchor Books, 1965.

    book reviews:
Anonymous, *Times Literary Supplement* (May 12, 1966):410;
P. Chiodi, *British Journal for the Philosophy of Science*
   15 (1964):166-168;
M. Cornforth, *Science and Society* 30 (1966):335-338;
J. H. Gill, *Philosophy and Phenomenological Research*
   27 (1966):137-138;
A. Narveson, *Dialogue* 5 (1966):101-102;
H. D. Sluga, *Philosophical Books* 7 (1966):22;
A. Stroll, *Journal of the History of Philosophy*
   5 (1967):190-193;
C. Wellman, *Philosophical Review* 76 (1967):385-387.

41.   Harward, Donald W. *Wittgenstein's Saying and Showing*
Themes. Bonn: Bouvier Verlag H. Grundmann, 1976.   71p.

42.   Hawkins, D. J. B. *Wittgenstein and the Cult of*
Language (The Aquinas Society of London--Aquinas Paper, 27).
London: Blackfriars, 1957.   14p.

   book reviews:
   J. Molloy, *The Clergy Review* 42 (1957):509-510;
   A. Shalom, *Études Philosophiques* 12 (1957):408.

43.   Henze, Donald F., and Saunders, John T. *The Private-*
Language Problem: A Philosophical Dialogue. New York:
Random House, 1967.

44.   Hester, Marcus B. *The Meaning of Poetic Metaphor.*
An Analysis in the Light of Wittgenstein's Claim that
Meaning is Use (De proprietatibus litterarum, series maior,
1).   's Gravenhage, Mouton, 1967.   229p.

   book review:
   D. Th. Wieck, *Journal of Aesthetics and Art Criticism*
      28 (1969-70):401.

45.   High, Dallas M. *Language, Persons, and Belief.*
Studies in Wittgenstein's Philosophical Investigations and
Religious Uses of Language. New York: Oxford Univ. Press,
1967.   216p.

   book reviews:
   Anonymous, *Choice* 5 (1968):1148;
   P. Dubois, *Revue Philosophique de la France et de*
      l'Etranger 99 (1974):366-367;
   S. Dunbar, *Religious Studies* (London) 4 (1968-69):294-
      297;
   G. Francescato, *Revue Belge de Philosophie et d'Histoire*
      (Brussels) 48 (1970):151-153;
   L. Griffiths, *Philosophy* 45 (1970):257-258;
   A. M., *Review of Metaphysics* 22 (1968):144-145;
   A. Plantinga, *Commonweal* 88 (1968):420f.

46.   Hudson, W. Donald. *Ludwig Wittgenstein. The Bearing*
of his Philosophy upon Religious Belief. Richmond
(Virginia): John Knox Press, 1968, 74p; London: Lutterworth
Press, 1968.

47. Hudson, W. Donald. *Wittgensteinian Fideism* (New
Studies in the Philosophy of Religion). New York:
Doubleday, Anchor Books, 1970.

48. Hudson, W. Donald. *Philosophical Approach to Religion*.
London: Macmillan, 1974.

    book reviews:
    T. E. Burke, *Religious Studies* 11 (1975):352-353;
    R. Butterworth, *The Heythrop Journal* 16 (1975):314-315.

49. Hudson, William Donald. *Wittgenstein and Religious
Belief* (New Studies in the Philosophy of Religion).
New York: St. Martin's Press, 1975, 206p; London: Macmillan,
1975.

    book reviews:
    R. Butterworth, *The Heythrop Journal* 17 (1976):453-455;
    A. Sell, *Philosophical Studies* (Maynooth) 25 (1977):
        380-382;
    P. H. Sherry, *Philosophical Books* 18 (1977):32-44.

50. Hunter, John Fletcher MacGregor. *Essays after Wittgenstein*. Toronto: Univ. of Toronto Press, 1973, 202p;
London: George Allen & Unwin, 1973.

    book reviews:
    R. Bambrough, *Canadian Journal of Philosophy* 7 (1977):
        869-876;
    S. Burns, *Dialogue* 14 (1975):341-343;
    V. M. Cooke, *International Philosophical Quarterly*
        15 (1975):122-124;
    I. Dilman, *Mind* 85 (1976):460-462;
    G. Hallett, *Gregorianum* 56 (1975):181-182;
    R. W. Newell, *Philosophy* 50 (1975):368-370;
    K. Nielsen, *Metaphilosophy* 7 (1976):241-264;
    G. K. Pletgher, *Modern Schoolman* 53 (1976):71-75;
    J. T. Price, *Foundations of Language* 13 (1975):307-308;
    B. Stroud, *Journal of Philosophy* 73 (1976):277-281.

51. Janik, Allan, and Toulmin, Stephen E. *Wittgenstein's
Vienna*. New York: Simon & Schuster, 1973, 314p; London:
George Weidenfeld & Nicolson, 1973, 314p.

    book reviews:
    W. W. Bartley, III, *Philosophy of the Social Sciences*
        5 (1975):88-91;
    J. Bouveresse, *Critique* 30 (1975):781-796;

J. W. Boyer, *Journal of Modern History* 47 (1976):699-
    711;
C. Henderson and V. Zeman, *Journal of the History of
    Philosophy* 14 (1976):118-121;
J. C. Nyiri, *Philosophischer Literaturanzeiger* 28
    (1975):95-99;
G. Steiner, *The New Yorker* (July 23, 1973).

52. Jones, O. R., ed. *The Private Language Argument.*
London: Macmillan; New York: St. Martin's Press, 1971.
284p.

   CONTENTS:
   Jones, O. R. "Editor's introduction." 13-26;
   Strawson, P. F. "Exposition and criticism of Wittgen-
       stein's *Investigations*." 27-32;
   Malcolm, Norman. "Exposition and criticism of Wittgen-
       stein's *Investigations*." 33-49;
   Ayer, A. J. "Could language be invented by a Robinson
       Crusoe?" 50-61;
   Rhees, Rush. Ibid. 61-75;
   Hervey, Helen. "Private language and private sensa-
       tions." 76-95;
   Garver, Newton. Ibid. 95-102;
   Mundle, C. W. K. "Behaviourism and the private lang-
       uage argument." 103-117;
   Holborow, L. C. Ibid. 117-131;
   Castañeda, Hector-Neri. "The private language argument
       as a *reductio ad absurdum*." 133-154;
   Chappell, V. C. Ibid. 155-168;
   Thomson, J. F. Ibid. 168-173;
   Castañeda, Hector-Neri. Ibid. 173-182;
   Thomson, Judith Jarvis. "The verification principle
       and the private language argument." 183-204;
   Kenny, Anthony. Ibid. 204-228;
   Rhees, Rush. "'Private experience' and 'sense data'.
       Note on the text." 229-232;
   Wittgenstein, Ludwig. "'Private experience' and
       'sense data'. Notes for lectures on 'private
       experience' and 'sense data'." 232-275.

   book review:
   H. G. Townsend, *The Heythrop Journal* 14 (1973):447-449.

53. Kaal, Hans, and McKinnon, Alastair. *Concordance to
Wittgenstein's* Philosophische Untersuchungen. Leiden:
E. J. Brill, 1975, xiii-596p.

   book reviews:
   Rolf George, *Dialogue* 16 (1978):545-546;
   Hubert Schwyzer, *Journal of the History of Philosophy*
       16 (1978):365-367.

54. Keightley, Alan W. *Wittgenstein, Grammar and God*.
London: Epworth Press, 1976. 176p.

55. Kenny, Anthony John Patrick. *Wittgenstein*. London:
Allen Lane, 1973, 240p; Cambridge (Massachusetts): Harvard
Univ. Press, 1973; Middlesex (England): Penguin Books, 1975.

book reviews:
K. Ameriks, *New Scholasticism* 49 (1975):94-118;
S. Brown, *Philosophy* 50 (1975):248-249;
S. A. M. Burns, *Dialogue* 13 (1974):196-198;
P. Byrne, *Religious Studies* 11 (1975):489-490;
A. Ellis, *Mind* 87 (1978):270-275;
G. Graham, *International Philosophical Quarterly* 15
    (1975):369-372;
A. Manser, *Mind* 84 (1975):616-621;
G. Megghe, *Erkenntnis* 9 (1975):145-152;
A. Palmer, *Philosophical Books* 15 (1974):6-8;
B. Stroud, *The Philosophical Review* 84 (1975):576-580.

56. Kielkopf, Charles F. *Strict Finitism. An Examination
of Ludwig Wittgenstein's* Remarks on the Foundations of
Mathematics (Studies in Philosophy, 15). The Hague:
Mouton, 1970. 192p.

57. Klemke, E. D., ed. *Essays on Wittgenstein*. Urbana:
Univ. of Illinois Press, 1971. 552p.

CONTENTS:
Part One: Wittgenstein's Ontology
Bergmann, G. "Ineffability, method, and ontology."
    3-24;
Bergmann, G. "The glory and the misery of Ludwig
    Wittgenstein." 25-43;
Bergmann, G. "Stenius on the *Tractatus*." 44-77;
Sellars, W. "Naming and saying." 78-103;
Klemke, E. D. "The ontology of Wittgenstein's
    Tractatus." 104-119;
Hochberg, H. "Material properties in the *Tractatus*."
    120-122;
Garver, N. "Wittgenstein's pantheism: A new light on
    the ontology of the *Tractatus*." 123-137;
Petrie, H. "Science and metaphysics: A Wittgensteinian
    interpretation." 138-171.
Part Two: Epistemology and Philosophy of Language
Hardin, C. L. "Wittgenstein on private language."
    173-186;
Garver, N. "Wittgenstein on private language." 187-
    196;
Todd, W. "Wittgenstein and private language." 197-213;

Castañeda, H.-N.   "The private-language argument."
  214-239;
Cook, J. W.   "Wittgenstein on privacy."   240-272;
Hunter, J. F. M.   "'Forms of life' in Wittgenstein's
  Philosophical Investigations."   273-297;
Gram, M. S.   "Privacy and language."   298-327;
Zabeeh, F.   "On language games and forms of life."
  328-373;
Hunter, J. F. M.   "Wittgenstein on meaning and use."
  374-393;
Oldenquist, A.   "Wittgenstein on phenomenalism, skep-
  ticism, and criteria."   394-423;
Stampe, D. W.   "Tractarian reflections on saying and
  showing."   423-445;
Part Three: Philosophy of Logic and Mathematics
Stroud, B.   "Wittgenstein and logical necessity."
  447-463;
Hochberg, H.   "Negation and generality."   464-484;
Hochberg, H.   "Facts, possibilities, and essences in
  the *Tractatus*."   485-533;
Hochberg, H.   "Arithmetic and propositional form in
  Wittgenstein's *Tractatus*."   534-542.

book review:
H. Mounce, *Mind* 81 (1972):618-620.

58.   Klenk, V. H.   *Wittgenstein's Philosophy of Mathematics*.
The Hague: Martinus Nijhoff, 1976, viii-128p.

58a.   Lazarowitz, Morris.   *The Language of Philosophy.
Freud and Wittgenstein*.   (Boston Studies in the Philosophy
of Science, 60) (Synthese Library, 117).   Boston-Dordrecht:
D. Reidel, 1977, xvi-209p.

59.   Lemoine, Roy Emanuel.   *The Anagogic Theory of Wittgenstein's* Tractatus (Janua linguarum Series Minor, 214).
The Hague-Paris: Mouton, 1975.   215p.

60.   Leinfellner, Elisabeth, ed.   *Wittgenstein and his
Impact on Contemporary Thought* (Proceedings of the 2nd
International Wittgenstein Symposium, Austria, 1977).
Boston-Dordrecht: Reidel, 1978.   550p.   [See Appendix for
contents]

    book review:
Pieranna Garavaso, "Il Secondo Simposio Internazionale
  su Wittgenstein."   *Verifiche* 6 (1977):893-896.

61. Leitner, Bernhard. *The Architecture of Ludwig Wittgenstein*. A documentation compiled by Bernhard Leitner with
excerpts from the family recollections by Hermine Wittgenstein. English text ed. by Dennis Young. Published for
the Press of the Nova Scotia College of Art and Design
[English and German text]. London: Studio International
Publications, 1973. 127p.

    book review:
    V. C. Aldrich, *Southwestern Journal of Philosophy*
      6 (1975):168-169.

62. Luckhardt, C. G., ed. *Wittgenstein: Sources and
Perspectives*. Ithaca (New York): Cornell Univ. Press,
1979. 349p.

    CONTENTS:
    Contributors, 7;
    Abbreviations, 9;
    Editor's introduction, 13;
    Pascal, Fania. "Wittgenstein: A personal memoir." 23;
    Wittgenstein, Ludwig. "Remarks on Frazer's *Golden
      Bough*." Trans. by John Beversluis. 61;
    Wittgenstein, Ludwig. "Letters to Ludwig von Ficker."
      Trans. by Bruce Gillette; ed. by Allan Janik. 82;
    von Wright, Georg Henrik. "The origin of Wittgenstein's
      Tractatus." 99;
    von Wright, Georg Henrik. "The origin and composition
      of Wittgenstein's *Investigations*." 138;
    Janik, Allan. "Wittgenstein, Ficker, and *Der Brenner*."
      161;
    Pears, David. "The relation between Wittgenstein's
      picture theory of propositions and Russell's theories
      of judgment." 190;
    Hacker, P. M. S. "Semantic holism: Frege and Wittgen-
      stein." 213;
    Baker, Gordon P. "*Verehrung und Verkehrung*: Waismann
      and Wittgenstein." 243;
    Linville, Kent. "Wittgenstein on 'Moore's Paradox'."
      286;
    Arrington, Robert L. "*Mechanism* and *Calculus*: Wittgen-
      stein on Augustine's theory of ostension." 303;
    Index of Wittgenstein's works cited, 339;
    Index of names, 341.

63. Malcolm, Norman. *Ludwig Wittgenstein: A Memoir*.
(With a biographical sketch by von Wright and a photograph.)
London: Oxford Univ. Press, 1958; revised ed., 1966.

    book reviews:
    W. H. Alamshah, *The Personalist* 44 (1963):106-107;
    M. A. Bertmann, *Modern Schoolman* 51 (1973-74):249-250;

N. Bobbio, *Rivista di Filosofia* 50 (1959):233-234;
K. Britton, *Philosophy* 35 (1959):277-278;
S. C., *Methodos* 10 (1958):92;
D. Campanale, *Rivista Critica di Storia della Filosofia*
   13 (1960):380-381;
J. Collins, *Cross Currents* 10 (1960):171-172;
J. Coulson, *Downside Review* 79 (1961):122-124;
A. C. Jackson, *Mind* 69 (1960):269-270;
J. R. Newman, *Scientific American* 201 (1959):149-158;
C. D. Rollins, *Journal of Philosophy* 56 (1959):280-283;
A. Shalom, *Etudes Philosophiques* 14 (1959):584; Ibid.,
   18 (1963):365;
G. Vlastos, *Philosophical Review* 69 (1960):105-108.

64.   Manser, A. R.   *The End of Philosophy: Marx and
Wittgenstein* (Inaugural lecture).   Southampton: University,
1973.   14p.

65.   Maslow, Alexander.   *A Study in Wittgenstein's* Tractatus.
Berkeley and Los Angeles: Univ. of California Press, 1961.

book reviews:
S. McCall, *Dialogue* 2 (1963):114-115;
G. C. Nerlich, *Philosophical Books* 1 (1960):13-16;
R. Rhees, *Philosophical Review* 72 (1963):213-220.

66.   Moran, John.   *Toward the World and Wisdom of Wittgenstein's* Tractatus (Studies in philosophy, 26).   The Hague:
Mouton, 1973.   126p.

book reviews:
L. Goldstein, *Philosophical Quarterly* 25 (1975):84-85;
G. C. Stine, *Philosophical Review* 84 (1975):570-575.

67.   Morawetz, Thomas.   *Wittgenstein and Knowledge.*
Amherst (Massachusetts): Univ. of Massachusetts Press, 1978.
159p.

68.   Morick, Harold, ed.   *Wittgenstein and the Problem of
Other Minds.*   New York, Maidenhead (England): McGraw-Hill,
1967, xxiii-231p.

CONTENTS:
Introduction, xiii-xxiii;
Strawson, P. F.   "Critical notice of Wittgenstein's
   Philosophical Investigations."   3-44;

Malcolm, N.   "Wittgenstein's *Philosophical Investiga-*
   tions."   45-81;
Ayer, A. J.   "Can there be a private language?"   82-96;
Perkins, M.   "Two arguments against a private language."
   97-118;
Moore, G. E.   "From 'Wittgenstein's lectures in 1930-
   1933'."   119-126;
Strawson, P. F.   "Persons."   127-153;
Wellman, C.   "Wittgenstein's conception of a criterion."
   154-169;
Chihara, C. S., and Fodor, J. A.   "Operationalism and
   ordinary language: A critique of Wittgenstein."
   170-202;
Geach, P.   "Could sensuous experience occur apart from
   an organism?"   205-210;
Geach, P.   "The fallacy of *Cogito, ergo sum*."   211-214;
Malcolm, N.   "The concept of dreaming."   215-227.

book reviews:
G. Frongia, *Giornale Critico della Filosofia Italiana*
   50 (1971):516-517;
H. Laycock, *Dialogue* 8 (1969-70):337-338;
P. Röper, *The Heythrop Journal* 10 (1969):198-202.

69.   Morrison, James C.   *Meaning and Truth in Wittgenstein's*
Tractatus (Janua linguarum, 64).   The Hague: Mouton, 1968.
148p.

book reviews:
D. L. Couprie, *Foundations of Language* 6 (1970):562-564;
E. Stenius, *Philosophical Review* 79 (1970):573-575.

70.   Mullin, A. A.   *Philosophical Comments on the Philos-*
ophies of C. S. Peirce and Ludwig Wittgenstein.   Urbana
(Illinois): Electrical Engineering Research Laboratory,
Engineering Experiment Station, Univ. of Illinois, 1961.

71.   Mundle, C. W. K.   *A Critique of Linguistic Philosophy.*
Oxford: Clarendon Press, 1976. [Part 2: Ludwig Wittgenstein, the Instigator of the Revolution in Philosophy,
153-260]

book reviews:
R. Abelson, *Metaphilosophy* 7 (1976):276-286;
D. Olin, *Philosophical Review* 82 (1973):246-249;
M. Shorter, *Philosophical Quarterly* 22 (1972):172-174;
M. Wencelius, *Etudes Philosophiques* (1972):283-285.

72. Naess, Arne. *Four Modern Philosophers*. Chicago: Univ. of Chicago Press, 1968. ["Ludwig Wittgenstein," 67-171]

book review:
A. Manser, *Mind* 80 (1971):623-626.

73. Pears, David Francis. *Ludwig Wittgenstein*. London: Fontana/Collins, 1971, 188p; New York: The Viking Press, 1970; Middlesex (England): W. Drayton; E. Rutherford (New Jersey): Penguin Books, 1977. 208p.

book reviews:
S. A. M. Burns, *Dialogue* 11 (1972):478-480;
A. García Suarez, *Teorema* (1972):99-103;
M. E. Levin, *Social Research* 40 (1973):192-207;
W. G. Lyons, *Metaphilosophy* 4 (1973):152-162;
B. Stroud, *Journal of Philosophy* 69 (1972):16-26;
E. Villanueva, *Crítica* 6 (1972):131-138.

74. Phillips, Derek L. *Wittgenstein and Scientific Knowledge. A Sociological Perspective*. London: Macmillan; Totowa (New Jersey): Rowman & Littlefield, 1977. 248p.

75. Pinsent, David. Excerpts on Wittgenstein from the *Diary* of David Pinsent, 1912-14. On Deposit at Trinity College, Cambridge University.

76. Pitcher, George, ed. *Wittgenstein: The* Philosophical Investigations (A collection of critical essays). New York: Doubleday, Anchor Books, 1966.

CONTENTS:
Preface, v;
Quinton, A. M. "Excerpt from *Contemporary British Philosophy*." 1-21;
Strawson, P. F. "Review of Wittgenstein's *Philosophical Investigations*." 22-64;
Malcolm, N. "Wittgenstein's *Philosophical Investigations*." 65-103;
Feyeraband, P. "Wittgenstein's *Philosophical Investigations*." 104-151;
Cavell, S. "The availability of Wittgenstein's later philosophy." 151-185;
Bambrough, R. "Universals and family resemblances." 186-204;
Khatchadourian, H. "Common names and 'family resemblances'." 205-230;

Albritton, R. "On Wittgenstein's use of the term
'criterion'." 231-250;
Ayer, A. J. "Can there be a private language?" 251-
266;
Rhees, R. "Can there be a private language?" 267-285;
Cook, J. W. "Wittgenstein on privacy." 286-323;
Donagan, A. "Wittgenstein on sensation." 324-251;
Kenny, A. "Cartesian privacy." 352-370;
Malcolm, N. "Knowledge of other minds." 371-383;
Chihara, C. S., and Fodor, J. A. "Operationalism and
ordinary language: A critique of Wittgenstein."
384-419;
Dummett, M. "Wittgenstein's philosophy of mathematics."
420-447;
Chihara, C. S. "Mathematical discovery and concept
formation." 448-468;
Chihara, C. S. "Wittgenstein and logical compulsion."
469-476;
Stroud, B. "Wittgenstein and logical necessity." 477-
496.

77. Pitcher, George. *The Philosophy of Wittgenstein*.
Englewood Cliffs (New Jersey): Prentice-Hall, 1964. 340p.

book reviews:
A. Ambrose, *Philosophy and Phenomenological Research*
25 (1965):423-425;
J. Bennett, *Philosophy* 41 (1966):86-87;
T. Binkely, *Philosophy and Phenomenological Research*
31 (1970-71):429-432;
A. Grabner-Harder, *Theologische Rundschau* 65 (1969):
380-381;
J. Griffin, *Mind* 74 (1965):438-441;
D. Gustafson, *Philosophy and Phenomenological Research*
28 (1967-68):252-258;
P. Hinst, *Philosophische Rundschau* 15 (1968):51-65;
J. F. M. Hunter, *Dialogue* 3 (1964-65):463-464;
D. Keyt, *Philosophical Review* 74 (1965):229-239;
J. M. B. Moss, *Philosophical Books* 6 (1966):20-23;
A. Narveson, *Philosophy of Science* 34 (1967):80-83;
G. Nuchelmans, *Foundations of Language* 1 (1965):552-
553;
R. Rhees, *Ratio* 8 (1966):180-193;
A. Shields, *The Personalist* 46 (1965):109;
S. Shoemaker, *Journal of Philosophy* 63 (1966):354-358;
E. Stenius, *Philosophical Quarterly* 6 (1966):373-374.

--- Pitkin, Hannah. See Fenichel, Hannah, *Wittgenstein
and Justice*, no. 27.

78.   Plochmann, G. K., and Lawson, J. B. *Terms in their Propositional Contexts in Wittgenstein's* Tractatus: An Index. Carbondale: Southern Illinois Univ. Press, 1962.

book reviews:
M. Black, *Philosophical Review* 72 (1963):265-266;
M. J. Fairbanks, *Modern Schoolman* 41 (1963-64):82-84;
C. W., *Ethics* 73 (1962-63):149.

79.   Pole, David. *The Later Philosophy of Wittgenstein.* London: The Athlone Press, Univ. of London, 1958.

book reviews:
Anonymous, *The Month* 21 (1959):256-257;
Anonymous, *Revue de Métaphysique et de Morale* 64 (1959): 489-490;
A. Bharati, *Zeitschrift für Philosophische Forschung* 16 (1962):158-164;
K. Britton, *Philosophy* 35 (1960):279-281;
J. G. Colbert, *Documentación Crítica Iberoamericana de Filosofía y Ciencias Afines* 3 (1966):152-154;
H. W. Jäger, *Philosophische Literaturanzeiger* 13 (1960): 28-30;
G. Nuchelmans, *Foundations of Language* 1 (1965):232-233;
J. Oroz, *Augustinus* 4 (1959):126;
J. Ruytinx, *Revue Internationale de Philosophie* 14 (1960):106-107;
A. Shalom, *Etudes Philosophiques* 14 (1959):237;
P. F. Strawson, *Philosophical Quarterly* 10 (1960):371-372;
J. Techmann, *Mind* 69 (1960):107.

---   Poulain, Jacques. See no. 111.

80.   Price, Jeffrey Thomas. *Language and Being in Wittgenstein's* Philosophical Investigations (Janua linguarum, Series minor, 178). The Hague: Mouton, 1973. 122p.

book review:
H. W. Baldwin, *Review of Metaphysics* 29 (1975):144-145.

81.   Rao, A. Pampapathy. *A Survey of Wittgenstein's Theory of Meaning.* Calcutta: Indian Univ. Press, 1965. 96p.

82.   Rhees, Rush. *Discussions of Wittgenstein*. London:
Routledge & Kegan Paul, 1970, 161p; New York: Schocken
Books, 1970.

   book reviews:
   R. Audi, *Philosophy Forum* 10 (1971):163-165;
   A. Bharati, *Zeitschrift für Philosophische Forschung*
      27 (1973):330-332;
   I. Dilman, *Philosophical Books* 11 (1970):23-28;
   M. Wolf, *Philosophical Studies* (Maynooth) 21: 287-291.

83.   Richardson, John T. E.   *The Grammar of Justification.
An Interpretation of Wittgenstien's Philosophy of Language.*
London: Chatto & Windus. Published for Sussex Univ. Press,
1976, 147p; New York: St. Martin's Press, 1976.

84.   Rollins, C. D., ed.   *Knowledge and Experience.*
Pittsburgh: Univ. of Pittsburgh Press, 1962. [Includes
two symposia on Wittgenstein]

   CONTENTS:
   Garver, Newton. "Wittgenstein on criteria." 55-71;
   Ginet, Carl. "Comments." 72-76;
   Siegler, F. A. "Comments." 77-80;
   Ziff, Paul. "Comments." 81-86;
   Garver, Newton. "Rejoinders." 86-87;
   Castañeda, H.-N. "The private-language argument."
      88-105;
   Chappell, V. C. "Comments." 106-118;
   Thomson, J. F. "Comments." 119-124;
   Castañeda, H.-N. "Rejoinders." 125-129.

85.   Sefler, G. F.   *Language and the World. A Methodologi-
cal-structural Synthesis within the Writings of M. Heidegger
and L. Wittgenstein.* Atlantic Highlands (New Jersey):
Humanities Press, 1974, xxxiii-228p.

   book review:
   K. Harries, *Philosophical Review* 85 (1976):422-426.

86.   Sherry, Patrick. *Religion, Truth and Language-games.*
New York: Barnes and Noble, 1977, x-234p.

87.   Shibles, Warren. *Wittgenstein. Language and Philos-*
ophy. Dubuque (Iowa): William C. Brown, 1969,100p; 3d ed.,
Whitewater (Wisconsin): The Language Press, 1974, viii-100p.

   book reviews:
   L. Hegensberg, *Convivium* (Spanish) 13 (1974):470-472;
   V. R. McKim, *New Scholasticism* 44 (1970):471;
   A. Pisani, *Rassegna di Scienze Filosofiche* 26 (1973):
     443-445.

88.   Specht, Ernst Konrad. *The Foundations of Wittgen-*
stein's Late Philosophy. Trans. from the German by
D. E. Walford. Manchester: Manchester Univ. Press, 1969,
viii-209p; New York: Barnes and Noble.

   book reviews:
   P. Feyeraband, *Philosophical Quarterly* 16 (1966):79-80;
   J. Hartnack, *Philosophical Review* 80 (1971):391-393;
   R. Castilla Lázaro, "Lenguaje y ontología. En torno
     al Wittgenstein de E. K. Specht." *Diálogos* 5 (1968):
     79-100;
   L. Pompa, *Philosophical Journal* 7 (1970):181-184.

89.   Stegmüller, Wolfgang. "Ludwig Wittgenstein." In
Main Currents in Contemporary German, English and American
Philosophy. Bloomington (Indiana): Indiana Univ. Press,
1970, 394-526.

90.   Stenius, E. *Wittgenstein's* Tractatus. Oxford: Basil
Blackwell, 1960.

   book reviews:
   Anonymous, *Times Literary Supplement* (December 23,
     1961):831 [See E. Stenius, Letter. *Times Literary*
     Supplement (February 17, 1961):105, comments on the
     review];
   G. Bergmann, *Theoria* 29 (1963):Part 2, 176-204.
     Reprinted in his *Logic and Reality.* Madison
     (Wisconsin): Wisconsin Univ. Press, 1964, 176-204;
   I. M. Copi, *Philosophical Review* 72 (1963):382-390;
   G. D. Duthie, *Philosophical Quarterly* 12 (1962):371-372;
   N. Garver, *Philosophy and Phenomenological Research*
     22 (1961-62):276-277;
   J. Jarvis, *Journal of Philosophy* 58 (1961):584-596;
   G. C. Nerlich, *Philosophical Books* 1 (1960):13-16;
   H. A. Nielsen, *Philosophical Studies* 10 (1960):265-266;
   G. Nuchelmans, *Foundations of Language* 2 (1966):270-271;
   E. Riverso, *Rivista Critica di Storia della Filosofia*
     15 (1962):255-256;
   A. Shalom, *Etudes Philosophiques* 16 (1961):277-278;

91. Van Hayek, F. A. Unfinished draft of a sketch of a
biography of Wittgenstein (written in 1953 for private
circulation). Informative account of Wittgenstein's life
up to 1929, unpublished.

92. Van Peursen, Cornelis Anthonie. *Ludwig Wittgenstein.
An Introduction to his Philosophy.* Trans. by Rex Ambler.
London: Faber & Faber, 1969, 120p; New York: E. P. Dutton,
1970, 122p.

  book reviews:
  S. Blackburn, *British Journal for the Philosophy of
    Science* 21 (1970):385-386;
  R. W. Newell, *Philosophical Quarterly* 20 (1970):275-
    276.

93. Vander Veer, Garrett L. *Philosophical Skepticism and
Ordinary Language Analysis.* Lawrence (Kansas): Regents
Press of Kansas, 1978, ix-277p.

94. Vesey, Godfrey, ed. *Understanding Wittgenstein*
(Royal Institute of Philosophy Lectures, Vol. 7, 1972-73).
London: Macmillan, 1974, xxii-285p; New York: St. Martin's
Press.

  CONTENTS:
  Kenny, A. "The ghost of the *Tractatus*." 1-13;
  White, R. M. "Can whether one proposition makes sense
    depend on the truth of another? (*Tractatus* 2.0211-2)"
    14-29;
  Rhees, R. "Questions on logical inference." 30-48;
  McGuinness, B. "The *Grundgedanke* of the *Tractatus*."
    49-61;
  Stock, G. "Wittgenstein on Russell's theory of judg-
    ment." 62-75;
  Williams, B. "Wittgenstein and idealism." 76-95;
  Griffiths, A. P. "Wittgenstein, Schopenhauer, and
    ethics." 96-116;
  Bambrough, R. "How to read Wittgenstein." 117-131;
  Teichman, J. "Wittgenstein on persons and human
    beings." 133-148;
  Vesey, G. "Other minds." 149-161;
  Dilman, I. "Wittgenstein on the soul." 162-192;
  Holborow, L. "The prejudice in favour of psychophysical
    parallelism." 193-207; [Zettel]
  Squires, R. "Silent soliloquy." 208-225;
  Ayer, A. J. "Wittgenstein on certainty." 226-245;
  Coope, C. "Wittgenstein's theory of knowledge." 246-
    284.

book reviews:
T. E. Burke, *Philosophical Books* 16 (1975):32-33;
A. Lichtigfeld, *Tijdschrift voor Filosofie* 37 (1975):
   540-544;
A. Manser, *Philosophy* 50 (1975):478-481;
R. W. Newell, *Philosophical Quarterly* 25 (1975):363-365.

95. Waismann, F. *The Principles of Linguistic Philosophy.*
R. Harré, ed. London: Macmillan; New York: St. Martin's
Press, 1968.

96. Welch, Cyril. *The Sense of Language.* The Hague:
Nijhoff, 1973. 184p.

97. Winch, Peter, ed. *Studies in the Philosophy of
Wittgenstein.* London: Routledge & Kegan Paul, 1969;
New York: Humanities Press, 1969, 210p.

   CONTENTS:
   Winch, P. "Introduction: The unity of Wittgenstein's
      philosophy." 1-19;
   Ishiguro, H. "Use and reference of names." 20-50;
   Rhees, R. "'Ontology' and identity in the *Tractatus*:
   A propos of Black's *Companion.*" 51-66;
   Shwayder, D. S. "Wittgenstein on mathematics." 66-116;
   Cook, J. W. "Human beings." 117-151;
   Reinhardt, L. R. "Wittgenstein and Strawson on other
      minds." 152-165;
   Manser, A. "Pain and private language." 166-183;
   Cioffi, F. "Wittgenstein's Freud." 184-209.

BOOKS IN FRENCH

98. Bouveresse, Jacques. *La parole malheureuse. De
l'alchimie linguistique à la grammaire philosophique.*
Paris: Les Editions de Minuit, 1971. 475p. [Ch. 3:
"Philosophie des mathématiques et thérapeutique d'une
maladie philosophique: Wittgenstein et la critique de
l'apparence 'ontologique' dans les mathématiques." (Orig.
published in *Cahiers pour l'Analyse*, no. 10, 1969); Ch. 4:
"Sur le 'finitisme' de Wittgenstein; Ch. 5: "La compétence,
l'usage et l'usage de la compétence."]

book review:
A. Kenny, *Archives de Philosophie* 37 (1974):343-345.

99. Bouveresse, Jacques. *Wittgenstein, la rime et la raison. Science, éthique et esthétique* (Coll. Critique). Paris: Editions de Minuit, 1973. 239p.

   book reviews:
   A. Kenny, *Archives de Philosophie* 37 (1974):343-345;
   G. Penco, *Proteus* 4 (1973):206-210.

100. Bouveresse, Jacques. *Wittgenstein et la philosophie.* Séance du 23 mars 1973. Exposé: M. J. Bouveresse; Discussion: R. P. Dubarle, Mme Dubouchet, Mlle Laffocrièrè, MM. Metlov, R. Poirier, D. Zaslawski. Note de M. M. Matschinski et réponse de M. J. Bouveresse. Paris: Armand Colin, 1973. *Bulletin de la Société française de Philosophie* 67 (1973):85-148.

101. Bouveresse, Jacques. *Le mythe de l'intériorité. Expérience, signification et langage privé chez Wittgenstein* (Critique). Paris: Editions de Minuit, 1976, xiv-702p.

   book review:
   G. Brykmann, *Revue Philosophique de la France et de l'Etranger* 102 (1977):1021.

102. Granger, Gilles-Gaston. *Ludwig Wittgenstein.* Présentation, choix de textes, bibliographie (Philosophes de tous les temps, 54). Paris: Seghers, 1969. 185p.

   book reviews:
   R. Blanché, *Journal de Psychologie Normale et Patho-logique* 67 (1970):232-233;
   P. Gochet, *Revue Internationale de Philosophie* 23 (1969):88-89, 371-378.

103. Granger, Gilles-Gaston, ed. *Wittgenstein et le problème d'une philosophie de la science.* Colloque d'Aix-en-Provence, 21-26 juillet 1969. Paris: Editions du Centre de la Recherche Scientifique, 1970. 225p. *Revue Internationale de Philosophie* 23 (1969):88-89, 151-378.

Les rapports comprennent:
McGuinness, B. F.   "Philosophy of science in the
   Tractatus;"
Specht, E. K.   "Wittgenstein und das Problem des
   a priori;"
Pariente, J.-C.   "Bergson et Wittgenstein;"
Imbert, Cl.   "L'héritage frégéen du *Tractatus*;"
Granger, G.-G.   "Wittgenstein et la métalangue;"
Clevelin, M.   "Elucidation philosophique et 'écriture
   conceptuelle' logique dans le *Tractatus*;"
von Wright, G. H.   "Wittgenstein's views on probability;"
Black, M.   "Verificationism and Wittgenstein's reflec-
   tions on mathematics;"
Vuillemin, J.   "Remarques sur 4.442 du *Tractatus*;"
Bouveresse, J.   "La notion de 'grammaire' chez le
   second Wittgenstein;"
Raggio, A. R.   "'Family resemblance predicates',
   modalités et réductionnisme;"
Fann, K. T.   "Supplement to the Wittgenstein bibliography." [Also in *International Philosophical
   Quarterly* 7 (1967):311-339]

book reviews:
J.-L. Kahn, *Revue des Questions Scientifiques* 141
   (1970):129-133;
A. Mercier, *Erasmus* 23 (1971):589-592.

104.   Hottois, Gilbert. *La philosophie du langage de
Ludwig Wittgenstein*.   Préface de J. Bouveresse (Université
Libre de Bruxelles. Faculté de Philosophie et Lettres,
63). Bruxelles: Editions de l'Université de Bruxelles,
1976. 220p.

   book reviews:
   A. Goldschläger, *La Pensee et les Hommes* 21 (1977-78):
      195-200;
   G. Hallett, *Gregorianum* 58 (1977):207-208;
   A. Reix, *Revue Philosophique de Louvain* 75 (1977):
      712-713.

105.   James, Dominique. *Le problème de l'erreur dans les*
Investigations Philosophiques *de Ludwig Wittgenstein*.
Basel: Verlag für Recht und Gesellschaft, 1974. [Ext. de:
Studia Philosophica 34 (1974):25-56]

106.   Janik, Allan S., et Toulmin, Stephen E. *Wittgen-
stein, Vienne et la modernité*. Traduit de l'américain par
Jacqueline Bernard (Perspectives critiques). Paris:
Presses Universitaires de France, 1978. 239p.

book review:
G. Even-Granboucan, *Revue de Métaphysique et de Morale* 84 (1979):258.

107. Kenny, Anthony. *Ce que Wittgenstein a vraiment dit.* Préface de Jean-François Malherbe. Traduction et adaptation de Jean-François Malherbe. (Marabout Université, 266. Connaître). Verviers: Marabout, 1975. 189p.

108. Lagache, Agnès. *Wittgenstein: La logique d'un dieu* (Collection Horizon philosophique). Paris: Editions du Cerf, 1975. 148p.

109. Leyvraz, Jean-Pierre. *La notion d'attente chez Wittgenstein.* Basel: Verlag für Recht und Gesellschaft, 1973. [Extr. de: *Studia Philosophica* 32 (1972):141-161]

110. Pears, David. *Wittgenstein* (Coll. Les maîtres modernes). Paris: Seghers, 1970. 256p.

book review:
R. Blanché, *Revue de Philosophie de la France et de l'Etranger* 97 (1972):118.

111. Poulain, Jacques. *Logique et religion. L'atomisme logique de L. Wittgenstein et la possibilité des propositions religieuses.* [Suivi de:] Logic and religion. A shortened and adapted version (Religion and reason, 7). The Hague-Paris: Mouton, 1973. 228p.

BOOKS IN GERMAN

112. Adler, Leo. *Ludwig Wittgenstein. Eine existenzielle Deutung.* Basel-München: S. Karger, 1976. 110p.

113. Bachmaier, P. *Wittgenstein und Kant: Versuch zum Begriff des Transzendentalen.* Frankfurt: Peter Lang, 1978. 213p.

114.   Bensch, Rudolf. *Ludwig Wittgenstein. Die apriorischen und mathematischen Sätze in seinem Spätwerk* (Abhandlungen zur Philosophie, Psychologie und Pädagogik, 79).
Bonn: Bouvier Verlag, 1973. 164p.

book reviews:
G. Hallett, *Gregorianum* 54 (1973):789-790;
V. Pittioni, *Conceptus* 7 (1973):96-99.

115.   Birnbacher, Dieter. *Die Logik der Kriterien.
Analysen z. Spätphilosophie Wittgensteins.* Hamburg:
Meiner, 1974, iv-155p.

116.   Borgis, Llona. *Index zu Ludwig Wittgensteins*
Tractatus Logico-Philosophicus und *Wittgenstein-Bibliographie.* Freiburg im Bresgau: Karl Alber Verlag, 1968.
112p.

book reviews:
M. Brander, *Freiburger Zeitschrift für Philosophie und
      Theologie* 16 (1970):226;
G. König, *Philosophy and History* 2 (1969):133-134;
R. Lay, *Theologie und Philosophie* 44 (1969):463-464;
J. P. Seibold, *Stromata* 26 (1970):137-138.

117.   Brand, Gerd. *Die grundlegenden Texte von Ludwig
Wittgenstein.* Frankfurt am Main: Suhrkamp, 1975. 217p.

book review:
W. Vossenkuhl, *Zeitschrift für Philosophische Forschung*
      31 (1977):467-470.

118.   Engelmann, P. *L. Wittgenstein. Briefe und
Begegnungen.* Brian F. McGuinness, hrsg. Wein-München:
Oldenburg, 1970. 127p.

book review:
A. Mercier, *Erasmus* 24 (1972):449-451.

119.   Fann, K. T. *Die Philosophie Ludwig Wittgensteins.*
Aus d. Engl. von Gisela Shaw (List-Taschenbücher der
Wissenschaft, 1642: Philosophie). München: List, 1971.
167p.

120. Gebauer, Gunter. *Wortgebrauch, Sprachbedeutung.*
Beitr. zu einer Theorie d. Bedeutung im Anschluss an. d.
spätere Philosophie Ludwig Wittgensteins (Grundfragen der
Literaturwissenschaft, 3). München: Bayerischer Schulbuch-
Verlag, 1971. 116p.

121. Giegel, Hans Joachim. *Die Logik der seelischen
Ereignisse. Zu Theorien von L. Wittgenstein und W. Sellars.*
Frankfurt am Main: Suhrkamp, 1969. 162p.

122. Hacker, P. M. S. *Einsicht und Täuschung. Wittgenstein über Philosophie u. d. Metaphysik d. Erfahrung.*
Übers. von Ursula Wolf. Frankfurt am Main: Suhrkamp, 1978.
422p.

123. Hartnack, Justus. *Wittgenstein und die moderne
Philosophie.* Aus d. Dan. von Rosemarie Lögstrup (Urban
Bücher). Stuttgart: Kohlhammer, 1962. 148p.

   book reviews:
   A. G. C., *Rivista di Filosofia* 53 (1962):357-358;
   E. Cassirer, *British Journal for the Philosophy of
      Science* 15 (1964-65):166-168;
   F. C. Copleston, *The Heythrop Journal* 7 (1966):321-325;
   W. von Del Negro, *Philosophischer Literaturanzeiger*
      15 (1962):267-269;
   J. H. Gill, *Philosophy and Phenomenological Research*
      27 (1966-67):137;
   J. B. Grize, *Revue de Théologie et de Philosophie* 13
      (1963):91;
   G. Hennemann, *Zeitschrift für Philosophische Forschung*
      20 (1966):338-341;
   T. Montúll, *Estudios Filosóficos* 12 (1963):563;
   G. Nuchelmans, *Foundations of Language* 2 (1966):270;
   M. Trinchero, *Rivista di Filosofia* 55 (1964):109-114.

124. Heinrich, R. *Einbildung und Darstellung. Zum
Kantianismus des frühen Wittgenstein.* Kastellaun,
Düsseldorf: A. Henn Verlag, 1977. 74p.

125. Kenny, Anthony. *Wittgenstein.* Aus d. Engl. von
Hermann Vetter (Suhrkamp-Taschenbücher Wissenschaft, 69).
Frankfurt am Main: Suhrkamp, 1974. 270p.

   book review:
   G. Megghe, *Erkenntnis* 9 (1975):139-143.

126.   Keyserling, A. *Der Wiener Denkstil.* Mach. Carnap.
Wittgenstein. Graz, 1965.

127.   Knüfermann, Bernhard. *Theorien Wittgensteins in der
Bildsprache* (Reihe A, 1). München: Willing, 1967. 140p.

128.   Lang, Martin. *Wittgensteins philosophische Grammatik.
Entstehung und Perspektiven der Strategie eines radikalen
Aufklärers.* 's-Gravenhage: Martinus Nijhoff, 1971, v-160p.

   book review:
   H. Parret, *Tijdschrift voor Filosofie* 34 (1972):594-595.

129.   Lubbe, Hermann. *Bewusstsein in Geschichten. Studien
zur Phänomenologie der Subjektivität: Mach, Husserl,
Schapp, Wittgenstein* (Rombach-Hochschulpaperback, 37).
Freiburg: Verlag Rombach, 1972. 174p.

   book review:
   R. Gralhoff, *Archiv für Rechts-und Sozialphilosophie*
      60 (1974):296-299.

130.   Marcuschi, Luiz Antônio. *Die Methode des Beispiels.
Unters. über d. method. Funktion d. Beispiels in d.
Philosophie, insbesondere bei Ludwig Wittgenstein* (Erlanger
Studien, 13). Erlangen: Palm und Enke, 1976, xvi-236p.

131.   Müller, Anselm Winfried. *Ontologie in Wittgensteins*
Tractatus (Abhandlungen zur Philosophie, Psychologie und
Pädagogik, 41). Bonn: Bouvier, 1967, xiii-250p.

   book review:
   E. Heintel, *Wiener Jahrbuch für Philosophie* 2 (1969):
      366-369.

132.   Pears, David. *Ludwig Wittgenstein.* Aus d. Engl. von
Ulrike von Savigny (dtv-Taschenbücher, 780: Moderne
Theoretiker). München: Deutscher Taschenbuch-Verlag, 1971.
195p.

133. Pitcher, George. *Die Philosophie Wittgensteins. Eine
krit. Einf. in d. Tractatus und d. Spätschriften.* Ubertr.
von Eike von Savigny. Freiburg im Bresgau-München: Karl
Alber Verlag, 1971. 195p.

> book review:
> J. Möller, *Theologische Quartalschaft* 119 (1969):198-
> 200.

134. Rossi-Landi, Ferrucio. *Sprache als Arbeit und Markt.*
München: Carl Hanser Verlag, 1972. 254p.

135. Schulz, Walter. *Wittgenstein: Die Negation der
Philosophie.* Stuttgart: Verlag Günther Neske Pfullingen,
1967. 113p.

> book reviews:
> A. Bharati, *Zeitschrift für Philosophische Forschung*
>   24 (1970):313-315;
> C. J. Boschheurne, *Streven* 21 (1967-68):821;
> W. von Del Negro, *Philosophischer Literaturanzeiger*
>   21 (1968):330-334;
> G. König, *Philosophy and History* 1 (1968):192-193;
> M. Presas, *Revista de Filosofía* (La Plata) (1969):52-
>   58;
> M. Presas, *Diálogos* (1969):341-345.

136. Shibles, Warren A. *Wittgenstein. Sprache und
Philosophie.* Dt. von Suzanne Mackiewicz (Bouvier dispu-
tanda, 5). Bonn: Bouvier Verlag, 1973. 172p.

137. Specht, Ernest Konrad. *Die sprachphilosophischen und
ontologischen Grundlagen im Spätwerk Ludwig Wittgensteins.*
Kantstudien, Ergänzungheft 84, Köln: Kölner Universitäts-
verlag, 1963.

> book reviews:
> N. Hilgenhager, *Archiv für Geschichte der Philosophie*
>   50 (1968):308-315;
> R. Norman, *Revue Philosophique de Louvain* 68 (1970):
>   401-405.

138. Stegmüller, Wolfgang. *Aufsätze zu Kant und Wittgenstein.* Darmstadt: Wissenschaftliche Buchges, 1970. 76p.

139. Stenius, Erik. *Wittgensteins* Traktatus. *Eine krit.*
Darlegung seiner Hauptgedanken. Aus d. Engl. von Wilhelm
Bader (Theorie. Reihe, 2). Frankfurt am Main: Suhrkamp,
1969. 310p.

140. Stetter, Christian. *Sprachkritik und Transformations-*
grammatik. Zur Bedeutung d. Philosophie Wittgensteins
§. d. sprachwiss. Theoriebildung. Düsseldorf: Pädagogischer
Verlag Schwann, 1974. 168p.

141. Studhalter, Kurt. *Ethik, Religion und Lebensform bei*
Ludwig Wittgenstein (Veröffentlichungen der Universität
Innsbruck, 82). Innsbruck: Universität Innsbruck, 1973.
78p.

142. Terricabras, J.-M. *Ludwig Wittgenstein. Kommentatur*
und Interpretationen. Frieberg-München: Karl Alber, 1978.
745p.

143. Wiggerhaus, Rolf, hrsg. *Sprachanalyse und Soziologie.*
Sie sozialwiss. Relevanz von Wittgensteins Sprachphilosophie.
(Suhrkamp-Taschenbücher Wissenschaft, 123). Frankfurt am
Main: Suhrkamp, 1975. 349p.

144. *Über Ludwig Wittgenstein.* With contributions by
Norman Malcolm, Peter Strawson, Newton Garver, and
Stanley Cavell. Frankfurt am Main: Suhrkamp, 1968.

145. *Wittgenstein: Schriften/Beiheft: Arbeiten über*
Wittgenstein. Mit Beitragen von I. Bachmann, et al.
Frankfurt am Main: Suhrkamp Verlag, 1960.

   CONTENTS:
   Bachmann, I. "Ludwig Wittgenstein. Zu einem Kapitel
      der jüngsten Philosophie-geschichte." 7-15;
   Cranston, M. "Bildnis eines Philosophen." 16-20;
   Ferrater Mora, J. "Wittgenstein oder die Destruktion."
      21-29;
   Feyeraband, P. "Ludwig Wittgenstein." 30-47;
   Heller, E. "Ludwig Wittgenstein. Unphilosophische
      Betrachtungen." 48-67;
   Russell, B. "Vorwort zum *Tractatus Logico-Philosophicus.*
      Übers. von Marcus Bierich." 68-81;
   von Wright, G. H. "Biographische Betrachtung." 82-99.

146. Wuchterl, Kurt. *Struktur und Sprachspiel bei
Wittgenstein* [Mit Bibliographie L. Wittgenstein] (Theorie,
Reihe 2). Frankfurt am Main: Suhrkamp Verlag, 1969. 220p.

  book review:
  T. Hanak, *Philosophischer Literaturanzeiger* 23 (1970):
    341-344.

147. Zimmermann, Jörg. *Wittgensteins sprachphilosophische
Hermeneutik* (Philosophische Abhandlungen, 46). Frankfurt
am Main: V. Klostermann, 1975, viii-318p.

BOOKS IN ITALIAN

148. Anscombe, G. E. M. *Introduzione al* Tractatus *di
Wittgenstein*. Trad. it. di E. Mistrelta (Collana di
filosofia e epistemologia). Roma: Ubaldini, 1966. 162p.

  book review:
  P. Cardoletti, *La Scuola Cattolica* 97 (1969):suppl.
    bibl. 158*-159*.

149. Antiseri, Dario. *Dopo Wittgenstein--Dove va la
filosofia analitica*. Roma: Edizioni Abete, 1967.

  book reviews:
  Fr. D'Agostino, *Rivista Internationale di Filosofia
    del Diritto* 48 (1971):163-164;
  U. Scarpelli, *Rivista di Filosofia* 59 (1968):88-92.

150. Barone, Francesco. *Il Neopositivismo logico*. Torino:
Edizioni di Filosofia, 1951.

151. Barone, Francesco. *Wittgenstein inedito* (Filosofia
della scienza, IV). Torino: Edizioni di Filosofia, 1953.
16p.

152. Bartley, William Warren, III. *Ludwig Wittgenstein,
maestro di scuola elementare*. Introduzione all'edizione
italiana di Dario Antiseri (Filosofia e problemi d'oggi,
42). Roma: Armando Armando, 1975. 203p.

153. Belohradsky, Vaclav. *Interpretazioni italiane di
Wittgenstein* (Studi sul pensiero filosofico e religioso dei
secoli XIX e XX, 21). Milano: Marzorati, 1972. 326p.

     book review:
     D. Rambaudi, *Giornale di Metafisica* 27 (1972):605-607.

154. Black, Max. *Manuale per il* Tractatus *di Wittgenstein*.
Trad. it. di R. Simone. Roma: Ubaldini, 1967. 438p.

     book reviews:
     Anonymous, *Ethica* 7 (1968):234-235;
     P. Cardoletti, *La Scuola Cattolica* 97 (1969):suppl.
       bibl. 160*-161*;
     A. Moreno, *Sapientia* 25 (1970):73-74;
     M. Trinchero, *Rivista di Filosofia* 59 (1968):351-354;
     A. von Pinto, *Revista Portuguesa de Filosofia* 8 (1970):
       suppl. bibl. 107*-108*.

155. Campanele, Domenico. *Studi su Wittgenstein*. Bari:
Ed. Adriatica, 1956, 275p; 2d ed., riveduta e aggiornata,
Bari: Adriatica, 1970, 264p.

     book review:
     A Babolin, *Rivista di Filosofia Neo-Scolastica* 63
       (1971):213-214.

156. Campanele, Domenico. *Problemi epistemologici de
Hume all'ultimo Wittgenstein*. Bari: Adriatica Editrice,
1961.

157. Cristaldi, Mariano. *Wittgenstein. L'ontologia
inibita*. Bologna: R. Patron, 1970. 394p.

158. Engelmann, P. *Lettere di Ludwig Wittgenstein con
ricordi*. Prefazione di Josef Schächter. Appendice di
Brian F. McGuinness. Trad. L. Roncaglia Cherubini
(Dimensioni, 11). Firenze: La Nuova Italia, 1970.

book reviews:
Br. Coppola, *Rivista critica di Storia della Filosofia*
24 (1971):153-154;
G. Frongia, *Giornale critico della Filosofia Italiana*
50 (1971):511-516;
U. Nuratore, *Rivista Rosminiana di Filosofia e di Cultura* 66 (1972):310-312;
M. Trinchero, *Rivista di Filosofia* 59 (1968):243-244.

159. Gargani, Aldo Giorgio. *Introduzione a Wittgenstein*
(I filosofi, 17). Roma: Laterza, 1973. 195p.

160. Gargani, Aldo Giorgio. *Linguaggio ed esperienza in Ludwig Wittgenstein* (Istituto di Filosofia dell'Università di Pisa). Pisa: Università degli studi, 1965. 58p.

161. Gargani, Aldo Giorgio. *Linguaggio ed esperienza in Ludwig Wittgenstein*. Firenze: F. Le Monnier, 1966, xii-504p.

book reviews:
M. Ferriana, *Rivista critica della Filosofia Italiana*
24 (1969):101-104;
A. M., *Review of Metaphysics* 22 (1968):144-145;
A. K. Marietti, *Etudes Philosophiques* (1968):459;
V. Novielli, *Filosofia* 19 (1968):321-330;
P. P., *Giornale critico della Filosofia Italiana*
47 (1968):161-164;
M. Rieser, *Journal of the History of Philosophy*
8 (1970):108-111;
M. Trinchero, *Rivista di Filosofia* 59 (1968):225-230.

162. Gellner, Ernest A. *Parole e cose. Un contributo critico all'analisi del linguaggio e uno studio sulla filosofia linguistica*. Introd. di E. Paci, prefazione di B. Russell. Trad. di Bruno Oddera (La Cultura, 41). Milano: Il Saggiatore, 1961.

book reviews:
N. Dazzi, *Giornale critico della Filosofia Italiana*
41 (1962):575-578;
A. G. Gargani, *Filosofia* 3 (1962):686-692.

163. Hartnack, Justus. *Wittgenstein e la filosofia moderna*. Trad. di Alfredo Marini (I Gabbiani, 62). Milano: Il Saggiatore, 1967. 167p.

book review:
P. Cardoletti, *La Scuola Cattolica* 97 (1969):suppl.
bibl. 161*-162*.

164. Janik, Allan, e Toulmin, Stephen E. *La grande Vienna*
[*Wittgenstein's Vienna*]. *Nella Vienna di Schönberg, di
Musil, di Kokoschka e del dottor Freud. La formazione
intellettuale del grande filosofo Wittgenstein.* Trad.
Ugo Giacomini (Saggi). Milano: Garzanti, 1975. 311p.

165. *Ludwig Wittgenstein e il Circolo di Vienna.* Colloqui
annotati da Friedrich Waismann. Presentazione di
B. F. McGuinness. Ed. italiana a cura di Sabina de Waal
(Dimensioni, 36). Firenze: La Nuova Italia, 1975. 253p.

166. Malcolm, Norman. *Ludwig Wittgenstein.* Con una
notizia biografica di G. H. von Wright. Trad. Bruno Oddera
(I satelliti Bompiani, 40). 3d ed., Milano: Bompiani,
1974. 135p.

book review:
G. Bortolaso, *La Civilta Cattolica* 112 (1961):414-415.

167. Marconi, Diego. *Il Mito del linguaggio scientifico.*
Studio su Wittgenstein (Biblioteca di filosofia, Richerche,
3). Milano: Mursia, 1971. 164p.

168. Micheletti, Mario. *Lo schopenhauerismo di Ludwig
Wittgenstein* (Università di Parma. Istituto di scienze
religiose, Saggi, 5). Padova: La Garangola, 1973. 190p.

book reviews:
Anonymous, *Ethica* 7 (1968):235;
A. Babolin, *Rivista di Filosofia Neo-Scolastica*
    65 (1973):630-633;
F. Guerrero Brezzi, *Aquinas* 18 (1975):293-295;
L. L., *Rivista di Filosofia Neo-Scolastica* 60 (1968):
    329-330;
A. Pieretti, *Studia Patavina* 16 (1969):177-179;
F. Rossi, *Sapienza* 30 (1977):114-116;
B. Salmona, *Giornale di Metafisica* 25 (1970):142-144.

169. Musciagli, Dario. *Logica e ontologia in Wittgenstein.*
Proposta d'analisi su struttura e conoscenza nel Tractatus.
Lecce: Milella, 1974. 197p.

170. Novielli, Valeria. *Wittgenstein e la filosofia*
(Pubblicazioni della Facoltà di Lettere e Filosofia della
Università degli Studi di Bari, 7). Bari: Adriatica
Editrice, 1969. 144p.

    book reviews:
    S. C. Becci, *Giornale critico della Filosofia Italiana*
      49 (1970):586-588;
    E. Namer, *Revue de Philosophie de la France et de*
      l'Etranger 95 (1970):256;
    L. M. P., *Review of Metaphysics* 24 (1970-71):751-752;
    R. Simili, *Rivista di Filosofia* 61 (1970):102-104;
    L. Thiry, *Dialogue* 10 (1971):207-209.

171. Novielli, Valeria. *Un libro su Wittgenstein.*
[A. G. Gargani, *Linguaggio ed esperienza in L. Wittgen-
stein*] (Sguardi su la filosofia contemporanea, 98).
Torino: Edizioni di Filosofia, 1968. 12p.

172. Piana, Giovanni. *Interpretazione del* Tractatus *di
Wittgenstein.* Milano: Il Saggiatore, 1973. 172p.

173. Riverso, Emanuele. *Ludwig Wittgenstein e il simbolismo logico.* Napoli, 1956.

174. Riverso, Emanuele. *Il pensiero di Ludovico Wittgenstein* (Filosofia e Pedagogia). Napoli: Libreria Scientifica Editrice, 1964, 392p; 2d ed., interamente rifatta,
Napoli: Libreria Scientifica Editrice, 1970, 484p.

    book review:
    P. F. Strawson, *Mind* 75 (1966):447 (1st ed.).

175. Riverso, Emanuele. *La filosofia analytica in
Inghilterra.* Roma: Armando Armando, 1969. 340p.

    book reviews:
    H. Bernard-Maître, *Revue de Synthèse* 91 (1970):128-129;
    L. Thiry, *Dialogue* 10 (1971):597-598;
    A. Trione, *Logos* 2 (1970):356-362.

BOOKS IN SPANISH

176.   Fann, K. T.   *El concepto de filosofía en Wittgenstein.*
Trad. Miguel Angel Bertrán (Col. Filosofía y Ensayo).
Madrid: Tecnos, 1975.   200p.

177.   Ferrater Mora, José, et al.   *Las filosofías de
Ludwig Wittgenstein.*   Trad. Ricardo Jordana (Libros Tau).
Vilasar de Mar (Barcelona): Oikos-Tau, 1966.   224p.

178.   Hartnack, Justus.   *Wittgenstein y la filosofía
contemporánea.*   Prólogo y traducción de las versiones
alemana e inglesa del original danés, por Jacobo Muñoz
(Col. Ariel Quicenal, 68).   Barcelona: Ediciones Ariel,
1972.   210p.

179.   Kenny, Anthony.   *Wittgenstein.*   Trad. del inglés por
Alfredo Deaño (Biblioteca de Filosofía, I).   Madrid:
Revista de Occidente, 1974.   207p.

180.   Pears, David.   *Wittgenstein.*   Trad. del inglés por
José Planells (Col. Maestros del Pensamiento Contemporáneo,
5).   Barcelona: Grijalbo, 1973.   315p.

   book reviews:
   E. A. Rabossi, *Revista Latinoamericana de Filosofía*
      1 (1975):72-73;
   J. A. Serrano, *Revista de Filosofía* (México) 7 (1974):
      404-406;
   E. Villanueva, *Crítica* 6 (1972):131-138.

181.   Santos Camacho, Modesto.   *Ética y filosofía analítica.
Estudio historico-crítico* [Wittgenstein y Toulmin].
Pamplona: Ediciones Universidad de Navarra, 1975.   822p.

182.   Schulz, Walter.   *La negación de la filosofía.*   Trad.
castellana de José Montoya Saenz (Colección Molina de Ideas,
6).   Madrid: G. del Toro, 1970.   115p.

   book review:
   V. Muñoz, *Salmanticensis* 18 (1971):187.

183. *Teorema, Sobre el* Tractatus Logico-Philosophicus.
(*Teorema*, 1972, número monográfico). Valencia: Universidad
de Valencia, 1972. 166p.

CONTENTS:
Pears, D. "The ontology of the *Tractatus*." 49-58;
Wolniewicz, B. "The notion of fact as a modal
   operator." 59-66;
Lorenz, K. "Zur Deutung der Abbildtheorie in Wittgen-
   steins *Tractatus*." 67-90;
Favrholdt, D. "The relation between thought and
   language in Wittgenstein's *Tractatus*." 91-100;
Blasco, J. L. "El lenguaje ordinario en el *Tractatus*."
   101-112;
Spisani, F. "Il concetto di identità in Wittgenstein."
   113-115;
Suárez García, A. "Es el lenguaje del *Tractatus* un
   lenguaje privado?" 117-130;
Hartnack, J. "The metaphysical subject." 131-138;
Garrido, M. "La logica del mundo." 139-152;
Vera, F. "Bibliografia." 153-166.

184. Van Peursen, C. A. *Ludwig Wittgenstein. Introducción
a su filosofía.* Buenos Aires: Ediciones Carlos Lohlé,
1973. 133p.

185. Waismann, Friedrich. *Ludwig Wittgenstein y el
círculo de Vienna.* México: Fondo de Cultura Económica,
1974.

BOOKS IN OTHER LANGUAGES

186. Beerling, R. F. *Wittgenstein geeft te denken.
Zesentwintig commentaren en een inleiding.* Meppel: Boom,
1974. 176p.

187. Hartnack, Justus. *Wittgenstein og den moderne
filosofi.* Kobenhavn: Gyldendal, 1960. 154p.

book review:
A. Stigen, *Inquiry* 5 (1962):167-175.

188. Hubbeling, H. G. *Inleiding tot het denken van Wittgenstein* (Born Pockets. Hoofdfiguren van het menselijk denken, H 8). 2e druk., Amsterdam, Assen: Born, N. V., 1969. 120p.

book review:
W. A. de Pater, *Foundations of Language* 6 (1972):601-602.

189. Islam, 'Azmi. *Ludwig Wittgenstein*. Le Caire: Dar al-Ma'aref, s.d. 396p.

190. Janik, Allen, and Toulmin, Stephen. *Het Wenen van Wittgenstein*. Vert. uit het Amerikaans door Hans W. Bakx en Paul de Bruin. Meppel: Boom, 1976. 299p.

191. Kenny, Anthony. *Wittgenstein*. Vert. door Alice ter Meulen (Aula-boeken, 520. Filosofie). Utrecht, Antwerpen: Het Spectrum, 1974. 288p.

192. Naess, Arne. *Moderne filosoffer: Carnap, Wittgenstein, Heidegger, Sartre*. Copenhagen: Stjernebogerme Vintens Forlag, 1965.

193. Øfsti, Audun. *Språk og fornuft: Spørsmalet om subjektenes transcendentale enhetsett på bakgrunn av Wittgensteins senfilosofi*. Oslo-Bergen: Universitetsforlaget, 1976. 200p.

194. Pears, David. *Ludwig Wittgenstein*. Vert. uit het Engels door Mons Weijers (Oriëntatie op morgen). Amsterdam: Meulenhoff, 1973. 146p.

195. Pears, David. *As ideias de Wittgenstein*. Trad. de Octanny Silveira da Mota e Leonidas Hegenberg. São Paulo: Editoras Cultrix/USP, 1973. 191p.

196. Rossvaer, Viggo. *Kant og Wittgenstein*. Oslo: Universitet-forlaget, 1974, xii-471p.

197.   Shibles, Warren. *Wittgenstein, linguagem filosófica*.
Trad. de Leonidas Hegenberg e Octanny Silveira da Mota.
São Paulo: Cultrix, 1974.   157p.

198.   Van Peursen, C. A.   *Ludwig Wittgenstein* (Wijsgerige
monografieën).   Baarn: Het Wereldvenster, 1965.   112p.

   book reviews:
   M. Gosselin, *Dialoog* 6 (1965-66):251-252;
   A. Poncelet, *Streven* 19 (1965-66):710;
   H. Robbers, *Bijdragen* 27 (1966):454.

CHAPTER 2:
Dissertations

DOCTORAL DISSERTATIONS

199. Adler, Leo. "Ludwig Wittgenstein. Eine existenzielle Deutung." Basel, 1976, 110p. *Dissertation Abstracts European* 38, no. 3 (Spring 1978):2/3248c.

200. Allaire, Edwin B., Jr.. "A Critical Examination of Wittgenstein's *Tractatus*." Univ. of Iowa, 1960, 234p. *Dissertation Abstracts* 21: 1590A.

201. Allmaker, Ali Martin. "'Wholeness' in the Philosophy of the Later Wittgenstein and its Applicability to the Philosophy of Education." State Univ. of New York at Albany, 1972. *Dissertation Abstracts* 33 (1972):2603A.

202. Ameriks, Karlis Peter. "Cartesianism and Wittgenstein: The Legacy of Subjectivism in Contemporary Philosophy of Mind." Yale Univ., 1973. *Dissertation Abstracts* 34 (1973): 2690A.

203. Anderson, Leland Tyson. "Wittgenstein and the Logical Possibility of Immortality." Temple Univ., 1972. *Dissertation Abstracts* 33 (1972):356A.

204. Anthony, Clifford Hugh. "Language as a Mirror of the World in Wittgenstein's *Tractatus*." Univ. of Western Ontario (Canada), 1973. *Dissertation Abstracts* 35 (1974):508A.

205. Ard, David J. "Language, Reality and Religion in the Philosophy of Ludwig Wittgenstein." McMaster Univ. (Canada), 1978. *Dissertation Abstracts* 39 (1979):5570A.

206. Bell, David A. "Wittgenstein's Notion of Form of Life in the *Philosophical Investigations*." Univ. of North Carolina, 1976, 162p. *Dissertation Abstracts*, 38 (1977):838A.

207. Bell, Richard Henry. "Theology as Grammar: Uses of
Linguistic Philosophy for the Study of Theology with Special
Reference to Wittgenstein." Yale Univ., 1968. *Dissertation
Abstracts* 29: 4086A.

208. Benarab, G. "Die operativ-pragmatische Basis der
Sprachphilosophie Ludwig Wittgensteins. Eine Studie zur
Kontinuität Sprachphilosophie Wittgensteins." Hamburg, BRD.,
1973, 309p. *Dissertation Abstracts European* 37, no. 3
(Spring 1977).

209. Berlinski, David. "The Well-tempered Wittgenstein."
Princeton Univ., 1968, 171p. *Dissertation Abstracts* 29:
4045A.

210. Bildhauer, William M. "The Reality of God: An Investigation of the Adequacy of Wittgensteinian Fideism." Univ.
of Arizona, 1972. *Dissertation Abstracts* 33(1973):6394-6395A.

211. Bindeman, Steven. "The Role of Silence in the Philosophies of Martin Heidegger and Ludwig Wittgenstein."
Duquesne Univ., 1978, 233p. *Dissertation Abstracts* 39 (1978):
1631A.

212. Binkley, Timothy Glenn. "Wittgenstein's Language."
Univ. of Texas at Austin, 1970, 294p. *Dissertation Abstracts*
31 (1971):3591A.

213. Blocker, H. E. "An Examination of Problems Involved
in the Ascription of Emotive Features to Works of Art."
Univ. of California at Berkeley, 1966.

214. Bitar, Byron I. "Wittgenstein's Conception of Philosophy and the Problem of Private Language." Univ. of Virginia,
1977, 245p. *Dissertation Abstracts* 39 (1979):4317A.

215. Boer, Steven E. "Language Games. An Interpretation
and Critique of the Later Wittgenstein's Philosophy of
Language." Univ. of Michigan, 1973. *Dissertation Abstracts*
34 (1973):1961A.

216. Bogen, James B. "Aspects of the Development of
Wittgenstein's Philosophy of Language." Univ. of California
at Berkeley, 1968, 474p. *Dissertation Abstracts* 29: 1248A.

217. Buchanan, Rupert. "Wittgenstein's Discussion of
Sensation." Duke Univ., 1966, 260p. *Dissertation Abstracts*
27: 3900A.

218. Burlingame, Charles E. "On the Logic of 'Seeing as'
Locution." Univ. of Virginia, 1965.

219. Callopy, Bartholomew, J. "Wittgenstein and Religious
Discourse: Some Possibilities for Theological Investigation."
Yale Univ., 1972. *Dissertation Abstracts* 33: 2479A.

220.   Campbell, William E.   "Wittgenstein's Picture Theory
of Meaning."   Washington Univ., 1973.   *Dissertation Abstracts*
34 (1974):6038A.

221.   Carlson, John W.   "Wittgenstein on Language and Philo-
sophical Understanding: A Study of Continuities in his
Thought."   Univ. of Notre Dame, 1970, 285p.   *Dissertation
Abstracts*, 31: 4834A.

222.   Cavalier, Robert J.   "Wittgenstein, Ethics and the
Will: An Interpretation of the *Tractatus*."   Duquesne Univ.,
1978, 258p.   *Dissertation Abstracts* 39 (1978):1632A.

223.   Cavell, Stanley.   "The Claim to Rationality."   Harvard
Univ., 1961.

224.   Churchill, John H.   "Wittgenstein and Philosophy of
Religion."   Yale Univ., 1977, 342p.   *Dissertation Abstracts*
39 (1978):1653-1654A.

225.   Cohen, Trevor E.   "Criteria and the Problem of Other
Minds in Wittgenstein's Later Philosophy."   Univ. of New
South Wales (Australia), 1975.   *Dissertation Abstracts* 36
(1976):6143A.

226.   Cooke, Vincent M.   "Wittgenstein's Use of the Private
Language Discussion."   Univ. of Wisconsin, 1971, 117p.
Dissertation Abstracts 32: 3363A.

227.   Craft, Jimmy Lee.   Some Remarks on Socrates and
Wittgenstein."   Univ. of Texas at Austin, 1977, 195p.
Dissertation Abstracts 38 (1977):2843A.

228.   Crowe, Charles Lawson.   "A New Estimate of the Signif-
igance of Wittgenstein's *Tractatus* for the Analysis of
Theological Discourse."   Columbia Univ., 1961.   *Dissertation
Abstracts* 22: 3276A.

229.   d'Hert, I. "Wittgenstein's Relevance for Theology."
Univ. of Fribourg (Switzerland), 1974.

230.   Dipre, Gilio L.   "The Language Games of Wittgenstein:
A Prolegomenon to a Metaphysics of Being."   Saint Bonaventure
Univ., 1968, 184p.   *Dissertation Abstracts* 30: 5479A.

231.   Dunlop, Lowell Alverson.   "Sense, Nonsense et Sense-
lessness.   An Essay in the Continuity of the Thought of
Wittgenstein."   Marquette Univ., 1972.   *Dissertation Abstracts*
33 (1973):5774-5775A.

232.   Edwards, James Creighton. "Persuasion and Discovery:
A Study of Wittgenstein's Philosophy."   Univ. of North
Carolina at Chapel Hill, 1972.   *Dissertation Abstracts* 33
(1973):4470A.

233. Ellos, W. "Attitudes and Thought: A Study in Wittgensteinian Cognition." Pontifica Universitatis Gregoriana, 1975, 963p. *Dissertation Abstracts European* 37 (Autumn 1976):25.

234. Erde, Edmund Lyman. "Philosophy and Science. Wittgenstein and Chomsky: An Examination of the Current Theory of Innate Ideas." Univ. of Texas at Austin, 1970, 218p. *Dissertation Abstracts* 31: 1839A.

235. Fahrnkopf, Robert Leroy. "Wittgenstein on Universals." Univ. of British Columbia (Canada), 1973. *Dissertation Abstracts* 34 (1974):7820A.

236. Fann, Kuang Tih. "Wittgenstein's Conception of Philosophy." Univ. of Hawaii, 1967. *Dissertation Abstracts* 29: 634A.

237. Fay, Thomas A. "Heidegger on Logic: An Encounter of his Thought with Wittgenstein." Fordham Univ., 1971, 350p. *Dissertation Abstracts* 32: 1012A.

238. Fitzgerald, Gisela. "The Language of Private Sensations: Russell in Light of Wittgenstein's Private Langauge Remarks." Purdue Univ., 1973. *Dissertation Abstracts* 35 (1974):513-514A.

239. Fulmer, Gilbert Everett. "Wittgenstein, Relativism and Reason." Rice Univ., 1972. *Dissertation Abstracts* 33 (1972):1780A.

240. Garver, Newton. "Grammar and Cirteria." Cornell Univ., 1965.

241. Genova, Judith. "An Approach to Wittgenstein's Metaphysics." Brandeis Univ., 1970, 187p. *Dissertation Abstracts* 31: 2970A.

242. Gettner, Alan F. "Analytic Truth in the Philosophies of Quine and the Later Wittgenstein." Columbia Univ., 1971, 244p. *Dissertation Abstracts* 32: 3209A.

243. Gibbens, Helen Paxton. "Berkeley and Wittgenstein. Some Correlations." Univ. of Oklahoma, 1970, 169p. *Dissertation Abstracts* 31: 2437A.

244. Goff, Robert Allen. "The Language of Method in Wittgenstein's *Philosophical Investigations*." Drew Univ., 1967, 153p. *Dissertation Abstracts* 28: 1847A.

245. Goldblatt, David A. "Wittgenstein, Rules and Logical Necessity." Univ. of Pennsylvania, 1972. *Dissertation Abstracts* 33 (1972):1780A.

246. Goldenberg, P. S. "A Comparative Analysis of Wittgenstein's *Tractatus* and Samkara's Advaita Vedanta with an
Introduction to the Logic of Comparative Methodology."
Univ. of Hawaii, 1977, 248p. *Dissertation Abstracts* 38
(1977):2845A.

247. Grant, Brian E. J. "Wittgenstein on Pain and Privacy."
Univ. of California at Irvine, 1968, 137p. *Dissertation
Abstracts* 29: 3201A.

248. Griffith, William B. "Problems about Infinity.
Wittgenstein's Contributions." Yale Univ., 1963, 144p.

249. Gross, Damon J. "Wittgenstein's Criticism of Platonism
in Mathematics." Univ. of Iowa, 1978, 201p. *Dissertation
Abstracts* 39 (1978):3631-3632A.

250. Gustason, William. "Negation and Assertion in Frege
and the *Tractatus*." Univ. of Michigan, 1968.

251. Hardwick, Charles S. "Language Learning and Language
Games in Wittgenstein's Later Work." Univ. of Texas at
Austin, 1967, 217p. *Dissertation Abstracts* 28: 1849A.

252. Hargrove, Eugene Carroll. "Wittgenstein and Ethics."
Univ. of Missouri at Columbia, 1974. *Dissertation Abstracts*
36 (1975):1578A.

253. Harris, Charles Edwin, Jr. "Wittgenstein's Criticism
of Ostensive Explanation." Vanderbilt Univ., 1964, 218p.
Dissertation Abstracts 25: 5332A.

254. Hart, Wilbur D. "Wittgenstein: Philosophy, Logic and
Mathematics." Harvard Univ., 1969, 232p.

255. Hicks, J. R. "Language-games and Inner Experience."
Univ. College, London, 1961.

256. High, Dallas Milton. "Language and Belief: Studies
in Wittgenstein's *Philosophical Investigations*." Duke
Univ., 1965. *Dissertation Abstracts* 26: 1194A.

257. Hoagland, Sarah Lucia. "The Status of Common Sense:
G. E. Moore and Ludwig Wittgenstein: A Comparative Study."
Univ. of Cincinnati, 1975. *Dissertation Abstracts* 36 (1975):
2256-2257A.

258. Howard, Michael Stuart. "Objects and Social Context
in Some Language-games: A Study in Wittgenstein's Later
Philosophy." Cornell Univ., 1975. *Dissertation Abstracts*
36 (1976):6750-6751A.

259. Hurst, Elaine Lancia. "Wittgenstein's Concept of
'Person': A Developmental and Critical Study." Fordham
Univ., 1976. *Dissertation Abstracts* 37 (1976):1022A.

260.   Ishikawa, Yukinou.   "The Critical Philosophy of
Wittgenstein."   In process, Southern Illinois Univ. at
Carbondale, 1979.

261.   Janik, Allan S.   "Uncle Ludwig's Book on Ethics:
Wittgenstein's *Tractatus* Reconsidered."   Brandeis Univ.,
1970, 225p.   *Dissertation Abstracts* 32: 1016A.

262.   Kielkopf, Charles Francis.   "An Examination of Ludwig
Wittgenstein's *Remarks on the Foundations of Mathematics*."
Univ. of Minnesota, 1962, 195p.   *Dissertation Abstracts* 24:
329A.

263.   Kirby, Ronald V.   "The Other Mind Quandary."   Univ.
of California at Berkeley, 1966.

264.   Klenk, Virginia H.   "Wittgenstein's Philosophy of
Mathematics."   Univ. of Pittsburgh, 1972.   *Dissertation
Abstracts* 33 (1973):4477A.

265.   Kluge, Eike-Henner Wendelin.   "Functions and Things:
An Essay in the Metaphysics of Frege and Wittgenstein
(Volumes I and II)."   Univ. of Michigan, 1968, 380p.
Dissertation Abstracts 29: 2753A.

266.   Kreilkamp-Cudmore, Ann.   "Language as Wittgenstein's
Way of Life."   Boston Univ. Graduate School, 1973.
Dissertation Abstracts 33 (1973):6965A.

267.   Kristiansen, Magne W.   "Relationships Between the
Later Writings of Ludwig Wittgenstein and their Readers."
Yale Univ., 1974.   *Dissertation Abstracts* 35 (1975):4617A.

268.   La Fave, Sandra.   "The Conception of Instinct."
Claremont Graduate School, 1979, 366p.   *Dissertation
Abstracts* 39 (1979):6811A.

269.   Lanfear, Jimmy Ray.   "An Analysis of Wittgenstein's
Locution 'Meaning as Use.'"   Rice Univ., 1968, 223p.
Dissertation Abstracts 29: 1568A.

270.   Lawhead, William Fisher.   "Wittgenstein and Merleau-
Ponty on Language and Critical Reflection."   Univ. of Texas
at Austin, 1978.

271.   Lee, Myung-Hyun.   "The Later Wittgenstein's Reflection
on Meaning, Language and Forms of Life."   Brown Univ., 1974.
Dissertation Abstracts 35 (1975):7351A.

272.   Lemoine, Roy Emanuel.   "The Anagogic Theology of
Wittgenstein's *Tractatus*."   Florida State Univ., 1972.
Dissertation Abstracts 33 (1972):2427-2428A.

273.   Levin, Michael Eric.   "Wittgenstein's Philosophy of
Mathematics."   Columbia Univ., 1969, 526p.   *Dissertation
Abstracts* 30: 4494A.

274. Lewis, Harry A. "Criteria, Theory and Knowledge of Other Minds." Stanford Univ., 1967.

275. Long, Thomas A. "Wittgenstein. Criteria and Private Experience." Univ. of Cincinnati, 1965, 161p. *Dissertation Abstracts* 26: 4004A.

276. Macdonald, Douglas C. "Student Rights and Educational Freedom: A Philosophical Analysis of the Language of Court Decisions and the Writings of Paul Goodman and John Holt Viewed Through the Perspectives of Wittgenstein." Temple Univ., 1979, 257p. *Dissertation Abstracts* 39 (1979):6624A.

277. Martin, Dean Monroe. "Christian Consciousness: Its Emergence with the Mastery of Concepts within the Christian Community with Special Reference to L. Wittgenstein." Baylor Univ., 1972. *Dissertation Abstracts* 33(1973):5279A.

278. Martin, Margaret J. "The Views of Whitehead and Wittgenstein in *Process and Reality* and *The Tractatus Logico-philosophicus*." Southern Illinois at Carbondale, 1978, 163p. *Dissertation Abstracts* 39 (1978):922A.

279. Maslow, Alexander P. "A Study in Ludwig Wittgenstein's *Tractatus Logico-philosophicus*." Univ. of California at Berkeley, 1934.

280. McBride, Frank Abbott. "The Later Wittgenstein's Conception of Teaching." Michigan State Univ., 1972. *Dissertation Abstracts* 33 (1972):2428A.

281. McCauley, Leland Mason, III. "The Grammar of Social and Scientific Discourse and its Educational Value. A Study in Chomsky and Wittgenstein." Univ. of Pittsburgh, 1975. *Dissertation Abstracts* 36 (1975):2160-2161A.

282. McDonough, Richard Michael. "Wittgenstein and the Law of the Excluded Middle." Cornell Univ., 1975. *Dissertation Abstracts* 36 (1976):7475A.

283. Mollaneda, R. "Concrete Approach and Therapeutic Activity: Marcel and Wittgenstein on Doing Philosophy." Pontifica Universitatis Gregoriana, 1975, 446p. *Dissertation Abstracts European* 37 (Autumn 1976):1.

283a. Moran, John Henry. "Ludwig Wittgenstein's Philosophical Therapy." Fordham Univ., 1962, 443p. *Dissertation Abstracts* 23: 3420A.

284. Morick, Harold. Wittgenstein's Attack on the Privileged Access View of Thoughts and Feelings." Columbia Univ., 1966, 138p. *Dissertation Abstracts* 31: 426A.

285. Morrison, James Carlton. "Meaning and Truth in Wittgenstein's *Tractatus*." Pennsylvania State Univ., 1964, 176p. *Dissertation Abstracts* 25: 4752A.

286. O'Brien, George D. "Meaning and Fact: A Study in the Philosophy of Wittgenstein." Univ. of Chicago, 1961.

287. Park, Young S. "Wittgenstein's Version of Verifiability in the *Tractatus* ." Emory Univ., 1975. *Dissertation Abstracts* 36 (1976):4564A.

288. Penick, John Jacob. "Wittgenstein on Sensory Pyrrhonism." Univ. of North Carolina at Chapel Hill, 1975. *Dissertation Abstracts* 36 (1975):3773A.

289. Polk, John T. "Wittgenstein's Views on Philosophical Skepticism and Certainty." Fordham Univ., 1976. *Dissertation Abstracts* 37 (1976):1029A.

290. Premo, Blanche Lillie Kolar. "Wittgenstein's Notion of Description: From Logic to Grammar." Marquette Univ., 1974. *Dissertation Abstracts* 36 (1975):351-352A.

291. Price, Jeffrey Thomas. "Language and Being in Wittgenstein's *Philosophical Investigations* ." Pennsylvania State Univ., 1969, 141p. *Dissertation Abstracts* 31: 1845A.

292. Pushadham, P. "The 'Language Game' of Praising in Prayers." Pontifica Universitatis Gregoriana, 1975, 232p. *Dissertation Abstracts European* 37 (Spring 1977):479.

293. Quinn, Wylie S. "Kierkegaard and Wittgenstein: The 'religious' as a 'form of life'." Duke Univ., 1976, 222p. *Dissertation Abstracts* 37 (1977):7804A.

294. Raphael, Leyla. "Wittgenstein et Hertz: pour une lecture antipositiviste de Wittgenstein." McGill Univ., 1978. *Dissertation Abstracts* 39(1979):5556A.

295. Reeder, Harry D. "Public and Private Aspects of Language in Husserl and Wittgenstein." Univ. of Waterloo (Canada), 1977. *Dissertation Abstracts* 38 (1977):2852A.

296. Robinson, John Hayes. "Seeing the World Aright: A Study of Wittgenstein's Pretractarian Notebooks." Univ. of Notre Dame, 1975. *Dissertation Abstracts* 36 (1975):1585A.

297. Rolston, Howard Lee. "Wittgenstein's Concept of Family Resemblance." Harvard Univ., 1972, 276p.

298. Ruddick, Sara L. "Wittgenstein on Sensation Statement." Harvard Univ., 1963.

299. Savitt, Steven Frederick. "Frege and Wittgenstein on Identity, Logic and Number." Brandeis Univ., 1972, 172p. *Dissertation Abstracts* 32: 7047A.

300. Schenck, John R. "An Analysis of the Concepts of Curriculum Through Wittgenstein's Concept of Language-games." Washington State Univ., 1978, 158p. *Dissertation Abstracts* 39 (1979):4905A.

301. Schmucker, Larry Alan. "Wittgenstein's Remarks on Basic Views." Univ. of Texas at Austin, 1970, 263p. *Dissertation Abstracts* 32: 4066A.

302. Sefler, Geroge Francis. "The Structure of Language and its Relation to the World. A Methodological Study of the Writings of M. Heidegger and L. Wittgenstein." Georgetown Univ., 1970, 312p. *Dissertation Abstracts* 31: 2979A.

303. Sheridan, G. R. "The Privacy of Mind: An Essay on the Logic of Psychological Statements." Univ. of California at Los Angeles, 1966.

304. Sherman, Gail R. "Images of Power: The Investigation-after Wittgenstein-of 'the Multinational Corporation' as a Political Concept." Univ. of Wisconsin-Madison, 1978, 447p. *Dissertation Abstracts* 39 (1978):3119A.

305. Shwayder, D. S. "Wittgenstein's *Tractatus* : A Historical and Critical Commentary." Oxford Univ., 1954.

306. Schwyzer, H. R. G. "The Acquisition of Concepts and the Use of Language." Univ. of California at Berkeley, 1968.

307. Sievert, Donald Edward. "Austin, Wittgenstein and Strawson on Mind." Univ. of Iowa, 1967, 141p. *Dissertation Abstracts* 28: 3229A.

308. Smerud, Warren D. "Can There Be a Private Language? A Review of Some Principal Arguments." Univ. of Washington, 1967.

309. Smucker, Jan Arden. "A Study of the Problem of Determining Ontological Commitments in Wittgenstein's *Tractatus* ." Michigan State Univ., 1969, 278p. *Dissertation Abstracts* 31: 1326A.

310. Stawinski, Arthur Walter. "L. Wittgenstein and the Perceptual Foundations of Knowledge." Northwestern Univ., 1973. *Dissertation Abstracts* 34 (1974):4345A.

311. Steinman, Diane. "The Role of the Notion of Grammar in Wittgenstein's Later Work." Univ. of Minnesota, 1977, 232p. *Dissertation Abstracts* 38 (1977):3565A.

312. Stith, Robert Charles. "A Phenomenological Interpretation of Wittgenstein." Duquesne Univ., 1972. *Dissertation Abstracts* 33 (1972):2432A.

313. Stratton, John Reginald. "Analysis and Individuals. An Examination of the Notions of a Picture, Objects, and Sense in Wittgenstein's *Tractatus* ." Univ. of Toronto (Canada), 1969. *Dissertation Abstracts* 32 (1971):1572A.

314. Strickler, Nina. "The Problem of the Absolute: A Study of Spinoza, Hegel and Wittgenstein." De Paul Univ., 1973. *Dissertation Abstracts* 34 (1973):3475A.

315. Stripling, Scott. "The Picture Theory of Meaning. An Interpretation of Wittgenstein's *Tractatus Logico-philosophicus*." Pennsylvania State Univ., 1976. *Dissertation Abstracts* 37 (1976):1032A.

316. Sullivan, Thomas D. "The Problem of Universals in the Later Wittgenstein." St. John's Univ., 1969, 244p. *Dissertation Abstracts* 31: 804A.

317. Taylor, Ken Hewitt. "Wittgenstein and Melville: A Study in the Character of Meaning." Univ. of California at Santa Barbara, 1976, 222p. *Dissertation Abstracts* 38 (1977): 763A.

318. Temkin, Jack. "Wittgenstein on the Privacy of Sensation." Univ. of Wisconsin-Madison, 1976. *Dissertation Abstracts* 37(1976):2951A.

319. Thibodeau, Eugene Francis. "An Interpretation of Wittgenstein's Later (1929-1951) Philosophy of Mathematics." New York Univ., 1973. *Dissertation Abstracts* 34 (1973):826A.

320. Toland, William G. "The Later Wittgenstein and Classical Pragmatism: A Critical Appraisal." Univ. of North Carolina at Chapel Hill, 1967, 262p. *Dissertation Abstracts* 28: 4670A.

321. Tominaga, Thomas Toyashi. "A Wittgensteinian Inquiry into the Confusions Generated by the Question 'What is the Meaning of a Word?'" Georgetown Univ., 1973. *Dissertation Abstracts* 34 (1974):4335A.

322. Vaugh, Scott R. "Pedagogical Experience and Theory of Meaning in Dewey and Wittgenstein." Michigan State Univ., 1976, 161p. *Dissertation Abstracts* 37 (1977):7608A.

323. Verharen, Charles Coulter. "The Demarcation of Philosophy from Science and Art in the Methodology of Wittgenstein." Georgetown Univ., 1978.

324. Wallace, Kyle Lee. "Wittgenstein's Theory of Meaning." Univ. of Miami, 1969, 234p. *Dissertation Abstracts* 30: 3509A.

325. Weinbren, Grahame. "Mysticism, Solipsism, and Judgment: The Conception of the Mind in the *Tractatus* and some related problems." State Univ. of New York at Buffalo, 1976.

326. Whelan, John Matthew. "Private Language Reexamined." Univ. of Texas at Austin, 1976.

327. White, J. F. "Cartesian Privacy and the Problem of Other Minds." Univ. of Colorado, 1968.

328. Wider, Kathleen V. "A Kantian-Wittgensteinian Approach to the Problem of Other Minds." Wayne State Univ., 1978, 314p. *Dissertation Abstracts* 39 (1979):6177A.

329. Wiebenga, William Martin. "Wittgenstein's Theory of Meaning." Yale Univ., 1966, 284p. *Dissertation Abstracts* 27: 3087A.

330. Wolters, Richard Mark. "Wittgenstein's Ontology in his Early Works." Univ. of Massachusetts, 1974. *Dissertation Abstracts* 34 (1974):525a.

331. Womack, James. "Quine and Wittgenstein on Reference." New York Univ., 1976, 259p. *Dissertation Abstracts* 37 (1977):5891A.

332. Yoos, George E. "An Analysis of Three Studies of Pictorial Representation: M. C. Beardsley, E. H. Gombrich, and L. Wittgenstein." Univ. of Missouri-Columbia, 1971, 231p. *Dissertation Abstracts* 32: 3377A.

333. Young, Iris Marion. "From Anonymity to Speech: A Reading of Wittgenstein's Later Writing." Pennsylvania State Univ., 1974. *Dissertation Abstracts* 35 (1975):7358A.

334. Zweig, Arnulf. "Theories of Real Definition: A Study of the Views of Aristotle, C. I. Lewis, and Wittgenstein." Stanford Univ., 1960, 194p. *Dissertation Abstracts* 21 (1960):212A.

MASTER'S THESES

335. Amdur, Stephen. "Toward an Understanding of the Later Philosophy of Wittgenstein." Univ. of New Mexico, 1967.

336. Gibbs, B. R. "Wittgenstein and the Problem of Meaning." Univ. of Canterbury (New Zealand), 1961.

337. Ginnane, W. J. "Thought, Language and Behavior. With Particular Reference to the Later Works of Wittgenstein." Univ. of Melbourne (Australia), 1958.

338. Hilmy, Sameer S. "Irrationalism in the Philosophies of Heidegger and Wittgenstein." The American Univ., 1976, 123p. *Masters Abstracts* 14 (1976):247.

339. Sivasambu, N. "Some Problems in the *Tractatus* ." University College (London), 1961.

340. Sanderson, Donald G. "The Philosophical Methods of Wittgenstein's *Philosophical Investigations* ." Florida State Univ., 1969.

341. Shaw, J. W. "The Influence of the Later Philosophy of Wittgenstein upon the Philosophy of Mind." Bangor College (Wales), 1962.

CHAPTER 3:
Studies of Individual Works by Wittgenstein

1) *Nachlass*

342. *Nachlass*. The originals of the Wittgenstein papers are kept in the Wren Library, Trinity College, Cambridge, England. The total material microfilmed in twenty reels is available from Cornell University Library, Ithaca, New York. An account of the scope and character of the *Nachlass* is given by Georg Henrik von Wright in "Special Supplement: The Wittgenstein Papers," *Philosophical Review* 78 (1969):483-503. [As indicated in the Introduction, in the past decade, a large amount of Wittgenstein's *Nachlass* and several of his lectures and letters have been made available to the public. This includes the *Prototractatus*, *Remarks on the Foundations of Mathematics*, *Zettel*, *On Certainty*, and *On Colour*.]

2) "Notes on Logic" (September 1913)

343. Anscombe, G. E. M., Rhees, R., and von Wright, G. H. "A note on Costello's version of the 'Notes on Logic'." *Journal of Philosophy* 54 (1957):484.

344. Kurtz, Paul W. "Letter to the Editor concerning Wittgenstein's 'Notes on Logic'." *Journal of Philosophy* 59 (1962):78-79.

345. McGuinness, B. F. "B. Russell and L. Wittgenstein. 'Notes on Logic'." *Revue Internationale de Philosophie* 26 (1972):444-460.

3) *Notebooks 1914-1916*

346. Bernstein, R. J. "Notice of *Notebooks*." *Review of Metaphysics* 15 (1961):197.

347. Black, Max. "Critical Notice of *Notebooks*." *Mind* 73 (1964):132-141.

348. Bouveresse, Jacques. "La voie et le moyen." *Critique* 28 (1972):444-459.

349. Copi, I. M. "Review of *Notebooks*." *Journal of Philosophy* 60 (1963):764-768.

350. Davie, I. "Review of *Notebooks*, Anscombe, and Stenius." *Tablet* 215 (May 6, 1961):440.

351. Preus, R. D. "Review of *Notebooks*." *Concordia Theological Monthly* 33 (1962):120.

352. Riverso, E. "Review of *Notebooks*." *Rassegna di Scienze Filosofiche* 15 (1962):252.

353. Robinson, John H. "Seeing the World Aright: A Study of Wittgenstein's Pretractarian *Notebooks*." Ph.D. Dissertation, Univ. of Notre Dame, 1975. *Dissertation Abstracts* 36 (1975):1585A.

354. Trinchero, M. "Review of *Notebooks*." *Rivista di Filosofia* 55 (1964):495-497.

355. Weiler, G. "Review of *Notebooks*." *Philosophical Books* 2 (1961):16-18.

356. Wienpahl, Paul. "Wittgenstein's *Notebooks 1914-1916*." *Inquiry* 12 (1969):287-316.

357. Unsigned. "The essential nature of propositions." (Review of *Notebooks*.) *Times Literary Supplement* 60 (August 11, 1961):528.

4) *Tractatus Logico-Philosophicus*

A) Critical Studies

358. Agacinski, S. "Decoupages du *Tractatus*." In *Mimesis des Articulations*. S. Agacinski and J. Derrida, et al. Paris: Aubier-Flammarion, 1975, 17-53.

359. Allaire, Edwin B. "*Tractatus* 6.3751." *Analysis* 19 (1959):100-105. Reprinted in Copi and Beard. [See no. 14]

360.   Allaire, Edwin B.   "Types and formation rules: A note on *Tractatus* 3.334." *Analysis* 21 (1961):14-16.

361.   Allaire, Edwin B.   "The *Tractatus*: Nominalistic or realistic." In *Essays in Ontology*.   E. B. Allaire, et al., eds.   The Hague: Martinus Nijhoff, 1963, 148-165.   Reprinted in Copi and Beard. [See no. 14]

----   Allaire, Edwin B.   "A critical examination of Wittgenstein's *Tractatus*." [See no. 200]

362.   Anscombe, G. E. M.   "Mr. Copi on 'Objects, Properties and Relations in the *Tractatus*'." *Mind* 68 (1959):404. Reprinted in Copi and Beard. [See no. 14]

----   Anscombe, G. E. M.   *An Introduction to Wittgenstein's* Tractatus. [See nos. 3 and 148]

----   Anthony, Clifford H.   "Language as a mirror of the world in Wittgenstein's *Tractatus*. [See no. 204]

363.   Battistella, Ernesto H.   "Interpretación del atomismo lógico del *Tractatus* mediante la lógica modal relativa de von Wright." *Revista Venezolana de Filosofía* (Caracas) (1976):7-18.

364.   Beard, R. W.   "*Tractatus* 4.24." *Southern Journal of Philosophy* 2 (1964):14-17.

365.   Bergmann, Gustav.   "Stenius on the *Tractatus*." *Theoria* 29, Part 2 (1963):176-204.   Reprinted in his *Logic and Reality*.   Madison: Univ. of Wisconsin Press, 242-271.   Also reprinted in Klemke. [See no. 57]

366.   Bergmann, G.   "The glory and the misery of Ludwig Wittgenstein."   In Copi and Beard. [See no. 14]

367.   Bertman, Martin A.   "Non-extentional propositions in Wittgenstein." *International Logical Review* 3 (1972):73-77.

368.   Bickenbach, Jerome E.   "The status of the propositions in the *Tractatus*." *Dialogue* 13 (1974):763-772.

369.   Block, Irving.   "Hart on the *Tractatus*." [W. D. Hart, *The Whole Sense of the* Tractatus.] *International Logical Review* 6 (1975):145-157.

370.   Black, I.   "'Showing' in the *Tractatus*: The root of Wittgenstein and Russel's basic incompatability." *Russell* (Spring 1975):4-22.

371.   Black, Max.   "Wittgenstein's *Tractatus*." In *Language and Philosophy*.   Ithaca (New York): Cornell Univ. Press, 1949, 139-165.

---- Black, Max. A *Companion to Wittgenstein's* Tractatus.
[See no. 8]

372. Blasco, Joseph Ll. "El lenguaje ordinario en el
Tractatus." In *Teorema*, 1972, 101-112.

373. Bonessio di Terzet, Ettore. "Ontologia e linguaggio
nel *Tractatus* di Wittgenstein." *Rivista Rosminiana* 69
(1975):344-355.

374. Borgis, Llona. *Index zu Ludwig Wittgensteins*
Tractatus Logico-Philosophicus. [See no. 116]

375. Burgos, Rafael. "Sobre el concepto de objeto en el
Tractatus." *Critica* (Mexico) 2 (1968):71-89.

376. Campanale, Domenico. "Ludwig Wittgenstein: *Tractatus
Logico-Philosophicus*." *Rassegna di Scienze Filosofiche*
7 (1954):421-428.

379. Campanale, Domenico. "Linguaggio e ontologia nel
Tractatus di Wittgenstein." In *Il Problema Filosofico
del Linguaggio*. Acura del Centro di Studi Filosofici di
Gallarate. Padoua: Gregoriana, 1965, 13-19.

380. Canfield, John V. "*Tractatus* objects." *Philosophia*
(Israel) 6 (1976).

381. Cell, E. "The *Tractatus*: The limits of language."
In his *Language, Existence and God*. Introduction to
Moore and others. Abingdon, 1971, 117-140.

382. Chiodi, Pietro. "Essere e linguaggio in Heidegger
e nel *Tractatus* di Wittgenstein." *Rivista di Filosofia*
46 (1955):170-191.

383. Clavelin, Maurice. "Élucidation philosophique et
'écriture conceptuelle' logique dans le *Tractatus*." *Revue
Internationale de Philosophie* 23 (1969):237-256.
[Discussion: G. H. von Wright, M. Clavelin, G. G. Granger,
J. Vuillemin, A. R. Raggio, M. Black]

384. Clegg, J. S. "Logical mysticism and the cultural
setting of Wittgenstein's *Tractatus*." *Schopenhauer-Jahr-
buch* 59 (1978):29-47.

385. Cohen, Michael. "*Tractatus* 5.542." *Mind* 83 (1974):
442-444.

---- Copi, Irving M., and Beard, R. W., eds. *Essays
Wittgenstein's* Tractatus. New York: Macmillan, 1966, 414p;
London: Routledge & Kegan Paul. [See no. 14]

386. Copi, Irving M. "*Tractatus* 5.542." *Analysis* 18
(1958):102-104. Reprinted in Copi and Beard. [See no. 14]

387. Copi, I. M. "Objects, properties, and relations in
the *Tractatus*." *Mind* 67 (1958):146-165. Reprinted in
Copi and Beard. [See no 14]

388. Copi, I. M. "Frege and Wittgenstein's *Tractatus*."
Philosophia (Israel) 6 (1976).

389. Corral, Ana Maria. "La relacion Dios-mundo en el
Tractatus Logico-Philosophicus de Ludwig Wittgenstein."
Revista de Filosofía (México) 11 (1978):421-428.

390. Couprie, D. L. "Over de tautologie in Wittgenstein's
Tractatus." *Tijdschrift voor Filosofie* 26 (1964):106-139.

---- Crowe, Charles L. "A new estimate of the significance
of Wittgenstein's *Tractatus* for the analysis of theological
discourse." [See no. 228]

391. Cudahy, Brian J. "Portrait of the analyst as a
metaphysician. The ontological status of philosophy in
Wittgenstein's *Tractatus*." *Modern Schoolman* 43 (1965-66):
365-373.

392. Daniels, Charles B., and Davison, John. "Ontology
and method in Wittgenstein's *Tractatus*." *Noûs* 7 (1973):
233-247.

393. Dayton, Eric B. "*Tractatus* 5.54-5.5422." *Canadian
Journal of Philosophy* 6 (1976):275-285.

394. Elgin, Catherine Z. "Analysis and the picture theory
in the *Tractatus*." *Philosophical Research Archives* 2
(1976).

395. Elgin, C. Z. "The impossibility of saying what is
shown." *Southern Journal of Philosophy* 16 (1978):617-628.

396. Evans, E. "*Tractatus* 3.1432." *Mind* 64 (1955):259-
260. Reprinted in Copi and Beard. [See no. 14]

397. Favrholdt, David. *An Interpretation and Critique of
Wittgenstein's* Tractatus. Copenhagen: Munksgaard, 1964;
New York: Humanities Press, 1966. 228p.

398. Favrholdt, D. "*Tractatus* 5.542." *Mind* 73 (1964):
557-562. [A new interpretation of the passage 5.541-5.542
in the *Tractatus*]

399. Favrholdt, David. "The relation between thought and
language in Wittgenstein's *Tractatus*." *Teorema*, 1972,
91-100.

400. Fay, Thomas A. "Wittgenstein's critique of metaphysics in the *Tractatus*." *Philosophical Studies* (Ireland)
20 (1972):51-61.

---- Finch, Henry L. *Wittgenstein--The Early Philosophy*. *An Exposition of the* Tractatus. New York: Humanities Press, 1971. 291p. [See no. 28]

---- Ganguly, S. *Wittgenstein's* Tractatus. [See no. 32]

401. García Suárez, Alfonso. "Es el lenguaje del *Tractatus* un lenguaje privado?" *Teorema*, 1972, 117-130.

402. Garrido, M. "La lógica del mundo." *Teorema* 1972, 139-152.

403. Garver, Newton. "Wittgenstein's pantheism: A new light on the ontology of the *Tractatus*." In Klemke. [See no. 57]

404. Gava, Giacomo. "Il solipsismo nel *Tractatus* di Wittgenstein." In *Posizione e criterio del discorso filosofico*. A cura di Carlo Giacon. (Pubblicazioni dell'Istituto di Storia della Filosofia e del Centro per Ricerche di Filosofia Medioevale.) Bologna: R. Patrón, 1967, 61-78.

405. Ghins, Michel. "La forme et le sens dans le *Tractatus* de Wittgenstein." *Revue Philosophique de Louvain* 75 (1977): 453-480.

406. Giacomini, Ugo. "Interpretazioni del *Tractatus* di Wittgenstein." *Aut Aut* (1963):63-75.

407. Ginet, Carl. "An incoherence in the *Tractatus*." *Canadian Journal of Philosophy* 3 (1973-74):143-151.

---- Goldenberg, Daniel S. "A comparative analysis of Wittgenstein's *Tractatus* and Samkara's *Advaita Vedanta*. [See no. 246]

408. Granger, G. G. "L'argumentation du *Tractatus*. Systèmes philosophiques et métastructures." In *Hommage à Martial Gueroult. L'histoire de la philosophie, ses problèmes, ses méthodes*. Textes de Leslie J. Beck, Yvon Belaval, Jean-Louis Bruch, Fernand Brunner, Henry Duméry, Victor Goldschmidt, Henri Gouhier, G.-G. Granger, Heinz Heimsoeth, Jean Hyppolite, Ch. Perelman, Pierre-Maxime Schuhl, Livio Teixeira, Jules Vuillemin. Paris: Librairie Fischbacher, 1964, 139-154.

409. Granger, G. G. "Le probleme de l'espace dans le *Tractatus*." *L'Age de la Science* 1 (1968):181-195.

410. Granger, G. G. "Sur le concept du langage dans le *Tractatus*." *Word* 23 (1967):196-207.

411. Gustason, William. "*Tractatus* 2.0201-2.0212." *Canadian Journal of Philosophy* 4 (1974-75):515-527.

412.   Hacker, P. M. S.   "Laying the ghost of the *Tractatus*."
Review of Metaphysics 29 (1975):96-116.

413.   Hackstaff, L. H.   "A note on Wittgenstein's truth-
function-generating operation in *Tractatus* 6."   *Mind* 75
(1966):255-256.

414.   Hallett, Garth.   "Is there a picture theory of
'language' in the *Tractatus*?"   *The Heythrop Journal* 14
(1973):314-321.

415.   Harlan, Robert.   "Wittgenstein's critical project."
Graduate Faculty Philosophy Journal 6 (1977):209-240.

416.   Harrison, A.   "Representation and conceptual change."
In *Royal Institute of Philosophy.   Philosophy and the Arts*.
Vol. 3, 1968-69, 106-131.   (Published 1970)

417.   Hart, W. D.   "The whole sense of the *Tractatus*."
Journal of Philosophy 68 (1971):273-288.

418.   Hartnack, Justus.   "The metaphysical subject."
Teorema, 1972, 131-138.

---- Harward, Donald W.   *Wittgenstein's Saying and Showing
Themes*.   [See no. 41]

419.   Hawkins, D. J. B.   "Wittgenstein and the cult of
language."   In *Crucial Problems of Modern Philosophy*.
Univ. of Notre Dame Press, 1962, 66-79.

420.   Heil, John.   "*Tractatus* 4.0141."   *Philosophy and
Phenomenological Research* 38 (1978):545-548.

421.   Hochberg, H.   "Material properties in the *Tractatus*."
In Klemke.   [See no. 57]

422.   Hochberg, H.   "Facts, possibilities and essences in
the *Tractatus*."   In Klemke.   [See no. 57]

422a.   Hope, V.   "The picture theory of meaning in *Tractatus*
as a development of Moore's and Russell's theories of
judgment."   *Philosophy* 44 (1969):140-148.

423.   Huby, Pamela M.   "Is *Tractatus* 5.542 more obscure in
English than it is in German?"   *Philosophy* 44 (1969):243.

424.   Iglesias, M. Teresa.   "Russell's introduction to
Wittgenstein's *Tractatus*."   *Russell* (1977):21-38.

425.   Imbert, Cl.   "L'héritage frégéen du *Tractatus*."
Revue Internationale de Philosophie 23 (1969):205-218.
[Discussion: J. Vuillemin, Cl. Imbert, G. G. Granger,
M. Black, A. R. Raggio, G. H. von Wright, M. Clavelin, 218-
222]

426. Jünger, F. G. "Satzsinn und Satzbedeutung. Gedanken zu den *Schriften* von Ludwig Wittgenstein." *Merkur* 15 (1961):1009-1023. Reprinted in his *Sprache und Denken*. Frankfurt am Main, 1962.

427. Kainz, Howard P. "Wittgenstein's *Tractatus*: Some metaphilosophical considerations." *Journal of Thought* 9 (1974):172-178.

428. Kenny, A. "The ghost of the *Tractatus*." In Vesey. [See no. 94]

429. Keyt, David. "A new interpretation of the *Tractatus* examined." *Philosophical Review* 74 (1965):229-239.

430. Keyt, David. "Wittgenstein's picture theory of language." In Copi and Beard. [See no. 14]

430a. Klemke, E. D. *Essays on Wittgenstein*. Part 1: Wittgenstein's Ontology. [See no. 57]

431. Klemke, E. D. "The ontology of Wittgenstein's *Tractatus*." In Klemke. [See no. 57]

432. Kluge, Eike-Henner. "Objects as universals: A re-appraisal of the *Tractatus*." *Dialogue* (Canada) 12 (1973):64-77.

433. Koenne, Werner. "Rekursive Techniken und der *Traktatus*." *Conceptus* 11 (1977):289-305.

434. Kozlova, M. S. "Logic and reality. Critical analysis of Ludwig Wittgenstein's conception of logical reflection of reality in his *Tractatus Logico-Philosophicus*." *Voprosy Filosofii* (1965):95-105. [In Russian with an English summary]

435. Laguna, Theodore de. "Review of *Tractatus*." *Philosophical Review* 33 (1924):103-109. Reprinted in Copi and Beard. [See no. 14]

436. Lemoine, Roy Emanuel. *The Anagogic Theory of Wittgenstein's* Tractatus. (Janua linguarum, Series Minor, 214). The Hague, Paris: Mouton, 1975. 215p.

437. Lewy, C. "A note on the text of the *Tractatus*." *Mind* 76 (1967):416-423.

438. Leyvraz, Jean-Pierre. "A propos des objets simples dans le *Tractatus*." In *Proceedings of the XIV International Congress of Philosophy*, Vol. 2, Vienna, 254-262.

439. Long, Peter. "Are predicates and relational expressions incomplete?" *Philosophical Review* 78 (1969):90-98. [On *Tractatus* 3.1432]

440. Lorenz, Kuno. "Zur Deutung der Abbildtheorie in Wittgensteins *Tractatus*." *Teorema* 1972, 67-90.

441. Ludwig, Jan. "'Substance' and 'simple objects' in *Tractatus* 2.02ff." *Philosophical Studies* (Dordrecht) 29 (1976):307-318.

442. Ludwig, J. "Zero-remarks and the numbering system of the *Tractatus*." *Journal of Critical Analysis* (Jersey City, N.J.) 6 (1975):21-29.

443. Malherbe, Jean-François. "Interprétations en conflit à propos du *Traité* de Wittgenstein." *Revue Philosophique de Louvain* 76 (1978):180-204.

444. Margáin, Hugo. "¿Lo indecible dicho? Una invitación a la muerte." *Crítica* 7 (1975):109-119. [L. Villoro, *Lo indecible en el* Tractatus]

---- Martin, Margaret J. "The views of Whitehead and Wittgenstein in *Process and Reality* and the *Tractatus*." [See no. 278]

---- Maslow, Alexander. *A Study of Wittgenstein's* Tractatus. [See no. 65]

445. Matson, Wallace I. "Wittgenstein's *Tractatus* and 'The Later Wittgenstein'." In his *A History of Philosophy*. New York: American Book Co., 1968, 466-469, 486-490.

446. McGuinness, F. "Pictures and form in Wittgenstein's *Tractatus*." *Archivio di Filosofia* (1956):207-228. [Filosofia e simbolismo]

447. McGuinness, F. "Raffigurazioni e forma nel *Tractatus* di Wittgenstein." (Trad. di A. Gianquinto). *Archivio di Filosofia* (1956):229-247. [Filosofia e simbolismo]

448. McGuinness, B. F. "The mysticism of the *Tractatus*." *Philosophical Review* 75 (1966):305-328.

449. McGuinness, B. F. "Philosophy of science in the *Tractatus*." *Revue Internationale de Philosophie* 23 (1969): 155-164. [Discussion: M. Black, G. G. Granger, B. F. McGuinness, J. Hartnack, J. Vuillemin, 164-166]

450. McGuinness, B. F. "Pictures and form in Wittgenstein's *Tractatus*." In Copi and Beard. [See no. 14]

451. McGuinness, B. F. "The Grundgedanke of the *Tractatus*." In Vesey. [See no. 94]

452. Miller, David. "The uniqueness of atomic facts in Wittgenstein's *Tractatus*." *Theoria* 43 (1977):174-185.

453. Moller, J. G. "Om bestemmelsen af etiske saetninger ifolge Wittgensteins *Tractatus*." *Svensk Teologisk Kvartalskrift* 44 (1968):96-104.

454. Montoya Sáenz, José. "La filosofía de 'lo mistico' en el *Tractatus* de Wittgenstein." *Anales del Semenario de Metafísica* (1969):59-74.

---- Moran, John. *Toward the World and Wisdom of Wittgenstein's* Tractatus. [See no. 66]

455. Moreno, Alberto. "Sistema y silencio en el *Tractatus* de Ludwig Wittgenstein." *Sapientia* 25 (1970):11-20.

456. Moreno, Arley R. "Conhecimento cientifico do individual e comentários filosóficos. Uma análise do *Tractatus*." *Trans/form/ação* 1 (1974):71-77.

---- Morrison, James C. *Meaning and Truth in Wittgenstein's* Tractatus. [See no. 69]

---- Müller, A. W. *Ontologie in Wittgenstein's* Tractatus. [See no. 13]

456a. Musciagli, Dario. *Logica e ontologia in Wittgenstein. Proposta d'analisi su struttura e conoscenza nel* Tractatus. Lecce: Milella, 1974. 197p.

457. Narveson, Anne. "The ontology of the *Tractatus*." *Dialogue* 3 (1964):273-283.

458. Noonan, H. W. "*Tractatus* 2.0211-2.0212." *Analysis* 36 (1975-76):147-149.

459. Norman, J. "Russell and *Tractatus* 3.1432." *Analysis* 29 (1968-69):190-192.

460. Nuchelmans, Gabriël. "*Tractatus* 4.113." *Mind* 80 (1971):106-107.

---- Park, Young S. "Wittgenstein's version of verifiability in the *Tractatus*." [See no. 287]

461. Passmore, J. A. "Some Cambridge philosophers and Wittgenstein's *Tractatus*." In *A Hundred Years of Philosophy*, 345-368.

462. Pears, David. "Relation between Wittgenstein's picture theory of propositions and Russell's theories of judgment." *Philosophical Review* 86 (1977):177-196.

463. Pears, David. "Wittgenstein's treatment of solipsism in the *Tractatus*." In his *Questions in the Philosophy of Mind*. London: Duckworth, 1975.

464. Pears, David. "The ontology of the *Tractatus*."
Teorema, 1972; *Sobre el* Tractatus, monograph devoted to
Tractatus, 49-58.

465. Peterson, R. G. "A picture is a fact: Wittgenstein
and *The Naked Lunch*." *Twentieth Century Literature* 12
(1966):78-86.

---- Piana, Giovanni. *Interpretazione del* Tractatus *di
Wittgenstein*. [See no. 172]

---- Pitcher, George. *Die Philosophie Wittgenstein*.
[See no. 133]

466. Plochmann, George Kimball. "Verdad, tautología y
verificación en el *Tractatus* de Wittgenstein." *Diánoia*
(México) 14 (1968):122-142.

---- Plochmann, G. K., and Lawson, J. B. *Terms in their
Propositional Contexts in Wittgenstein's* Tractatus.
[See no. 78]

467. Poulain, Jacques. "La possibilité des propositions
ontologiques dans le *Tractatus Logico-Philosophicus*."
Études Philosophiques (1973):529-552.

468. Proctor, G. L. "Scientific laws and scientific
objects in the *Tractatus*." In Copi and Beard. [See no. 14]

469. Rabossi, Eduardo A. "El *Tractatus* y la filosofia
crítica." *Revista Latinoamericana de Filosofía* (Buenos
Aires) 1 (1975):109-132.

470. Ramsey, Frank. "Critical notice of the *Tractatus*."
Mind 32 (1923):465-478. Reprinted in his *Foundations of
Mathematics*. London: Routledge & Kegan Paul, 1931.
Also reprinted in Copi and Beard. [See no. 14]

471. Rhees, Rush. "The *Tractatus*: Seeds of some misunderstandings." *Mind* 72 (1963):213-220.

472. Rhees, Rush. "Miss Anscombe on the *Tractatus*."
Philosophical Quarterly 10 (1960):21-31.

473. Rhees, Rush. "Critical notice of Cornforth's *Science
Versus Idealism*." *Mind* 56 (1947):374-392. [Criticizes
Cornforth's criticism of the *Tractatus*]

474. Rhees, Rush. "Ontology and identity in the *Tractatus*."
In Winch. [See no. 97]

475. Rosenberg, Jay F. "New perspectives on the *Tractatus*."
Dialogue 4 (1966):506-517.

476. Russell, Bertrand. "Introduction to *Tractatus*, in
Wittgenstein: *Tractatus Logico-Philosophicus*."

477. Schiavone, Michele. "Il pensiero filosofico di
Ludwig Wittgenstein alla luce del *Tractatus Logico-
Philosophicus*." *Rivista di Filosofia Neo-Scolastica* 47
(1955):225-252.

478. Schwyzer, H. R. G. "Wittgenstein's picture-theory
of language." In Copi and Beard. [See no. 14]

479. Sellars, W. "Naming and saying." In Copi and
Beard. [See no. 14]

---- Shwayder, D. S. "Wittgenstein's *Tractatus*: A
historical and critical commentary." [See no. 305]

480. Shwayder, D. S. "On the picture theory of language."
In Copi and Beard. [See no. 14]

481. Slovenko, Ralph. "The opinion rule and Wittgenstein's
Tractatus." *ETC* 24 (1967):289-303. [A review of general
semantics]

482. Spiess, Reinhard. "Observations concerning Yeats'
"Last Poems" and Wittgenstein's *Tractatus Logico-Philosophicus*." *Revue des Lettres vivantes-Tijdschrift voor
Levende Talen* 42 (1976):83-86. [Wittgenstein's influence
on Yeats]

483. Spisani, Franco. "Il concetto di identita in
Wittgenstein." *Teorema*, 1972, 113-115.

484. Spisani, Franco. "The concept of identity in
Wittgenstein." *Systematics* 10 (1972):119-121.

---- Stenius, Erik. *Wittgenstein's* Tractatus. [See nos.
90 and 139]

485. Stenius, Erik. "Uppbyggnaden av Wittgenstein's
Tractatus Logico-Philosophicus." *Ajatus* 19 (1955):121-138.

486. Stenius, Erik. "Wittgenstein's picture-theory."
In Copi and Beard. [See no. 14]

487. Stenius, Erik. "The sentence as a function of its
constituents in Frege and in the *Tractatus*." In *Essays on
Wittgenstein in Honour of G. H. von Wright* (Acta Philos.
Fenn. 28 (1976)). Amsterdam: North-Holland, 1976, 71-84.

488. Stolte, Dieter. "Logic is die Hölle--Zu Wittgensteins
Schriften." *Der Monat* 14 (1961):66-70.

---- Stratton, John R. "Analysis and individuals. An
examination of the notions of a picture, objects, and sense
in Wittgenstein's *Tractatus*." [See no. 313]

489. Suszko, Roman. "Ontologia w *Trakfacie* L. Wittgen-
steina." *Studia Filozoficzne* (Warszawa) 68 (1952):97.

490. Suszko, Roman. "Ontology in the *Tractatus* of L.
Wittgenstein." *Notre Dame Journal of Formal Logic* 9 (1968):
7-33.

491. *Teorema. Sobre el* Tractatus Logico-Philosophicus.
1972.

> CONTENTS:
> Wittgenstein, Ludwig. "Notes on logic - Notas sobre
>   lógica (Versión castellana de Josep Ll. Blasco y
>   Alfonso García Suárez)." 6-47;
> Pears, David. "The ontology of the *Tractatus*." 49-58;
> Wolniewicz, Boguslaw. "The notion of fact as a modal
>   operator." 59-66;
> Lorenz, Kuno. "Zur Deutung der Abbildtheorie in
>   Wittgensteins *Tractatus*." 67-90;
> Favrholdt, David. "The relation between thought and
>   language in Wittgenstein's *Tractatus*." 91-100;
> Blasco, Josep Ll. "El lenguaje ordinario en el
>   *Tractatus*." 101-112;
> Spisani, Franco. "Il concetto di identità in Wittgen-
>   stein." 113-115;
> García Suárez, Alfonso. "¿Es el lenguaje del *Tractatus*
>   un lenguaje privado?" 117-130;
> Hartnack, Justus. "The metaphysical subject." 131-138;
> Garrido, M. "La lógica del mundo." 139-152;
> Vera, Francisco. Bibliografía. 153-166.

492. Trentman, John. "A note on *Tractatus* 4.12 and logical
form." *Graduate Review of Philosophy* (Univ. of Minnesota)
4 (1962):29-33.

493. Verhack, Ignace. "De filosofie van de logica van
Wittgensteins *Tractatus*." *Tijdschrift voor Filosofie*
37 (1975):617-651. [Summary: The philosophy of logic in
Wittgenstein's *Tractatus*, 652]

494. Verhack, Ignace. "Wittgenstein's deictic metaphysics:
An uncommon reading of the *Tractatus*. *International
Philosophical Quarterly* 18 (1978):433-444.

495. Villoro, Luis. "Lo indecible en el *Tractatus*.
Crítica 7 (1975):5-39.

496. Villoro, Luis. "El *Tractatus* desenmascarado (Réplica
a Margáin)." *Crítica* 7 (1975):105-114. [H. Margáin,
" Lo indecible dicho?"]

497. von Wright, Georg H. "The origin of Wittgenstein's
Tractatus." In *Wittgenstein: Sources and Perspectives*.
C. G. Luckhardt, ed. Ithaca (New York): Cornell Univ.
Press, 1979, 99-137.

498. Vuillemin, Jules. "Remarques sur 4.442 du *Tractatus*."
Revue Internationale de Philosophie 23 (1969):299-313.
[Discussion: B. F. McGuinness, J. Vuillemin, G. G. Granger,
M. Black, A. R. Raggio, 313-318]

499. Wasmuth, Ewald. "Ludwig Wittgensteins tystnad. Om
'det mystiska' i *Tractatus Logico-Philosophicus*." *Credo*
36 (1955):118-125. [The silence of L. Wittgenstein. On
'the mystical' in *Tractatus Logico-Philosophicus*]

500. Weissman, David. "Ontology in the *Tractatus*."
Philosophy and Phenomenological Research 27 (1966-67):475-
501.

501. Weissman, David. "Platonism in the *Tractatus*."
Idealistic Studies 2 (1972):51-80.

501a. White, R. M. "Can whether one proposition makes
sense depend on the truth of another? (*Tractatus* 2.0211-2)."
In Vesey. [See no. 94]

502. Wolniewicz, Boguslaw. "The notion of fact as a modal
operator." *Teorema*, 1972, monograph devoted to *Tractatus*,
59-66. [See no. 491]

                         B)   Reviews

503. Apostel, L. "Review of *Tractatus*." *Revue Internationale de Philosophie* 9 (1955):439.

504. Bacelar e Oliveira, J. *Revista Portuguesa de Filosofia* 12 (1956):109-110.

505. Bernard-Maitre, H. "Wittgenstein, *Tractatus Logico-
Philosophicus*." *Revue de Synthèse* 85 (1964):163-164.
[Trad. par P. Klossowski, 1961]

506. Bernstein, R. J. "Notice of *Tractatus*." *Review of
Metaphysics* 15 (1962):681.

507. Bochenski, I. M. *Freiburger Zeitschrift für Philosophie und Theologie* 1 (1954):316-317.

508. Blanche, R. "Wittgenstein, *Tractatus Logico-Philosophicus*." *Revue Philosophique de la France et de
l'Etranger* 86 (1961):521. [Testo... e note a cura di
G. C. M. Colombo, 1954]

509. Campanini, G. "Wittgenstein, *Tractatus*." *Rivista
Internazionale della Filosofia del Diritto* 4 (1964):811-
813. [Italian trans. trad. A. G. Conte]

510. Cardoletti, P. "Wittgenstein, *Tractatus Logico-
Philosophicus*." *La Scuola Cattolica* 97 (1969):Suppl.
bibl. 155*-156*. [Trad. di A. G. Conte, 1964]

511. Chastaing, Maxime. "Review of *Tractatus*." *Revue
Philosophique* 158 (1968):133-135.

512. Conte, Amendo G. "L. Wittgenstein: *Tractatus Logico-Philosophicus*." *Rivista de Filosofia* 53 (1962):92. [Trans. Pears and McGuinness]

513. Conte, Amendo G. "Wittgenstein: *Tractatus Logico-Philosophicus*." *Rivista de Filosofia* 53 (1962):222. [Trans. Pierre Klossowski]

514. Conte, Amendo G. "Wittgenstein, *Schriften, Tractatus Logico-Philosophicus*." *Rivista di Filosofia* 53 (1962): 356-357.

515. Drudis Baldrich, R. "Wittgenstein: *Tractatus Logico-Philosophicus* e *Quaderni 1914-1916*." *Aporia* 1 (1964-65):316-317.

516. Drudis Baldrich, R. "Wittgenstein: *Tractatus Logico-Philosophicus*." *Arbor* 33 (1956):452-456.

517. Eichner, Hans. "Review of the new translation of *Tractatus*." *Dialogue* 1 (1962):212-126.

518. Fabrat, A. *Pensamiento* 11 (1955):99.

519. Gadamer, Hans-G. *Philosophische Rundschau* 11 (1963): 41-45.

520. Geach, P. T. "Review of *Tractatus* as translated into English by Pears and McGuinness." *Philosophical Review* 72 (1963):264-265.

521. Geach, P. T. "Review of Colombo's Italian translation of *Tractatus*." *Philosophical Review* 66 (1957):556-559.

522. Gianquinto, A. *Rassegna di Scienze Filosofiche* 4 (1955):245-248.

523. Golffing, Francis. "Review of Wittgenstein's *Schriften*." *Books Abroad* 36 (1962):405.

524. Grize, J.-B. *Revue de Théologie et de Philosophie* 11 (1961):293-294.

525. Henschen-Dahlquist, Ann-Mari. "Review of Swedish translation of *Tractatus*." *Journal of Symbolic Logic* 29 (1964):134f.

526. Jacob, André. "Review of the *Tractatus*." *Etudes Philosophiques* 16 (1961):447.

527. Jarvis, J. "Review of the new translation of *Tractatus*." *Journal of Philosophy* 52 (1962):332-335.

528. Keyser, C. J. "A short notice of Wittgenstein's *Tractatus*." *Bulletin of the American Mathematical Society* 30 (1924):179-181.

529. MacGregor, G. "Notice of the *Tractatus*." *Personalist* 43 (1962):559-560.

530. McNicholl, A. *Angelicum* 33 (1956):96-98.

531. Montagnes, B. *Revue des Sciences Philosophiques et Théologiques* 46 (1962):713. [Trad. P. Klossowski]

532. Platzeck, E.-W. *Antonianum* 30 (1955):211.

533. Plochmann, G. K. "Review of the new translation of *Tractatus*." *Modern Schoolman* 40 (1962):65-67.

534. Pöggeler, O. *Philosophischer Literaturanzeiger* 15 (1962):304-307.

535. Rescher, Nicholas. "Review of *Tractatus*." *Modern Schoolman* 33 (1956):120-122.

536. Ryffel, H. "Wittgenstein, *Schriften, I-II*." *Studia Philosophica* 28 (1968):191-194.

537. Trinchero, M. "Review of *Tractatus*." *Rivista di Filosofia* 55 (1964):495-497.

538. Urmson, J. O. "Review of the new translation of *Tractatus*." *Mind* 72 (1963):298-300.

539. Weiler, G. "Review of the new translation of the *Tractatus*." *Philosophical Books* 3 (1962):25.

540. (Unsigned) "Review of Ogden's translation of the *Tractatus*." *Times Literary Supplement* (December 21, 1922): 854. Reprinted as "Ludwig Wittgenstein: 1922" in *Times Literary Supplement* August 28, 1953):xlviii.

541. (Unsigned) "Notice of *Tractatus*." *Personalist* 4 (1923):207-208.

542. (Unsigned) *Civiltà Cattolica* 106 (1955):422-423.

543. (Unsigned) "Review of the *Tractatus*." *Scientific American* 207 (1962):274.

544. (Unsigned) "Wittgenstein in Red." *Times Literary Supplement* (January 19, 1962):45. [Review of the new English translation of *Tractatus*]

545. (Unsigned) "Notice of the new translation of *Tractatus*. *Twentieth Century* 170 (1962):192.

5) *Wörterbuch für Volksschulen*

546.   Rest, Walter.   "Über Wittgenstein's *Wörterbuch für Volksschulen.*"   *Rundschau* 16 (1962):680-686.

6) Lecture on Ethics

547.   Klemke, E. D.   "Wittgenstein's lecture on Ethics."   *Journal of Value Inquiry* 9 (1975):118-127.

7) *Philosophische Grammatik - Philosophical Grammar*

548.   Baker, G. P., and Hacker, P. M. S.   "*Philosophical Grammar.*"   *Mind* 84 (1976):269-294.

549.   Goldstein, L.   *Philosophical Quarterly* 25 (1975): 279-281.

550.   Kenny, Anthony.   "From the big transcript to the *Philosophical Grammar.*"   In *Essays on Wittgenstein in Honour of G. H. von Wright* (Acta Philos. Fenn. 28 (1976)). Amsterdam: North-Holland, 1976, 41-53.

551.   King-Farlow, John.   "Wittgenstein's *Philosophical Grammar.*"   *Metaphilosophy* 7 (1976):265-275.

552.   Miller, Richard W.   "Wittgenstein in transition.   A review of the *Philosophical Grammar.*"   *Philosophical Review* 86 (1977):520-544.

553.   Stenius, Erik.   "*Schriften, IV: Philosophische Grammatik.*"   *Philosophical Quarterly* 21 (1971):376-377.

554.   Todd, D. D.   *Philosophy and Rhetoric* 8 (1975):260-262.

8) *Philosophische Bemerkungen - Philosophical Remarks*

555.   Blanché, R.   "*Schriften, II: Philosophische Bemerkungen.*"   *Revue Philosophique de la France et de l'Etranger* 96 (1971):253-254.

556.   Flusser, V.   "Wittgenstein, *Schriften, II: Philosophische Bemerkungen.*"   *Revista Brasileira de Filosofia* 16 (1966):129-132.

557.   Hampshire, Stuart.   "Out of the World.   A review of *Philosophische Bemerkungen.*"   *New Statesmen* 71 (1966): 163-164.

558. Malcolm, Norman. "Wittgenstein's *Philosophische Bemerkungen*." *Philosophical Review* 76 (1967):220-229.

559. Riverso, Emanuelle. "Les analyses sémantiques des *Philosophische Bemerkungen* de Wittgenstein." *Revue Internationale de Philosophie* 21 (1967):508-521.

560. Stein, Ernst. "Die Teufelsaustreibung aus der Sprache Ludwig Wittgenstein: dem reinen Zweifel ausgeliefert." *Die Zeit* (March 19, 1965):12. [A review of *Philosophische Bemerkungen* with a sketch of Wittgenstein by his friend Michael Drobil]

561. Stenius, Erik. "Review of *Bemerkungen*." *Philosophical Quarterly* 16 (1966):371-372.

562. Sluga, H. D. "Review of *Bemerkungen*." *British Journal for the Philosophy of Science* 17 (1967):339-341.

563. von Morstein, Petra. "Philosophie-Verwalterin der Grammatik über die Schriften des 'mittleren' Wittgenstein." *Die Welt: Der Literatur* 2 (1965):216. [Review of *Philosophische Bemerkungen*]

564. Weiler, Gershon. "Review of *Bemerkungen*." *Australasian Journal of Philosophy* 43 (1965):412-415.

565. (Unsigned) "Wittgenstein's yard-stick." *Times Literary Supplement* (December 9, 1965):1163. [Review of *Philosophische Bemerkungen*]

9) *Blue and Brown Books*

566. Ambrose, Alice. "The Yellow book notes in relation to *The Blue Book*." *Crítica* 9 (1977):3-20.

567. Ayer, A. J. "'Wittgenstein.' Review of *Blue and Brown Books* and Malcolm's *Memoir*." *Spectator* 201 (1958):654.

568. Bouwsma, O. K. "*The Blue Book*." *Journal of Philosophy* 58 (1961):141-162. Reprinted in his *Philosophical Essays*. Univ. of Nebraska Press, 1965, 175-201. Also reprinted in Fann.

569. Campanale, D. "Linguaggio ordinario e linguaggio scientifico in *The Blue Book* e in *The Brown Book*." *Annali della Facoltà di Lettere e Filosofia dell'Università di Bari* 6 (1960):397-415.

570. Deledalle, G. "Review of *Blue and Brown Books* and *Investigations*." *Etudes Philosophiques* 14 (1959):107-108.

571.   Delpech, Léon-Jacques.   "Wittgenstein: *Le Cahier Bleu et le Cahier Brun*." *Etudes Philosophiques* (1965):562-563.

572.   Engel, S. Morris. *Wittgenstein's Doctrine of the Tyrrany of Language. An Historical and Critical Examination of his* Blue Book. With an introduction by Stephen Toulmin. Reprint of the original ed. The Hague: Nijhoff, 1975, xvii-145p.

573.   Fitzpatrick, P.   "Review of *The Blue and Brown Books*." *Tablet* 212 (November 29, 1958):482.

574.   Garver, Newton.   "Reivew of *Blue and Brown Books*." *Philosophy and Phenomenological Research* 21 (1961):576-577.

575.   Hampshire, Stuart.   "'The Proper Method.' A review of *The Blue and Brown Books*." *New Statesmen* 56 (1958): 228-229. Reprinted in his "Wittgenstein," in *Modern Writers and Other Essays*. New York: Knopf, 1970, 130-135.

576.   Keisel, G.   "*The Blue and Brown Books*." *British Journal for the Philosophy of Science* 11 (1960-61):238-251.

577.   Lorenzen, Paul.   "Notice of *Blue and Brown Books*." *Philosophische Rundschau* 7 (1959):160.

578.   Margolin, Jean-Claude.   "*Le Cahier Bleu et le Cahier Brun*."   *Revue de Synthèse* 87 (1966):266-269.

579.   Morel, G.   "*Le Cahier Bleu et le Cahier Brun*." *Etudes* 322 (1965):890.

580.   Newman, J. R.   "Review of *Blue and Brown Books*." *Scientific American* 201 (1959):149-158.

581.   Pacifico.   "*Il Libro Blu* and *Il Libro Marrone*." In *Dizionario Letterario delle Opere di Tutti i Tempi e di Tutte le Letterature*. Appendice, Vol. 1. Milano: Bompiani Editrice, 1964.

582.   Pole, David.   "Review of *Blue and Brown Books*." *Philosophy* 34 (1959):367-368.

583.   Rhees, Rush.   "Preface to *Blue and Brown Books*." In Wittgenstein's *Blue and Brown Books*. Oxford: Blackwell; New York: Harper, 1958, v-xiv.

584.   Schoonbrood, C.   "Wittgenstein's *Blue Book*--Het Keerpunt in de Analytische Filosofie." *Bijdragen: Tijdschrift voor Filosofie en Theologie* 23 (1962):1-11.

585.   Strawson, P. F.   "*The Blue and Brown Books*." *Philosophical Quarterly* 10 (1960):371-372.

586.   Warnock, G. J.   "Review of *Blue and Brown Books*." *Mind* 69 (1960):283-284.

587. Wienpahl, Paul. "Wittgenstein's *Blue and Brown Books*." Part 1, *Inquiry* 15 (1972)267-319; Part 2, *Inquiry* 15 (1972):434-457.

588. Zuurdeeg, W. F. "Review of *Blue and Brown Books*." *Journal of Religion* 40 (1960):54-55.

589. (Unsigned) "Meaning and understanding." *Times Literary Supplement* (January 16, 1959):36. [Review of the *Blue and Brown Books*]

10) *Bemerkungen über die Grundlagen der Mathematik - Remarks on the Foundations of Mathematics*

590. Ambrose, A. "Proof and the theorem proved." *Journal of Philosophy* 55 (1958):901-902.

591. Ambrose, A. "Proof and the theorem proved." *Mind* 68 (1959):435-445. [See Castañeda, 1961, no. 598]

592. Ambrose, A. "Review of *Remarks on the Foundations of Mathematics*." *Philosophy and Phenomenological Research* 18 (1957):262-265.

593. Anderson, A. R. "Mathematics and the language game." RM 11 (1957-58):446-458. Reprinted in *Philosophy of Mathematics*. P. Benacerraf and H. Putnam, eds. Englewood Cliffs (New Jersey): Prentice-Hall, 1964, 481-490.

594. Ayer, A. J. "Review on *Remarks on the Foundations of Mathematics*." *The Spectator* (March 1957).

595. Bennett, J. "On being forced to a conclusion." *Proceedings of the Aristotelian Society, Supplement* 35 (1961):15-31. [See Wood, 1961, no. 623]

596. Bernays, P. "Comments on Ludwig Wittgenstein's *Remarks on the Foundations of Mathematics*." *Ratio* 2 (1959-60):1-22. Reprinted in *Philosophy of Mathematics*, P. Benacerraf and H. Putnam, eds., 1964, 510-528.

597. Berry, G. D. W. "Review of *Remarks*." *Philosophical Forum* 16 (1958-59):73-75.

598. Castañeda, H.-N. "On mathematical proofs and meaning." *Mind* 70 (1961):385-390. [See Ambrose, 1959, no. 591]

599. Chihara, C. S. "Wittgenstein and logical compulsion." *Analysis* 21 (1960-61):136-140. [Reply to Nell, see no. 616]

600. Chihara, C. S. "Wittgenstein and logical compulsion." *Philosophical Review* 72 (1963):17-34.

601.   Collins, J.   "Review of *Remarks*."   *Modern Schoolman*
35 (1957-58):147-150.

602.   Cowan, J. L.   "Wittgenstein's philosophy of logic."
Philosophical Review 70 (1961):362-375.

603.   Dummett, M.   "Wittgenstein's philosophy of mathematics."   *Philosophical Review* 68 (1959):324-348.   Reprinted
in *Philosophy of Mathematics*.   Benacerraf and Putnam, eds.,
491-509.

604.   Duthie, G. D.   "Critical study of *Remarks*."
Philosophical Quarterly 7 (1957):368-373.

605.   Engel, S. Morris.   "Wittgenstein's *Foundations* and
its reception."   *American Philosophical Quarterly* 4 (1967):
257-268.

606.   Goodstein, R. L.   "Critical notice of *Remarks*."
Mind 66 (1957):549-553.

607.   Hadot, P.   "Remarks on the *Foundations of Mathematics*."
Critique 15 (1959):972-983.

608.   Kielkopf, Charles F.   *Strict Finitism.   An Examination of Ludwig Wittgenstein's* Remarks on the Foundations
of Mathematics.   The Hague: Mouton, 1970.

609.   Kreisel, G.   "Wittgenstein's *Remarks*."   *British
Journal for the Philosophy of Science* 9 (1958):135-158.
[With Anscombe's corrections to her translation]

610.   Kreisel, G.   "Remarks on the *Foundations of Mathematics*."   *British Journal for the Philosophy of Science*
11 (1960-61):238-252.

611.   Levison, A. B.   "Wittgenstein and logical laws."
[Abstract]   *Journal of Philosophy* 59 (1962):677-678.

612.   Levison, A. B.   "Wittgenstein and logical laws."
Philosophical Quarterly 14 (1964):345-354.

613.   Levison, A. B.   "Wittgenstein and logical necessity."
Inquiry 7 (1964):367-373.

614.   Lewis, C. J.   "Review of *Remarks*."   *Thought* 32 (1957):
446-448.

615.   McBrien, V. O.   *New Scholasticism* 32 (1958):269-271.

616.   Nell, E. J.   "The hardness of the logical 'must'."
Analysis 21 (1960-61):68-72.   [See Chihara, 1960-61, no. 599]

617.   Shalom, A.   "Review of *Remarks*."   *Etudes Philosophiques* 12 (1957):433.

618. Stegmüller, W. *Philosophische Rundschau* 13 (1965-66): 138-152.

619. Stroud, B. "Wittgenstein and logical necessity." *Philosophical Review* 74 (1965):504-518.

620. Swanson, J. W. "A footnote to Mrs. Lazerowitz on Wittgenstein." *Journal of Philosophy* 56 (1959):678-679. [See Ambrose, 1958, no. 592]

621. Tessari, A. "Osservazioni sopra i *Fondamenti della Matematica*." *Bolletino Filosofico* 5 (1971):119-121.

622. Wisdom, J. O. "Esotericism." *Philosophy* 34 (1959): 338-354.

623. Wood, O. P. "On being forced to a conclusion." *Proceedings of the Aristotelian Society, Supplement* 35 (1961):35-44. [Reply to Bennett, 1961, no. 595]

624. (Unsigned) "Review of *Remarks*." *Choice* 3 (1966):666.

11) *Lectures and Conversations on Aesthetics, Psychology and Religious Belief*

625. Beardsley, M. C. "Review of *Lectures and Conversations*." *Journal of Aesthetics* 26 (1968):554.

626. Bouveresse, Jacques. "La voie et le moyen." *Critique* 28 (1972):441-459.

627. Cardoletti, P. "*Lezioni e Conversazioni sull'Etica...*" *La Scuola Cattolica* 97 (1969):Suppl. bibl. 157*-158*.

628. Collins, J. "Review of *Lectures and Conversations*." *Modern Schoolman* 44 (1967):421-423.

629. Collins, J. "*Lectures and Conversations on Aesthetics, Psychology...*" *Cross Currents* 17 (1967):217-218.

630. Davenport, Guy. "More of Wittgenstein." *National Review* 20 (1968):249-252.

631. Deledalle, G. "*Lectures and Conversations on Aesthetics...*" *Etudes Philosophiques* (1969):429.

632. Engel, S. Morris. "Wittgenstein's *Lectures and Conversations*." *Dialogue* 7 (1968-69):108-121.

633. Flew, Anthony. "Review of *Lectures and Conversations*." *Spectator* (September 16, 1966):355.

634. Gargani, A. G. "*Lezioni e Conversazioni sull'Etica...*" *Rivista Critica di Storia della Filosofia* 23 (1968):475-477.

635.   Griffiths, L.   "*Lectures and Conversations...*"
Mind 79 (1970):464-466.

636.   Hofstadter, Albert.   "Wittgenstein's *Lectures and
Conversations*." *Journal of Value Inquiry* 3 (1969):63-71.

637.   Leonardi, P.   "*Lezioni e Conversazioni sull'Etica...*"
Studia Patavina 18 (1971):202-206.

638.   Locke, Don.   "Review of *Lectures and Conversations*."
London Magazine 6 (1966):119f.

639.   Morick, Harold.   "Review of *Lectures and Conversations*."
International Philosophical Quarterly 8 (1968):651-653.

640.   Osborne, H.   "Review of *Lectures and Conversations*."
British Journal of Aesthetics 6 (1966):385-387.

641.   Radford, Colin.   "Religious belief and contradiction."
Philosophy 50 (1975):437-444.

642.   Shalom, Albert.   "A propos d'une publication récente
de Wittgenstein (*Lectures and Conversations*)." *Dialogue*
6 (1967):103-113.

643.   (Unsigned)   "The language of language." *Times
Literary Supplement* (November 3, 1966):1006. [Review of
Lectures and Conversations]

644.   (Unsigned)   "Review of *Lectures and Conversations*."
Choice 3 (1966):783.

12)   *Philosophische Untersuchungen* -
Philosophical Investigations

[See also, Section 6: Items Arranged by Subjects -
Criterion, Dreams and Dreaming, Family Resemblances,
Forms of Life, Games, Language, (Other) Mind, Pain,
Privacy, Private Language, Sensation, Universals]

645.   Albritton, R.   "On Wittgenstein's use of the term
'criterion'." *Journal of Philosophy* 56 (1959):845-857.

646.   Ambrose, A.   "Review of *Investigations*." *Philosophy
and Phenomenological Research* 15 (1954-55):111-115.

647.   Ammerman, R. R.   "Wittgenstein's later methods."
[Abstract] *Journal of Philosophy* 58 (1961):707-708.

648.   Anscombe, G. E. M.   "Note on the English version of
Wittgenstein's *Philosophische Untersuchungen*." *Mind* 62
(1953):521-522.

649.   Arnhart, Larry.   "Language and nature in Wittgenstein's
Philosophical Investigations."   *Journal of Thought* 10
(1975):194-199.

650.   Aune, B.   "On the complexity of avowals."   In
Philosophy in America.   M. Black, ed.   Ithaca (New York):
Cornell Univ. Press, 1965, 35-57.

651.   Ayer, A. J.   "Can there be a private language?"
Proceedings of the Aristotelian Society, Supplement 28
(1954):63-76.   Reprinted in his *The Concept of a Person and
other Essays*.   London: Macmillan; New York: St. Martin's
Press, 1963, 36-51.   [See Rhees, 1954, no. 764]

652.   Ayer, A. J.   "Can there be a private language?"
In Pitcher.   [See no. 76]

653.   Bambrough, J. R.   "Universals and family resemblances."
Proceedings of the Aristotelian Society 61 (1960-61):207-
222.

654.   Bambrough, J. R.   "Principia metaphysica."   *Philosophy*
39 (1964):97-109.

655.   Bambrough, J. R.   "Universals and family resemblances."
In Pitcher.   [See no. 76]

656.   Barone, F.   "Wittgenstein: *Philosophical Investigations*."   *Filosofia* 4 (1953):680-691.

657.   Barone, F.   "Review of *Investigations*."   *Giornale
Critico della Filosofia Italiana* 33 (1954):108-117.

658.   Barone, F.   "Wittgenstein inedito."   *Filosofia della
Scienza* (Torino) 4 (1953):5-16.

659.   Berggren, D.   "Language games and symbolic forms."
[Abstract]   *Journal of Philosophy* 58 (1961):708-709.

660.   Black, Carolyn.   "*Philosophical Investigations*.
Remark 43 revisited."   *Mind* 83 (1974):596-598.

661.   Britton, K.   "Feelings and their expression."
Philosophy 32 (1957):97-111.

662.   Buck, R. C.   "Non-other minds."   In *Analytical
Philosophy*.   R. J. Butler, ed.   Oxford: Basil Blackwell,
1962, 187-210.

663.   Burnheim, J.   "Review of *Investigations*."   *Philosophical Studies* (Irish) 4 (1954):114-115.

664.   Cameron, J.   "The glass of language: The testament
of Wittgenstein."   *Tablet* 202 (July 4, 1953):11-12.
[Review of *Investigations*]

665.   Campanale, D.   "*Investigazioni Filosofiche*."   In
*Dizionario Lettario delle Opere di Tutti i Tempi e di
Tutte le Lettarature*, Appendice, Vol. 1.   Milano: Bampiania
Editrice, 1964.

666.   Campbell, K.   "Family resemblance predicates."
American Philosophical Quarterly 2 (1965):238-244.

667.   Cardoletti, P.   "*Ricerche Filosofiche*."   *Scuola
Cattolica* 97 (1969):Suppl. bibl. 157*-157*.   [Ed. ital. a
cura di M. Trinchero]

668.   Carney, J. D.   "Private language: The logic of
Wittgenstein's argument."   *Mind* 69 (1960):560-565.
[Reply to Wellman, 1959, see no. 793]

669.   Carney, J. D.   "Is Wittgenstein impaled on Miss
Hervey's dilemma?"   *Philosophy* 38 (1963):167-170.
[Reply to Hervey, 1961.   See reply by Hervey, 1963, no. 720]

670.   Castañeda, H.-N.   "Knowledge and certainty."   *Review
of Metaphysics* 18 (1965):508-547.   [Review of N. Malcolm,
Knowledge and Certainty.   Sec. V, 528-535, is a criticism
of Malcolm's "Wittgenstein's *Philosophical Investigations*."]

671.   Castañeda, H.-N.   "The private-language argument."
In Rollins.   [See no. 768]

672.   Cavell, S.   "The availability of Wittgenstein's later
philosophy."   *Philosophical Review* 71 (1962):67-93.
[Contains criticism of Pole, 1958, see no. 761]   Also in
Pitcher.   [See no. 76]

673.   Cavell, S.   "Existentialism and analytical philosophy."
Daedalus 93 (1964):946-974.

674.   Chappell, V. C.   "Comments."   [On H.-N. Castañeda's
"The private-language argument"]   In Rollins.   [See no. 768]

675.   Chappel, V. C.   "The concept of dreaming."
Philosophical Quarterly   13 (1963):193-213.

676.   Chihara, C. S., and Fodor, J. A.   "Operationalism and
ordinary language: A critique of Wittgenstein."   *American
Philosophical Quarterly* 2 (1965):281-295.

677.   Collins, J.   "Review of *Investigations*."   *Thought* 29
(1954-55):288-289.

678.   Conte, A. G.   "Notice of the French edition of
Investigations."   *Rivista di Filosofia* 53 (1962):222.

679.   Cook, J. W.   "Wittgenstein on privacy."   *Philosophical
Review* 74 (1965):281-314.

680. Copeland, J. W. "Review of *Investigations*."
Philosophical Forum 12 (1954):112.

681. Cunningham, G. W. "Notice of *Investigations*." *Ethics*
64 (1954):330.

682. Daly, C. B. "New light on Wittgenstein." Part 1,
Philosophical Studies (Ireland) 10 (1960):5-49; Part 2,
Ibid., 11 (1961-62):28-62.

683. Davie, I. "Review of *Investigations*." *Downside
Review* 72 (1954):119-122.

684. Dazzi, Nino, and Simone, Raffaele. "*Philosophische
Untersuchungen*." *Rivista di Filosofia* 63 (1972):59-74.

685. Deledalle, G. "*Philosophical Investigations*."
Etudes Philosophiques 14 (1959):107-108.

686. Deledalle, G. "The *Philosophical Investigations*."
Etudes Philosophiques (1969):417. (G. Pitcher, ed.)

687. Evans, E. "Notes on *Philosophical Investigations*."
Indian Journal of Philosophy 2 (1960):31-39.

688. Fairbanks, M. J. "Language-games and sensationalism."
Modern Schoolman 40 (1962-63):275-281.

689. Feibleman, James K. "Reflections after Wittgenstein."
Sophia 23 (1955):322-328.

690. Feyeraband, Paul. "Wittgenstein's *Philosophical
Investigations*." *Philosophical Review* 64 (1955):449-483.
Reprinted in Pitcher and in Fann. [See nos. 76 and 23]
Also in *Readings in Semantics*. F. Zabeeh, E. D. Klemke
and A. Jacobson, eds. Chicago: Univ. of Illinois Press,
1974. 853p. [Contains P. Fayeraband's review of
Philosophical Investigations]

691. Filho, Baltazar Barbosa. "Nota sobre o conceito de
jogo-de-linguagem nas *Investigaçoes Filosoficas* de
Wittgenstein." *ITA, Humanidades* 9 (1973):75-104.

692. Finch, Henry Leroy. *Wittgenstein--the Later Philosophy. An Exposition of the* Philosophical Investigations.
Atlantic Highlands (New Jersey): Humanities Press, 1977.
284p.

693. Findlay, J. N. "Wittgenstein's *Philosophical Investigations*." *Philosophy* 30 (1955):173-179. Reprinted in
his *Language, Mind and Value*. New York: Humanities Press,
1963; London: George Allen & Unwin, 1963, p. 197-208.

694. Findlay, J. N. "Wittgenstein's *Philosophical Investigations*." *Revue Internationale de Philosophie* 7 (1953):
201-216.

695. Fodor, J. A. "Of words and uses." *Isis* 4 (1961):
190-208.

696. Furberg, Mats. "An attempt at a table of contents
of Wittgenstein's *Philosophical Investigations*, Part 1."
In *Analyser och Argument*. Ann-Mari Henschen-Dahlquist, ed.
Uppsala: Univ. of Uppsala, 1966.

697. Garver, N. "Wittgenstein on private language."
Philosophy and Phenomenological Research 20 (1959-60):
389-396.

698. Garver, N. "Wittgenstein on criteria." In Rollins.
[See no. 768]

699. Gasking, D. "Avowals." In *Analytical Philosophy*,
R. J. Butler, ed. Oxford: Basil Blackwell, 1962, 154-169.
[See reply by Lean, no. 735]

700. Gert, B. "Wittgenstein and logical positivism."
[Abstract] *Journal of Philosophy* 58 (1961):707.

701. Gert, B. "Wittgenstein and private language."
[Abstract] *Journal of Philosophy* 61 (1964):700.

702. Giacomini, U. "Il problema del linguaggio nella
seconda *Ricerca Filosofica* di Wittgenstein." *Aut Aut*
69 (1962):238-244.

703. Gill, Jerry H. "Wittgenstein's *Philosophical Investigations*: An annotated Table of Contents." *International
Philosophical Quarterly* 7 (1967):305-310.

704. Ginet, C. "Comments." [To N. Garver, "Wittgenstein
on criteria] In Roller. [See no. 768]

705. Goff, R. "Language of method in Wittgenstein's
Philosophical Investigations." [Precis of dissertation]
Drew Gateway 40 (1970):149-150.

706. Gruender, D. "Wittgenstein on explanation and
description." *Journal of Philosophy* 59 (1962):523-530.

707. Gustafson, D. F. "Privacy." *Southern Journal of
Philosophy* 3 (1965):140-146. [Comments on Castañeda, in
Rollins, see no. 768]

708. Gustafson, D. F. "On Pitcher's account of *Investigations* 43." *Philosophy and Phenomenological Research*
28 (1967):252-258.

709. Hall, Roland. "Review of *Philosophical Investigations*
3d Edition." *Philosophical Quarterly* 17 (1967):362-363.

710. Hallett, Garth L. *A Companion to Wittgenstein's*
Philosophical Investigations. Cornell Univ. Press, 1977.

711. Hallie, P. P. "Wittgenstein's grammatical-empirical distinction." *Journal of Philosophy* 60 (1963):565-578.

712. Hallie, P. P. "Wittgenstein's exclusion of metaphysical nonsense." *Philosophical Quarterly* 16 (1966):97-112.

713. Hamilton, R. "Review of *Investigations*." *Month* 11 (1954):116-117.

714. Hampshire, S. "'A Great Philosopher.' A review of the *Investigations*." *Spectator* 190 (May 22, 1953):682.

715. Hardin, C. L. "Wittgenstein on private languages." *Journal of Philosophy* 56 (1959):517-528.

716. Harries, Karsten. "Two conflicting interpretations of language in Wittgenstein's *Investigations*." *Kantstudien* 59 (1968):397-409.

717. Heath, P. L. "Wittgenstein investigated." *Philosophical Quarterly* 6 (1956):66-71.

718. Heinemann, F. H. "Review of *Philosophical Investigations*." *Hibbert Journal* 52 (1953):89-90.

719. Hervey, H. "The private language problem." *Philosophical Quarterly* 7 (1957):63-79.

720. Hervey, H. "The problem of the model language game in Wittgenstein's later philosophy." *Philosophy* 36 (1961): 333-351. [See reply by Carney, 1963, no. 669]

721. Hervey, H. "A reply to Dr. Carney's challenge." *Philosophy* 38 (1963):170-175.

722. Hintikka, Jaakko. "Tutkimus filosofiasta." [A study of philosophy] (Review of Ludwig Wittgenstein, *Philosophical Investigations*) *Suomalainen Suomi* (1955):206-211.

723. Hintikka, Jaakko. "Tutkimus kielestä." [A study of language] (Review of Ludwig Wittgenstein, *Philosophical Investigations*) *Suomalainen Suomi* (1955):273-277.

724. Hunter, J. F. M. "'Forms of life' in Wittgenstein's *Philosophical Investigations*." *American Philosophical Quarterly* 5 (1968):233-243. [Reply in Klemke, see no. 57]

725. Hunter, J. F. M. "Some grammatical states." *Philosophy* 52 (1977):155-166.

726. Hunter, John F. M. "A scholar's Wittgenstein." *Philosophical Review* 87 (1978):259-274. [On Garth Hallet's *A Companion to Wittgenstein's* Philosophical Investigations. See no. 38]

727. Hutten, E. H. "Review of *Investigations*." *British Journal for the Philosophy of Science* 4 (1953):258-260.

728. Kaal, Hans, and McKinnon, Alastair. *Concordance to Wittgenstein's* Philosophische Untersuchungen. Leiden: E. N. Brill, 1975.

729. Kenny, A. "Aquinas and Wittgenstein." *Downside Review* 77 (1959):217-235.

730. Kenny, A. "Cartesian privacy." In Pitcher, 352-370. [See no. 76]

731. Kerr, F. "Language as hermaneutic in the later Wittgenstein." *Tijdschrift voor Filosofie* 27 (1965):491- 520.

732. Khatchadourian, H. "Common names and 'family resem- blance'." *Philosophy and Phenomenological Research* 18 (1957-58):341-358. [Reply in Pitcher, see no. 76]

733. Klein, J. Theodore. "Wittgenstein's analysis of the use of 'I' in the *Philosophical Investigations*." *Modern Schoolman* 51 (1973-74):47-53.

734. Kretzmann, N. "Maupertuis, Wittgenstein, and the origin of language." [Abstract] *Journal of Philosophy* 54 (1957):776.

735. Lean, M. E. "Mr. Gasking on avowals." In *Analytical Philosophy*, R. J. Butler, ed. Oxford: Basil Blackwell, 1962, 169-186. [Reply to Gasking, see no. 699]

736. Levi, A. W. "Wittgenstein as dialectitian." *Journal of Philosophy* 61 (1964):127-138.

737. Lieb, Irwin C. "Wittgenstein's *Investigations*." *Review of Metaphysics* 8 (1954):125-143.

738. Linsky, L. "Wittgenstein on language and some prob- lems of philosophy." *Journal of Philosophy* 54 (1957): 285-293.

739. Llewellyn, J. E. "On not speaking the same language." *American Journal of Philology* 40 (1962):35-48, 127-145.

740. Long, T. A. "The problem of pain and contextual implication." *Philosophy and Phenomenological Research* 26 (1965-66):106-111. (Comments on Malcolm's "Wittgen- stein's *Philosophical Investigations*")

741. Lubbe, H. "*Philosophische Untersuchungen*." *Kantstudien* 52 (1960-61):220-243.

742. Luckhardt, C. G. "Wittgenstein: *Investigations* 50." *Southern Journal of Philosophy* 15 (1977):81-90.

743. Malcolm, N. "Knowledge of other minds." *Journal of Philosophy* 55 (1958):969-978. Reprinted in *The Philosophy of Mind*, V. C. Chappell, ed. Englewood Cliffs (New Jersey): Prentice-Hall, 1962, 151-159. Also in Malcolm, *Knowledge and Certainty*, Englewood Cliffs (New Jersey): Prentice-Hall, 1963, 130-140.

744. Malcolm, Norman. "Wittgenstein's *Philosophical Investigations*." *Philosophical Review* 63 (1954):530-559. Reprinted in *The Philosophy of Mind*, V. C. Chappell, ed. Englewood Cliffs (New Jersey): Prentice-Hall, 1962, 74-100. Also reprinted, in slightly revised form, in Malcolm's *Knowledge and Certainty: Essays and Lectures*, Englewood Cliffs (New Jersey): Prentice-Hall, 1963, 96-129. And reprinted in T. O. Buford's *Essays on Other Minds*, Univ. of Illinois Press, 1970, 208-246. Also in Pitcher, in Fann, and in Morick [see nos. 76, 23 and 68].

745. Malcolm, Norman. "Wittgenstein's conception of first person psychological sentences as 'expressions'." *Philosophical Exchange* 2 (1978):59-72.

746. Mandelbaum, M. "Family resemblances and generaliza- tion concerning the arts." *American Philosophical Quarterly* 2 (1965):219-228.

747. Melden, A. I. "My kinaesthetic sensations advise me...." *Analysis* 18 (1957-58):43-48.

748. Mora, J. F. "Wittgenstein: A symbol of troubled times." *Philosophy and Phenomenological Research* 14 (1953-54):89-96.

749. Mundle, C. W. K. "'Private language' and Wittgen- stein's kind of behaviourism." *Philosophical Quarterly* 16 (1966):35-46.

750. Munson, T. N. "Wittgenstein's phenomenology." *Philosophy and Phenomenological Research* 23 (1962-63):37-50.

751. Nakhnikian, George. "Review of *Investigations*." *Philosophy of Science* 21 (1954):353-354.

752. Nielson, H. A. "Wittgenstein on language." *Philosophical Studies* (Ireland) 8 (1958).

753. Nolet, Y. "Review of *Untersuchungen*." *Revue Philo- sophique de Louvain* 66 (1968):132-133. [*Philosophische Untersuchungen,* trans. by G. E. M. Anscombe, 2d ed.]

754. Olscamp, P. J. "Wittgenstein's refutation of skepticism." *Philosophy and Phenomenological Research* 26 (1965-66):239-247.

755. Passmore, J. *A Hundred Years of Philosophy*. London:
Duckworth, 1957, ch. 18: "Wittgenstein and ordinary
language philosophy," 425-458.

756. Paul, G. A. "Wittgenstein." In *The Revolution in
Philosophy*, A. J. Ayer, ed. London: Macmillan; New York:
St. Martin's Press, 1956, 88-96.

757. Paul, R. "B's perplexity." *Analysis* 25 (1964-65):
176-178.

758. Perkins, M. "Two arguments against a private language." *Journal of Philosophy* 62 (1965):443-459.

759. Pitcher, George, ed. *Wittgenstein: The* Philosophical
Investigations (A collection of critical essays).
New York: Doubleday, Anchor Books, 1966.

760. Pitcher, G. "Wittgenstein, nonsense, and Lewis
Carroll." *The Massachusetts Review* 6 (1965):591-611.

761. Pole, D. *The Later Philosophy of Ludwig Wittgenstein*.
London: Univ. of London, The Athlone Press, 1958. [See
Cavell, 1962, no. 672]

762. Price, Jeffrey T. *Language and Being in Wittgenstein's*
Philosophical Investigations. Mouton, 1973.

763. Rankin, K. W. "Wittgenstein on meaning, understanding, and intending." *American Philosophical Quarterly*
3 (1966):1-13.

764. Rhees, R. "Can there be a private language?"
Proceedings of the Aristotelian Society, Supplement 28
(1954):77-94. Reprinted in *Philosophy and Ordinary
Language*, C. E. Caton, ed. Urbana: Univ. of Illinois,
1963, 90-107. [Reply to Ayer, 1954, see no. 651]

765. Rhees, R. "Wittgenstein's builders." *Proceedings
of the Aristotelian Society* 60 (1959-60):171-186. In Fann.
[See no. 23]

766. Rembert, Andrew. "Wittgenstein on learning the
names of inner states." *Philosophical Review* 84 (1975):
236-248.

767. Richman, R. J. "Something common." *Journal of
Philosophy* 59 (1962):821-830.

768. Rollins, C. D., ed. *Knowledge and Experience:*
Proceedings of the 1962 Oberlin Colloquium in Philosophy.
Univ. of Pittsburgh Press, no date.

     CONTENTS:
     Garver, N. "Wittgenstein on criteria." 55-71;
     Ginet, C. "Comments." 72-76;

        Siegler, F. A.   "Comments."   77-80;
        Ziff, P.   "Comments."   81-85;
        Garver, N.   "Rejoinders."   86-87;
        Castañeda, H.-N.   "The private language argument."
          88-105;
        Chappell, V. C.   "Comments."   106-118;
        Thomson, J. F.   "Comments."   118-124;
        Castañeda, H.-N.   "Rejoinders."   125-132.

769.   Rorty, R.   "Pragmatism, categories, and language."
Philosophical Review 70 (1961):197-223.

770.   Scholz, H.   "Wittgenstein: *Philosophische Untersuchungen*."   *Philosophische Rundschau* 1 (1953):193-197.

771.   Shirley, Edward S.   "Hintikka on *Investigations* 265."
Southwestern Journal of Philosophy   7 (1976):67-73.

772.   Siegler, F. A.   "Comments."   [To N. Garver's "Wittgenstein on criteria"]   In Rollins.   [See no. 768]

773.   Smart, H. R.   "Language games."   *Philosophical
Quarterly* 7 (1957):224-235.

774.   Stern, K.   "Private language and skepticism."
Journal of Philosophy 60 (1963):745-759.

775.   Stocker, M. A. G.   "Memory and the private language
argument."   *Philosophical Quarterly* 16 (1966):47-53.

776.   Strawson, P. F.   "Critical notice of *Philosophical
Investigations*."   *Mind* 63 (1954):70-99.   Reprinted in
Pitcher and in Morick.   [See nos. 76 and 68]

777.   Strawson, P. F.   "Wittgenstein's *Philosophical Investigations*."   In his *Freedom and Resentment and Other Essays*.
London: Methuen; New York: Barnes and Noble, 1974, 133-168.

778.   Suter, R.   "Augustine on time with some criticisms
from Wittgenstein."   *Revue Internationale de Philosophie*
16 (1962):378-394.

779.   Tanburn, N. P.   "Private languages again."   *Mind*
72 (1963):88-102.

780.   Thomson, J. F.   "Comments."   [To H.-N. Castañeda's
"The private-language argument"]   In Rollins.   [See no. 768]

787.   Thomson, Judith Jarvis.   "Private languages."
American Philosophical Quarterly 1 (1964):20-31.

788.   Thyssen, Johannes.   "Sprachregelung und Sprachspiel.
Kritische Bemerkungen zu Wittgensteins *Philosophischen
Untersuchungen*."   *Zeitschrift für Philosophische Forschung*
20 (1966):3-22.

789. Todd, W. "Private languages." *Philosophical Quarterly* 12 (1962):206-217.

790. Torretti, Roberto. "Las *Investigaciones* de Wittgenstein y la posibilidad de la filosofía." *Diálogos* 5 (1968): 35-59.

791. Vandamme, F. "*Philosophical Investigations*, 2d ed." *Communication and Cognition* 2, no. 3 (1969):17-28; no. 4: 9-23.

792. Warnock, G. J. "The philosophy of Wittgenstein." In *Philosophy in the Mid-Century* Vol. 2. R. Klibansky, ed. Firenze: La Nuova Italia Editrice, 1958, 203-207.

793. Wellman, C. "Wittgenstein and the egocentric predicament." *Mind* 68 (1959):223-233.

794. Wellman, C. "Our criteria for third-person psychological sentences." *Journal of Philosophy* 58 (1961):281-293.

795. Wellman, C. "Wittgenstein's conception of a criterion." *Philosophical Review* 71 (1962):433-447.

796. Wheatley, J. "'Like'." *Proceedings of the Aristotelian Society* 62 (1961-62):99-116.

797. White, Alan. "Wittgenstein's *Philosophical Investigations*." In his *G. E. Moore, A Critical Exposition*. Oxford: Basil Blackwell, 1958, 225-236.

798. Wisdom, J. "A feature of Wittgenstein's technique." *Proceedings of the Aristotelian Society, Supplement* 35 (1961):1-14.

799. Wolgast, E. H. "Wittgenstein and criteria." *Isis* 7 (1964):348-366.

800. Wollheim, Richard. "Review of *Investigations*." *New Statesman and Nation* 46 (1953):20-21.

801. Wollheim, Richard. "Las *Investigaciones Filosóficas* de Ludwig Wittgenstein." *Notas Est. Filos.* 5 (1954):31-36.

802. von Wright, Georg Henrik. "The origin and composition of Wittgenstein's *Investigations*." In *Wittgenstein: Sources and Perspectives*, C. G. Luckhardt, ed. Cornell Univ. Press, 1979, 138-160.

803. Workman, A. J. "Review of *Investigations*." *Personalist* 36 (1955):292-293.

804. (Unsigned) "Wittgenstein: *Philosophical Investigations*." In *Masterpieces of World Philosophy in Summary Form*, Frank N. Magill, ed. New York: Harper & Brothers, 1961, 1160-1166.

805.   (Unsigned)   "A philosophical vocation."   *Times Literary Supplement* (August 28, 1953):xlviii-l.

13)   *Zettel*

806.   Amdur, Stephen, and Horine, Samuel A.   "An index of philosophically relevant terms in Wittgenstein's *Zettel*. *International Philosophical Quarterly* 10 (1970):310-321.

807.   Bernstein, J. R.   "Review of *Zettel*."   *Review of Metaphysics* 22 (1968):158.

808.   Davenport, Guy.   "Review of *Zettel*."   *National Review* 20 (1968):249-252.

809.   Gustafson, D. F.   "Review of *Zettel*."   *Philosophy* 43 (1968):161-164.

810.   Hunter, John F. M.   "Wittgenstein and materialism." *Mind* 86 (1977):514-531.

811.   Llewelyn, J. E.   "*Zettel*."   *Philosophical Quarterly* 18 (1968):176-177.

812.   Louch, A. R.   "*Zettel*."   *Journal of the History of Philosophy* 6 (1968):98-100.

813.   Morick, H.   "*Zettel*."   *International Philosophical Quarterly* 9 (1969):151-152.   [G. E. M. Anscombe, ed.]

814.   Novielli, V.   "*Zettel*."   *Filosofia* 20 (1969):643-645. [G. E. M. Anscombe, ed.]

815.   Vesey, G. N. A.   "Wittgenstein on the myth of mental processes."   *Philosophical Review* 77 (1968):350-355. [Review article on *Zettel*]

816.   Warnock, Mary.   "Review of *Zettel*."   *Listener* 78 (1967):55.

817.   (Unsigned)   "Review of *Zettel*."   *Choice* 5 (March 1968):66.

818.   (Unsigned)   "Review of *Zettel*."   *Yale Review* 57 (Autumn 1967):viii.

14)   *On Certainty*

819.   Almond, P. C.   "Winch and Wittgenstein."   *Religious Studies* 12 (1976):473-482.

820.   Black, Carolyn.   "Taking."   *Theoria* 40 (1974):60-75.

821. Bogen, James. "Wittgenstein and skepticism."
Philosophical Review 83 (1974):364-373.

822. Derksen, A. A. *"Über Gewissheit."* *Bijdragen* 31
(1970):196-199. [G. E. M. Anscombe, ed.]

823. Dilman, Ilham. "On Wittgenstein's last notes (1950-51)
On Certainty." *Philosophy* 46 (1971):162-168.

824, Finch, Henry Leroy. "Wittgenstein's last word:
Ordinary certainty." *International Philosophical Quarterly*
15 (1975):383-395.

825. Gill, Jerry H. "Saying and showing. Radical themes
in Wittgenstein's *On Certainty."* *Religious Studies* 10
(1974):279-290.

826. Hudson, W. D. "Language-games and presuppositions."
Philosophy 53 (1978):894-899.

827. Moreau, Pierre François. *Nouvelle Revue Française*
no. 294 (1977):105-106.

828. Palmer, A. *"On Certainty."* *Mind* 81 (1972):453-457.
[G. E. M. Anscombe, ed.]

829. White, A. R. *"On Certainty."* *Philosophical Books*
11 (1970):30-32. [G. E. M. Anscombe, ed.]

830. Zimmermann, Jürg. *Zu Wittgensteins* Über Gewissheit.
Versuch eines Überblicks. (SA. aus: *Studia Philosophica*
36 (1977):226-239.) Basel: Verlag für Recht und Gesellschaft, 1977, 226-239.

15) *Prototractatus*

831. Devaux, P. "Review of *Prototractatus*." *Revue
Internationale de Philosophie* 26 (1972):573-575.

831a. Hart, W. D. "Review of *Prototractatus*." *Journal
of Philosophy* 70 (1973):19-24.

832. Newell, R. W. "Review of *Prototractatus*." *Philosophy*
48 (1973):97-99.

833. Rhees, Rush. "Review of *Prototractatus*." *Philosophical Review* 82 (1973):530-531.

834. Winch, Peter. "Review of *Prototractatus*." *Philosophical Books* 13 (1972):36-38.

835. Wolf, M. "Review of *Prototractatus*." *Philosophical
Studies* (Maynooth) 21: 284-285.

836. Wolter, A. B. "Review of *Prototractatus*." *Review of Metaphysics* 25 (1971-72):575-576.

16) *Remarks on Colour*

837. Harrison, Bernard. "*Remarks on Colour*." *Philosophy* 53 (1978):564-566. [G. E. M. Anscombe, ed.]

17) *Philosophical Remarks*

838. Carlston, J. "Review of *Philosophical Remarks*." *Modern Schoolman* 54 (1977):423-424.

839. Lucchese, I. "Review of *Osservazioni Filosofiche*." *Rassegna di Scienze Filosofiche* 30 (1977):123-124.

840. Stock, Guy. "*Philosophical Remarks*." *Philosophical Quarterly* 26 (1976):178-180.

841. White, A. R. "Review of *Philosophical Remarks*." *Metaphilosophy* 8 (1977):72-74.

18) *Lectures on the Foundations of Mathematics*

842. Bouveresse, Jacques. "Le paradis de Cantor et le purgatoire de Wittgenstein." *Critique* 33 (1977):316-351. [C. Diamond, ed. *Wittgenstein's* Lectures on the Foundations of Mathematics]

843. Chihara, Charles S. "Wittgenstein's analysis of the paradoxes in his *Lectures on the Foundations of Mathematics*." *Philosophical Review* 86 (1977):365-381.

844. Goldstein, L. "Review of *Lectures on the Foundations of Mathematics*." *Philosophical Quarterly* 27 (1977):370-371.

845. Morrison, P. G. "Review of *Lectures on the Foundations of Mathematics*." *Philosophy and Phenomenological Research* 37 (1976-77):584-586.

846. Wrigley, Michael. "Wittgenstein's philosophy of mathematics." *Philosophical Quarterly* 27 (1977):50-59.

19) Letters and Conversations

847. Antiseri, Dario. "Prefazione" to *Lettere a Ludwig von Ficker*. A cura di Georg Henrik von Wright, con la collaborazione di Walter Methlagl. Roma: A. Armando, 1974. 149p.

848. Bell, David. "Wittgenstein: Letters to Russell."
[Review] *Russell* (Journal of the Bertrand Russell Archives)
15 (1974):26-28.

849. Boschheurne, C. J. "Letters from L. Wittgenstein."
Streven 21 (1967-68):821-822.

850. Conte, A. G. "Notice of *Schriften/Beiheft*." *Rivista
di Filosofia* 53 (1962):356-358.

851. Edwards, James C. "Wittgenstein: Letters to Russell."
Philosophical Review 85 (1976):271-274.

852. Eichner, H. "*Schriften, III*: Wittgenstein und der
Wiener Kreis." *Dialogue* 7 (1968-69):494-495.

853. Goldstein, L. "Letters to Russell." *Philosophical
Quarterly* 25 (1975):279-280.

854. Griffin, N. "Letters to Russell." *Australasian
Journal of Philosophy* 53 (1975):102.

855. Hallett, Garth. "Review of letters to Ogden."
The Heythrop Journal 15 (1974):347-348.

856. Keyt, D. "Letters from Ludwig Wittgenstein."
Dialogue 8 (1969-70):128-131.

857. Murray, M. "Reply to Waismann's 'Notes on talks with
Wittgenstein'." *Philosophical Review* 83 (1974):501-503.
[See Waismann below, no. 862]

858. Nolet, Y. "Review of *Schriften III*." *Revue Philosophique de Louvain* 66 (1968):333-334. [B. F. McGuinness,
ed., *Schriften III: Wittgenstein und der Wiener Kreis*]

859. Stenius, Erik. "Review of letters to Ogden." *Philosophical Quarterly* 25 (1975):62-68. [Wittgenstein's
Letters to C. K. Ogden]

860. Titze, H. "Briefe an L. von Ficker." *Philosophischer
Literaturanzeiger* 23 (1970):344-348. [G. H. von Wright, ed.]

861. Trinchero, M. "Letters from L. Wittgenstein..."
[Review] *Rivista di Filosofia* 59 (1968):243-244.

862. Waismann, Friedrich. "Notes on talks with Wittgenstein." *Philosophical Review* 74 (1965):12-16. [See
Murray above, no. 857]

863. Wolf, Maria. "Review of letters to Ogden."
Philosophical Studies (Maynooth) 22 (1974):275-279.

CHAPTER 4:
General Discussion
of the Works
# of Wittgenstein

864. Abbagnano, N. "L'ultimo Wittgenstein." *Rivista di Filosofia* 44 (1953):447-456.

865. Achinstein, Peter, and Barker, Stephen. *Legacy of Logical Positivism: Studies in the Philosophy of Science.* Baltimore: Johns Hopkins Press, 1969.

866. Ackermann, Inge. "Wittgenstein's fairy tale." *Analysis* 38 (1978):159-160.

867. Albrecht, E. "Zur Kritik der Auffassungen Ludwig Wittgensteins über das Verhältnis von Sprache, Logik und Erkenntnistheorie." *Deutsche Zeitschrift für Philosophie* 16 (1968):813-829.

868. Albritton, R. "Knowledge and doubt." In Isenberg lecture delivered at Michigan State Univ., Nov. 8, 1968.

869. Allaire, Edwin B. "Things, relations and identity." *Philosophy of Science* 34 (1967):260-272.

870. Alston, William P. "Introduction to Part IX: Ordinary language philosophy." In *Readings in 20th Century Philosophy.* W. P. Alston and G. Nakhnikian, eds. New York: The Free Press, 1963, 495-512.

871. Alston, William P., et al. *Origenes de la filosofia analitica: Moore, Russell, Wittgenstein.* Trad. Carmen García Trevijano (Col. Filosofia Ensayo). Madrid: Editorial Tecnos, 1976, 176p.

872. Ambrose, Alice. "Invention and discovery." In her *Essays in Analysis*, 66-87. [See no. 2]

873. Ambrose, Alice, and Lazerowitz, M. "Wittgenstein: Philosophy, experiment and proof." In *British Philosophy in the Mid-century*. C. A. Mace, ed. London: George Allen & Unwin, 1966, revised.

874. Améry, J. "Ludwig Wittgenstein im Rückblick." (Zum 25 Todestag 29.4.1976) *Merkur* (Stuttgart) 30 (1976): 991-995.

875. Améry, Jean. "An den Grenzen des Scharfsinns. Zu den Vermischten Bermerkungen Ludwig Wittgensteins." *Neue Rundschau* 90 (1979):86-95.

876. Ammerman, R. R. "Wittgenstein's later methods." [Abstract] *Journal of Philosophy* 58 (1961):707-708.

877. Anscombe, G. E. M. "The question of linguistic idealism." In *Essays on Wittgenstein in Honour of G. H. von Wright* (Acta. Philos. Fenn., 28 (1976)). Amsterdam: North-Holland, 1976, 188-215.

878. Anderson, Perry. "Components of the national culture." *New Left Review* 50 (1968):21-25. [On Wittgenstein]

879. Antonelli, Maria Teresa. "A proposito del último Wittgenstein: Observaciones sobre el convencionalismo." *Crisis* 3 (1956):473-484.

880. Apel, K.-O. "Wittgenstein und das Problem des hermeneutischen Verstehens." *Zeitschrift für Theologie und Kirche* 63 (1966):49-87.

881. Arrington, Robert L. "*Mechanism* and *Calculus*: Wittgenstein on Augustine's theory of ostension." In *Wittgenstein: Sources and Perspectives*. C. G. Luckhardt, ed. Ithaca (New York): Cornell Univ. Press, 1979, 303-338.

882. Aune, Bruce. "Knowing and merely thinking." *Philosophical Studies* 12 (1960):53-58.

883. Aune, Bruce. "On the complexity of avowals." In *Philosophy in America*. M. Black, ed. Ithaca (New York): Cornell Univ. Press, 1965, 35-57.

884. Aune, Bruce. "Does knowledge have an indubitable foundation?" In his *Knowledge, Mind and Nature*. New York: Random House, 1967, 31-62.

885. Baier, Kurt. "Ludwig Wittgenstein." *Meanjin* (March 1960):84-87.

886. Baker, Gordon P. "*Verehrung und Verkehrung*: Waismann and Wittgenstein." In *Wittgenstein: Sources and Perspectives*. C. G. Luckhardt, ed. Ithaca (New York): Cornell Univ. Press, 1979, 243-285.

887.   Bambrough, J. R.   "Principia metaphysica." *Philosophy* 39 (1964):97-109.

888.   Barone, Francesco. "Ludwig Wittgenstein." In *Enciclopedia Filosofica* (Venezia: Istituto per la colla-borazione culturale) 4 (1957).

889.   Barone, Francesco. "Wittgenstein inedito." *Filosofia della Scienza* 4 (1953):5-16.

890.   Barone, Francesco. "El solipsismo linguistico di Ludwig Wittgenstein." *Filosofia* 2 (1951):543-570.

891.   Begelman, D. A.   "Wittgenstein." *Behaviorism* 4 (1976): 201-207.

892.   Bell, Julian.   "An epistle on the subject of the ethical and aesthetic beliefs of Herr Ludwig Wittgenstein." In *Whips and Scorpions: Specimens of Modern Satiric Verse, 1914-1931*. Sherard Vines, ed.   London: Wishart, 1932, 21-30. Reprinted in Copi and Beard. [See no. 14]

893.   Benacerraf, Paul, and Putnam, Hilary.   "Wittgenstien." A section in their introduction to *Philosophy of Mathematics* (selected readings), 25-38.

894.   Bennett, Jonathan.   "On being forced to a conclusion." *Proceedings of the Aristotelian Society* Suppl. 35 (1961): 15-34.

895.   Benton, Ted.   "Winch, Wittgenstein and Marxism." *Radical Philosophy* 13 (1976).

896.   Bergmann, Gustav.   "The glory and the misery of Ludwig Wittgenstein." In his *Logic and Reality*. Wisconsin Univ. Press, 1964, 225-241. Reprinted in Copi and Beard. [See no. 14] Italian trans. by A. G. Conte in *Rivista di Filosofia* 52 (1961):387-406.

897.   Bouveresse, Jacques.   "Les derniers jours de l'humanité [Ludwig Wittgenstein]." *Critique* 31 (1975):753-805.

898.   Bouveresse, Jacques.   "Savoir, croire et agir [Wittgenstein]." In *Savoir, faire, espérer: les limites du la raison, I-II*.   (Publications des Facultés universitaires Saint Louis, 5) Bruxelles: Facultés universitaires Saint Louis, 1976, 19-41.

899.   Brunton, J. A.   "Logical wedges and the turning of spades. Some comments on Wittgenstein, philosophers he has influenced and verificationism." *Second Order. An African Journal of Philosophy* (Ile Ife) 3 (1974):3-28.

900.   Bubner, Rudiger. "Die Einheit in Wittgensteins Wandlungen." *Philosophische Rundschau* 15 (1968):161-184.

901.   Buck, R. C.   "Non-other minds."   In *Analytical Philosophy*.   R. J. Butler, ed.   Oxford: Basil Blackwell, 1962, 187-210.

902.   Bunting, I. A.   "Some difficulties in Stnius' account of the independence of atomic states of affairs."   *Australasian Journal of Philosophy* 43 (1965):368-375.

903.   Burr, Ronald.   "Wittgenstein's later language-philosophy and some issues in philosophy of mysticism."   *International Journal for Philosophy of Religion* 7 (1976):261-287.

904.   Butchvarov, P.   "Meaning-as-use and meaning-as-correspondence."   *Philosophy* 35 (1960):314-325.

905.   Cacciari, Massimo.   *Krisis.   Saggio sulla crisi del pensiero negativo da Nietzsche a Wittgenstein*.   (I fatti e le idee, 322).   Milan: Feltrinelli, 1976, 188p.

906.   Campanale, D.   "Il mondo in Wittgenstein."   *Rassegna di Scienze Filosofiche* 9 (1956):38-76.

907.   Campanale, D.   "La filosofia in Wittgenstein."   *Rassegna di Scienze Filosofiche* 8 (1955):417-461.

908.   Campanale, D.   "La teoria della raffigurazione in Wittgenstein."   *Rassegna di Scienze Filosofiche* 9 (1956): 159-207.

909.   Campanale, D.   "Ludwig Wittgenstein."   In *Les grands courants de la pensée contemporaine*.   Milan: Marzorati Editrice, 1964, 1525-1551.

910.   Camponigri, A. Robert.   *A History of Western Philosophy*.   Vol. 5.   Notre Dame (Indiana)-London: Univ. of Notre Dame Press, 1971, 314-321 et passim.

911.   Castañeda, Héctor-Neri.   "El atomismo sintáctico en la filosofia posterior de Wittgenstein y la naturaleza de las cuestiones filosóficas."   [Abstract]   *Revista Latinoamericana de Filosofía* 2 (1976):103-120.

912.   Cavell, Stanley.   "The availability of Wittgenstein's later philosophy."   *Philosophical Review* 71 (1962):67-93.   Reprinted in Pitcher.

913.   Cavell, Stanley.   *The Claim of Reason.   Wittgenstein, Skepticism, Morality, and Tragedy*.   New York: Oxford Univ. Press, 1979.

914.   Clarke, Bowman L.   *Language and Natural Theology*.   New York: Humanities Press, 1967.

915.   Cohen, Mendel.   "Wittgenstein's anti-essentialism."   *Australasian Journal of Philosophy* 46 (1968):210-214.

916. Colombo, G. C. M. "Epilogue on Wittgenstein."
The Month 18 (1957):356-358.

917. Cook, Monte. "Wittgenstein's appeal to particular
cases. *Modern Schoolman* 54 (1976-77):56-66.

918. Cooper, Neil. "Inconsistency." *Philosophical Quarterly*
16 (1966):54-58.

919. Copleston, Frederick C. *A History of Philosophy*. Vol.
8: *Bentham to Russell*. London: Burns & Oates Ltd., 1966.
"Epilogue," 495-504 et passim.

920. Cordua, Carla. "La teoria de los elementos últimos
en Wittgenstein." [Abstract] *Revista Latinoamericana de
Filosofía* 2 (1976):197-213.

921. Cornforth, Maurice C. "The philosophy of Wittgenstein."
In his *Science and Idealism*. New York: International
Publishers, 1947, 141-166.

922. Cornforth, Maurice C. "A therapy for theories." In
his *Marxism and the Linguistic Philosophy*. New York:
International Publishers, 1965, 133-154.

923. Cornman, James W. "Uses of language and philosophical
problems." *Philosophical Studies* 15 (1964):11-16.

924. Cornman, James W. "Private languages and private
entities." *Australasian Journal of Philosophy* 46 (1968).

925. Cornman, James W. *Metaphysics, Reference and Language*.
New Haven: Yale Univ. Press, 1966.

926. Cornman, James W. *Materialism and Sensations*.
New Haven: Yale Univ. Press, 1971.

927. Coulson, J. "Philosophy and integrity." *Downside
Review* 79 (1961):122-127. [On Wittgenstein and Gellner]

928. Coulter, Jeff. "Transparence of mind: The availability
of subjective phenomena." *Philosophy of the Social Sciences*
7 (1977).

929. Cox, Charles H., and Cox, Jean W. "The mystical
experience. With an emphasis on Wittgenstein and Zen."
Religious Studies 12 (1976):483-491.

930. Cranston, Maurice. "Ludwig Wittgenstein." *World
Review* (December 1951):21-24.

931. Cranston, Maurice. "Bildnis eines Philosophen."
Monat 4 (1952):495-497. Reprinted in *Wittgenstein:
Schriften/Beiheft*, 16-20.

932. Cranston, Maurice. "Vita e morte di Wittgenstein."
Aut Aut (1952):239-245.

933. Cranston, Maurice. "Literature of ideas." In *Craft
of Letters in England*. J. Lehmann, ed. Boston: Houghton
Mifflin, 1957, 205-207.

934. Daly, G. B. "New light on Wittgenstein." *Philosophical
Studies* (Maynooth) Part I, 10 (1960):5-49; Part II, 11 (1961):
28-62.

935. Daly, G. B. "Logical positivism, metaphysics and
ethics, I: Ludwig Wittgenstein." *Irish Theological Quarterly*
23 (1956):111-150.

936. Daniel, Stephen H. "Wittgenstein on field and stream."
Auslegung 4 (1977):176-198.

937. Davis, D. "Limits. An essay on Yvor Winters and Ludwig
Wittgenstein." *Poetry Nation* (Manchester) 4 (1977):21-25.

938. Davis, John W. "Is philosophy a sickness or a therapy?"
Antioch Review 23 (1963):5-23.

939. Deaño, Alfredo. "Filosofia, lenguaje y communicacion."
Convívium no. 37 (1971):23-54.

940. Delius, Harold. "Was sich überhaupt sagen lasst lasst
sich klar sagen. Gedanken zu einer Formulierung Ludwig
Wittgensteins." *Archiv für Philosophie* 8 (1958):211-254.

941. Diamond, Cora. "Secondary sense." *Aristotelian
Society Proceedings* 67 (1966-67):189-208.

942. Diamond, Cora. "Riddles and Anselm's riddle."
Aristotelian Society 51 (1977):143-168.

943. Disco, Cornelius. "Ludwig Wittgenstein and the end of
wild conjectures." *Theory and Society* 3 (1976).

944. Dommeyer, Frederick. *Current Philosophical Issues:
Essays in Honor of Curt John Ducasse*. Springfield (Illinois):
Thomas, 1966.

945. Drudius, Baldrich R. "Ludwig Wittgenstein y su obra
filosofía." *Theoría* (Madrid) 1 (1952):51-54.

946. Drury, M. O'C. "Some notes on conversations with
Wittgenstein." In *Essays on Wittgenstein in Honour of
G. H. von Wright* (Acta Philos. Fenn. 28 (1976)). Amsterdam:
North-Holland, 1976, 22-40.

947. Dufrenne, Mikel. "Wittgenstein et la philosophie."
Études Philosophiques 20 (1965):281-306.

948. Dummett, Michael. *Truth and Other Enigmas*. Cambridge
(Massachusetts): Harvard Univ. Press, 1978.

949. Elgin, C. Z. "The impossibility of saying what is
shown [Wittgenstein]." *Southern Journal of Philosophy*
16 (1978):617-627.

950. Ellis, Anthony. "Kenny and the continuity of Wittgenstein's philosophy [A. Kenny, *Wittgenstein*]." *Mind* 87
(1978):270-275.

951. Engel, S. Morris. "Thought and language." *Dialogue*
3 (1964):160-170.

952. Engel, S. Morris. "Reason, morals and philosophic
irony." *The Personalist* 45 (1964):533-555.

953. Erickson, Stephen A. "Meaning and language." *Man and
World* 1 (1968):563-586.

954. Esposito, Joseph L. "Play and possibility." *Philosophy
Today* 18 (1974):137-146.

955. Fabril, Albrecht. "Ludwig Wittgenstein." *Merkur*
7 (1953):1193-1196.

956. Fahrenback, H. "Positionen und Probleme gegenwärtigen
Philosophie, II: Philosophie der Sprache." *Theologische
Rundschau* n.s. 36 (1971):125-141; Ibid., 221-243.

957. Farrell, B. A. "An appraisal of therapeutic positivism." Part I, *Mind* 55 (1946):25-48; Part II, *Mind* 55
(1946):133-150.

958. Feibleman, J. K. "Reflections after Wittgenstein's
Philosophical Investigations." In his *Inside the Great
Mirror*, 203-216.

959. Ferrater Mora, José. "Wittgenstein o la destrucción."
Realidad (Buenos Aires) 3 (1949):129-140.

960. Ferrater Mora, José. "Wittgenstein oder die Destruktion." *Monat* 4 (1952). Reprinted in *Wittgenstein:
Schriften/Beiheft*, 21-29.

961. Ferrater Mora, José. "Wittgenstein, a symbol of
troubled times." *Philosophy and Phenomenological Research*
14 (1953):89-96. [In Fann]

962. Ferrater Mora, José. "Wittgenstein, simbolo de una
epoca angustiada." *Theoria* (Madrid) 2 (1954):33-38.

963. Ferrater Mora, José. "Del uso." *Diálogos* 5 (1968):
61-78.

964. Feyerabend, Paul. "Wittgenstein und die Philosophie."
Wissenschaft und Weltbild 7 (1954):212-220, 283-292.

965. Feyerabend, Paul. "Ludwig Wittgenstein." *Merkur*
8 (1954):1021-1038. Reprinted in *Wittgenstein: Schriften/
Beiheft*, 30-47.

966. Filiasi Carcano, Paolo. "Il secondo Wittgenstein."
In *La filosofia dal '45 ad oggi*. A cura di Valerio Verra
(Saggi, 65). Torino: Eri, Edizioni RAI Radio-Televisione
Italiana, 1976, 239-251.

967. Finch, Henry Le Roy. "Wittgenstein's last word:
ordinary certainty. *International Philosophical Quarterly*
15 (1975):383-395.

968. Findlay, J. B. "Some reactions to recent Cambridge
Philosophy." *Australasian Jorunal of Psychology and
Philosophy* 18 (1940):193-211; 19 (1941):1-13.

969. Findlay, John N. *Language, Mind and Value: Philosophical Essays*. London: George Allen & Unwin, 1963. 259p.

970. Findlay, John N. "Wittgenstein's philosophical
investigations." *Revue Internationale de Philosophie*
7 (1953):201-216.

971. Findlay, John N. "Ordinary, revisionary, and
dialectical strategies in philosophy: A plea for the
re-introduction of a logic of aspects." *Erkenntnis* 11
(1977):275-290.

972. Fisher, Mark. "Reason, emotion, and love." *Inquiry*
20 (1977):189-203.

973. Flam, Leopold. *La philosophie au tournant de notre
temps*. Bruxelles: Presses Universitaires de Bruxelles, 1970.

974. Fleming, Noël. "Recognizing and seeing as."
Philosophical Review 66 (1957):161-179.

975. Fleming, Noël. "Seeing the soul." *Philosophy* 53
(1978):33-50.

976. Fodor, Jerry, and Katz, Jerrold. "The availability
of what we say." *Philosophical Review* 72 (1963):57-71.

977. Forgie, J. William. "Wittgenstein on naming and
ostensive definition. *Studi Internazionale di Filosofia*
8 (1976):13-26.

978. Foster, Lawrence, and Swanson, J. W., eds. *Experience
and Theory*. Amherst: Univ. of Massachusetts Press, 1970.

979. Freeman, James B., and Daniels, Charles B. "Maximal propositions and the coherence theory of truth." *Dialogue* 17 (1978):56-71.

980. Frege, W. C. *Doen of Laten?* Amsterdam/Baarn: Moussault, 1974. 94p.

981. Freundlich, R. "Logik und Mystik." *Zeitschrift für Philosophische Forschung* 7 (1953):554-570.

982. Fulmer, Gilbert. "Reasoning in a 'primitive' society." *Metaphilosophy* 8 (1977):164-171.

983. Funke, Gerhard. "Einheitssprache, Sprachspiel und Sprachauslegung bei Wittgenstein." *Zeitschrift für Philosophische Forschung* 22 (1968):1-30 and 216-247.

984. Gabriel, Leo. "Logische Magie. Ein Nachwort zum Thema Wittgenstein." *Wissenschaft und Weltbild* 7 (1954): 288-293.

985. Gale, Richard M. "Could logical space be empty?" In *Essays on Wittgenstein in Honour of G. H. von Wright* (Acta Philos. Fenn. 28 (1976)). Amsterdam: North-Holland, 1976, 85-104.

986. Gallacher, Hugh P. "Met Wittgenstein tussen twijfel en zekerheid." *Algemeen Nederlands Tijdschrift voor Wijsbegeerte en Psychologie* 69 (1977):73-94.

987. Garavaso, Pieranna. "Il fondamento unitario del pensiero di Wittgenstein dal *Tractatus* alle *Ricerche Filosofiche*." *Verifiche* 6 (1977):49-88.

988. Gasking, D. A. T. "Avowals." In *Analytical Philosophy*. R. J. Butler, ed. Oxford: Basil Blackwell, 1962, 154-169.

989. Gellner, Ernest. *The Devil in Modern Philosophy*. London: Routledge, 1974.

990. Gellner, Ernest. *Legitimation of Belief*. Cambridge Univ. Press, 129-138 et passim.

991. Germana, Joseph. "Wittgenstein: Wittgenstein." *Behaviorism* 5 (1977):61-62.

992. Giacomini, Ugo. "Wittgenstein oggi." *Aut Aut* (1972): 415-419.

993. Gilson, E.-T. Langan. "Ludwig Wittgenstein." In *Recent Philosophy*. E.-T. Langan Gilson and A. A. Maurer. New York: Random House, 1962, 521-530.

994. Ginet, Carl. "Wittgenstein's claim that there could not be just one occasion of obeying a rule." In *Essays on Wittgenstein in Honour of G. H. von Wright* (Acta Philos. Fenn. 28 (1976)). Amsterdam: North-Holland, 1976, 154-165.

995.   Goff, Robert A.   "The Wittgenstein game."   *Christian
Scholar* 45 (1962).

996.   Goodman, R. B.   "An analysis of two perceptual
predicates."   *Southwestern Journal of Philosophy* 7 (1976):
35-53.

997.   Griffiths, A. Phillips.   "Wittgenstein and the four-
fold root of the principle of sufficient reason."
Proceedings of the Aristotelian Society 50 (suppl. 1976):
1-20.

998.   Gross, Barry.   *Analytic Philosophy. An Historical
Introduction.*   New York: Pegasus, 1970, 141-180.

999.   Gruender, D.   "Wittgenstein on explanation and description."   *Journal of Philosophy* 59 (1962):523-530.

1000.   Gruender, D.   "Language, society, and knowledge."
Antioch Review 28 (1968):187-212.

1001.   Grünfeld, Joseph.   "Raising the ghost in the machine."
Science et Esprit 27 (1975):91-105.

1002.   G. N.   "Ludwig Wittgenstein (1889-1951)."   *Wijsgerig
Perspectief of Maatschappij en Wetenschap* 1 (1960-61):
246-250.

1003.   Hacker, P. M. S.   "Semantic holism: Frege and
Wittgenstein."   In *Wittgenstein: Sources and Perspectives.*
C. G. Luckhardt, ed.   Ithaca (New York): Cornell Univ.
Press, 1979, 213-242.

1004.   Hadot, P.   "Wittgenstein, philosophe du language."
Critique (1959):866-881 and (1959):972-983.

1005.   Haller, Rudolf.   "Österreichische Philosophie."
Conceptus 11 (1977):57-66.

1006.   Hallett, Garth L.   "A oposição de Wittgenstein à
filosofia 'cientifica'."   (Trad. por Agenor Joao Ferrari).
Pres. filos. (1975):36-47.

1007.   Hallie, Philip P.   "Wittgenstein's grammatical-
empirical distinctions."   *Journal of Philosophy* 60 (1963):
565-578.

1008.   Hallie, Philip P.   "Wittgenstein's exclusion of
metaphysical nonsense."   *Philosophical Quarterly* 16 (1966):
97-112.

1009.   Hamburg, Carl.   "Whereof one cannot speak."   *Journal
of Philosophy* 50 (1953):662-664.

1010.   Hamlyn, D. W.   "Categories, formal concepts and
metaphysics."   *Philosophy* 34 (1959):111-124.

1011. Hampshire, Stuart. "Wittgenstein." In his *Modern Writers and Other Essays*. New York: Knopf, 1970, 130-137.

1012. Hannay, Alastair. "Was Wittgenstein a psychologist?" *Inquiry* 7 (1964):379-386.

1013. Harrison, Bernard. *Meaning and Structure: An Essay in the Philosophy of Language*. New York: Harper & Row, 1972.

1014. Harrison, Frank R. "Wittgenstein and the doctrine of identical minimal meaning." *Methodos* 14 (1962):61-74.

1015. Hartnack, Justus. "Me and my body." In *Essays on Wittgenstein in Honour of G. H. von Wright* (Acta Philos. Fenn. 28 (1976)). Amsterdam: North-Holland, 1976, 241-249.

1016. Hawkins, D. J. B. *Crucial Problems of Modern Philosophy*. Englewood Cliffs (New Jersey): Hawthorn Books, 1963.

1017. Heath, P. L. "Wittgenstein investigated." *Philosophical Quarterly* 6 (1956):66-71.

1018. Heller, Erich L. "Wittgenstein: Unphilosophical notes." *Encounter* (September 1959):40-48. Reprinted in his *An Artist's Journey into the Interior and Other Essays*. New York: Random House, 1965; and in Fann [see no. 23]. German version appeared in *Merkur* 13 (1958); and in *Wittgenstein: Schriften/Beiheft*.

1019. Hertzberg, Lars. "On the factual dependence of the language-game." In *Essays on Wittgenstein in Honour of G. H. von Wright* (Acta Philos. Fenn. 28 (1976)). Amsterdam: North-Holland, 1976, 126-153.

1020. Hinst, P. "Die Früh- und Spätphilosophie L. Wittgensteins." *Philosophische Rundschau* 15 (1968):51-65. [Review on Pitcher]

1021. Holmes, Arthur F. *Christian Philosophy in the 20th Century: An Essay in Philosophical Methodology*. Nutley (New Jersey): Craig Press, 1969.

1022. Hottois, Gilbert. "Esquisse comparative de la réception de la psychanalyse comme 'art sémantique' dans la philosophie linguistique thérapeutique de Wittgenstein, Lazerowitz et Wisdom." *Annales de L'Institut de Philosophie* (1975):177-205.

1023. Hudson, W. D. "Wittgenstein on fundamental propositions." *Southwestern Journal of Philosophy* 7 (1977): 7-22.

1024. Hunter, John F. M. Wittgenstein on describing and making connections. *Philosophical Quarterly* 26 (1976): 243-250.

1025. Hunter, John F. M. "Wittgenstein on inner processes
and outward criteria." *Canadian Journal of Philosophy*
7 (1977):805-817.

1026. Hunter, John F. M. "Some grammatical states."
Philosophy 52 (1977):155-166.

1027. Kazemier, B. H. "Wittgenstein in het Geding (I)."
*Algemeen Nederlands Tijdschrift voor Wijsbegeerte en
Psychologie* 58 (1966).

1028. Keeling, L. Bryant, and Morelli, Mario F. "Beyond
Wittgensteinian fideism: An examination of John Hick's
analysis of religious faith." *International Journal for
the Philosophy of Religion* 8 (1977):250-262.

1029. Kemmerling, A. "Regel und Geltung im Lichte der
Analyse Wittgensteins." *Rechtstheorie* (Berlin) 6 (1975):
104-131.

1030. Kempski, Jürgen von. "Wittgenstein und Analytische
Philosophie." *Merkur* 15 (1961):664-676.

1031. Kempski, Jürgen von. "Wittgenstein y la filosofía
analítica." *Diálogos* 5 (1968):115-129.

1032. Kempski, Jürgen von. "Über Wittgenstein." *Neue
Deutsche Hefte* 82 (1961):43-60.

1033. Kempski, Jürgen von. "Anotaciones sobre Wittgenstein."
Diálogos 5 (1968):101-114.

1034. Kenny, Anthony. *Action, Emotion and Will*. New York:
Humanities Press, 1963. [Psych.]

1035. Kenny, Anthony. *Will, Freedom and Power*. Oxford:
Blackwell, 1976. 170p.

1036. Kenny, Anthony. "From the big typescript to the
Philosophical Grammar." In *Essays on Wittgenstein in
Honour of G. H. von Wright* (Acta Philos. Fenn. 28 (1976)).
Amsterdam: North-Holland, 1976, 41-53.

1037. Kolakowski, Leszek. "Ludwig Wittgenstein." In his
The Alienation of Reason. New York: Anchor Books, 1969,
174-177.

1038. Kolenda, K. "Wittgenstein's 'Weltanschaaung'."
Rice University Studies 50 (1961):23-37.

1039. Kohl, Herbert. "Wittgenstein returns." In his
The Age of Complexity. New York: A Mentor Book, 1965,
119-128.

1040. Kraft, Werner. "Ludwig Wittgenstein." *Wiener Zeitschrift für Philosophie, Psychologie, Pädagogik* 3 (1951): 161-163.

1041. Kraft, Werner. *Rebellen des Geistes*. Stuttgart: Kohlhammer, 1968. 162p.

1042. Kreisel, G. "Wittgenstein's theory and practice of philosophy." *British Journal for the Philosophy of Science* 11 (1960):238-252.

1043. Kreisel, G. "Der unheilvolle Einbruch der Logik in die Mathematik." In *Essays on Wittgenstein in Honour of G. H. von Wright* (Acta Philos. Fenn. 28 (1976)). Amsterdam: North-Holland, 1976, 166-187.

1044. Kuntz, P. G. "Order in language, phenomena, and reality: Notes on linguistic analysis, phenomenology and metaphysics." *The Monist* 49 (1965):107-136.

1045. Kutschera, Franz von. *The Philosophy of Language*. Trans. from the German by B. Terrell. Dordrecht: Reidel, 1975. [Chapter 2 on Wittgenstein]

1046. Kuzminski, Adrian. "Showing and saying: Wittgenstein's mystical realism." *Yale Review* 68 (1979):500-518.

1047. Lamb, David. "Hegel and Wittgenstein on language and sense-certainty." *Clio* 7 (1978):288-301.

1048. Lamb, David. "Preserving a primitive society: reflections on post-Wittgensteinian social philosophy." *Sociological Review* 25 (1977):689-719.

1049. Laycock, H. "Ordinary language and materialism." *Philosophy* 42 (1967):363-367.

1050. Lazerowitz, Morris. "Tiempo y terminología temporal." *Diálogos* 5 (1968):7-34.

1051. Leiber, Justin. *Structuralism, Skepticism and Mind in the Psychological Sciences*. Boston: G. K. Hall Twayne, 1978, 49-58, 124-138.

1058. Levi, Albert W. "Wittgenstein as dialectician." *Journal of Philosophy* 61 (1964):127-139. Reprinted in Fann. [See no. 23]

1059. Levi, Albert W. "G. E. Moore and Ludwig Wittgenstein." In his *Philosophy and Modern World*. Bloomington (Indiana): Indiana Univ. Press, 1959, 436-481.

1060. Levi, Albert W. "The biographical sources of Wittgenstein's ethics." *Telos* (Winter 1978-79):63-76.

1061. Levin, Michael E. "Wittgenstein in perspective
[D. F. Pears, *Ludwig Wittgenstein*]." *Social Research*
40 (1973):192-207.

1062. Levinson, Stephen C. "Activity types and language."
Pragmatics Microfiche 3, D1 (1978).

1063. Lewis, P. B. "Wittgenstein on seeing and inter-
preting." In *Impressions of Empiricism*. Godfrey Vesey, ed.
London: Macmillan, 1972. 237p. Royal Institute of
Philosophy Lectures 9 (1974-75).

1064. Lieb, Irwin C. "Wittgenstein's investigations."
Review of Metaphysics 8 (1954):125-143.

1065. Linsky, L. "Meaning and use." *Algemeen Nederlands
Tijdschrift voor Wijsbegeerte en Psychologie* 53 (1960):
201-207.

1066. Linsky, L. "Wittgenstein on language and some
problems of philosophy." *Journal of Philosophy* 54 (1957):
285-293. Reprinted in Fann.

1067. Linville, Kent. "Wittgenstein at criticism."
Southern Journal of Philosophy 17 (1979):85-94.

1068. Llewelyn, J. E. "On not speaking the same language."
Australasian Journal of Philosophy 40 (1962):35-48 and
127-145.

1069. Lucier, P. "Le statut du langage religieux dans la
philosophie de Ludwig Wittgenstein." *St. Rel./Sc. Rel.*
3 (1973):14-28.

1070. Lugton, Robert C. "Ludwig Wittgenstein: The logic
of language." *ETC* 22 (1965):165-192.

1071. Malcolm, Norman. "The privacy of experience." In
Epistemology: New Essays in the Theory of Knowledge.
Avrum Stroll, ed. New York: Harper & Row, 1967, 129-158.

1072. Malcolm, Norman. "Ludwig Wittgenstein." In
The Encyclopedia of Philosophy, Vol. 8. Paul Edwards, ed.
New York: Macmillan, The Free Press, 1967, 327-340.

1073. Malcolm, Norman. "Moore and Wittgenstein on the sense
of *I Know.*" In *Essays on Wittgenstein in Honour of G. H.
von Wright* (Acta Philos. Fenn. 28 (1976)). Amsterdam:
North-Holland, 1976, 215-240.

1074. Malcolm, Norman. "Wittgenstein's conception of first
person psychological sentences as 'expressions'."
Philosophic Exchange 2 (1978):59-72.

1075. Marcuse, Herbert. "The triumph of positive thinking: One-dimensional philosophy." In his *One-dimensional Man*. Boston: Beacon Press, 1961, 170-202.

1076. Mardiros, A. M. "Shapers of the modern outlook - Ludwig Wittgenstein: Philosopher." *Canadian Forum* 33 (1954):223-225.

1077. Marks, Charles E. "Ginet on Wittgenstein's argument against private rules [C. G. Ginet, *Wittgenstein's Argument that One Can Obey a Rule Privately*]." *Philosophical Studies* (Dordrecht) 25 (1974):261-271.

1078. Martinez Díez, Felicísimo. "El pensamiento de L. Wittgenstein sobre el lenguaje religioso y ético." *Studium* 15 (1975):463-490.

1079. Martland, T. R. "On 'The limits of my language mean the limits of my world'." *Review of Metaphysics* 29 (1975-76): 19-26.

1080. Mays, Wolfe. "Note on Wittgenstein's Manchester period." *Mind* 64 (1955):247-248.

1081. McGill, V. F. "An evaluation of logical positivism." *Science and Society* 1 (1936-37):45-80.

1083. McMullin, Ernan. "The analytical approach to philosophy." *Proceedings of the American Catholic Philosophical Association* 34 (1960):80-109.

1084. Mehta, Ved. "A battle against the bewitchment of our intelligence." *New Yorker*, December 9, 1961. Reprinted in his *The Fly and the Fly Bottle: Encounters with British Intellectuals*. Boston: Little, Brown, & Co., 1962.

1085. Mennell, S. "Ethnomethodology and the new methodenstreit." *Acta Sociologica* 18 (1975):287-302.

1086. Meyer, H. "La philosophie de Ludwig Wittgenstein." *Algemeen Nederlands Tijdschrift voor Wijsbegeerte en Psychologie* 48 (1956):44-53.

1087. Meyer, H. "Zin en onzin volgens Ludwig Wittgenstein." *Algemeen Nederlands Tijdschrift voor Wijsbegeerte en Psychologie* 48 (1956):202-208.

1088. Miller, J. "Wittgenstein's *Weltanschaaung*." *Philosophical Studies* (Maynooth) 13 (1964):127-140.

1089. Miller, Robert G. "Linguistic analysis and metaphysics." *Proceedings of the American Catholic Philosophical Association* 34 (1960):80-109.

1090. Mills, John F. "A meeting with Wittgenstein." *Times Literary Supplement* June 12, 1959, 353.

1091. Mohr, Richard D. "Family resemblance, platonism, universals." *Canadian Journal of Philosophy* 7 (1977):593-600.

1092. Montero Moliner, Fernando. "El analisis del
lenguaje y la reduccion eidetica." *Convivium* 34 (1971):
5-22.

1093. Moore, G. E. "'Truth possibilities', and Wittgenstein's sense of 'Tautology'." In his *Common place Book*.
London: George Allen & Unwin, 1962, 282-286.

1094. Mosier, Richard D. "Reflections on the philosophy
of Wittgenstein." *Philosophy of Education: Proceedings*
23 (1967):121-126.

1095. Munz, Peter. "Popper and Wittgenstein." In
The Critical Approach to Science and Philosophy. M. A.
Bunge, ed. New York: Free Press, 1964, 82-91.

1096. Murphy, John. "Another note on a misreading of
Wittgenstein." *Analysis* 29 (1968):62-64.

1097. Nagel, Ernest. "Impressions and appraisals of
analytic philosophy in Europe." *Journal of Philosophy*
33 (1936):5-53.

1098. Needham, Rodney. *Belief, Language and Experience*.
Chicago Univ. Press, 1972, xvii-269p.

1099. Nehlich, G. C. "If you can't be wrong, then you
can't be right." *Philosophical Quarterly* 17 (1967):300-307.

1100. Newell, R. W. *The Concept of Philosophy*. London:
Methuen, 1967, 145-152.

1101. Nielsen, Kai. "Remarks on a Wittgensteinian method.
An examination of J. F. M. Hunter's *Essays after Wittgenstein*." *Metaphilosophy* 7 (1976):241-264.

1102. Nolet de Brauwere, Y. "Coups de sonde dans la
philosophie anglaise contemporaine." *Revue Philosophique
de Louvain* 58 (1960):250-268.

1103. Northrop, F. S. C. "Language, mysticism and God."
In his *Man, Nature and God*. New York: Simon & Schuster,
1962, 238-245.

1104. Nygren, Anders. "From atomism to contexts of meaning in philosophy." In *Philosophical Essays* dedicated to
Gunnar Aspelin. Lund: GWK Gleerup Bokförlag, 1963, 122-136.

1105. Nyiri, J. C. "Wittgenstein's new traditionalism."
In *Essays on Wittgenstein in Honour of G. H. von Wright*
(Acta Philos. Fenn. 28 (1976)). Amsterdam: North-Holland,
1976, 503-512.

1106. Nyiri, J. C. "Zwei geistige Leitsterne: Musil und Wittgenstein." *Literatur und Kritik* 1/3 (1977):167-179.

1107. O'Brien, George. "The unity of Wittgenstein's thought." *International Philosophical Quarterly* 6 (1966): 45-70. Reprinted in Fann. [See no. 23]

1108. Olson, Raymond, et al., eds. *Contemporary Philosophy in Scandinavia*. Baltimore: Johns Hopkins Press, 1972.

1109. Orr, S. S. "Some reflections on the Cambridge approach to philosophy." *Australasian Journal of Psychology and Philosophy* 4 (1946):34-76, and 120-167.

1109a. Osheroff, Steven S. "Wittgenstein: Psychological disputes and common moves." *Philosophical Phenomenological Research* 36 (1975-76):339-363.

1110. Paci, Enzo. "Negatività e positività di Wittgenstein." *Aut Aut* (May 1952):252-256.

1111. Pagee, Samuel. "Of words and tools." *Inquiry* 10 (1967):181-195.

1112. Palmer, H. "The other logical constant." *Mind* 68 (1958):50-59.

1113. Passmore, John. "Some Cambridge philosophers: and Wittgenstein's *Tractatus* and 'Wittgenstein and ordinary language philosophy." In his *Hundred Years of Philosophy*. New York: Basic Books, 1966, 348-368, and 431-475. 2d ed., revised.

1114. Paul, G. A. "Wittgenstein." In *The Revolution in Philosophy*. A. J. Ayer, et al., eds. London: Macmillan, 1963.

1115. Payer, Peter. "Wittgensteins Sprachphilosophische Grundmetaphern." *Conceptus* 11 (1977):283-288.

1116. Pears, David F. "Logical atomism: Russell and Wittgenstein." In *The Revolution in Philosophy*. A. J. Ayer, et al., eds. London: Macmillan, 1956, 44-55.

1117. Pears, David F. "Wittgenstein and Austin." In *British Analytical Philosophy*. B. Williams and A. Montefiore, eds. London: Routledge & Kegan Paul, 1966, 17-39.

1118. Pears, David F. "The development of Wittgenstein's philosophy." *New York Review of Books*, January 16, 1969: 21-30.

1119. Pears, David F., ed. *Bertrand Russell: A Collection of Critical Essays*. Garden City: Doubleday Anchor Books, 1972.

1120. Peduzzi, O. "Wittgenstein in Inghilterra." *Aut Aut*
(May 1954):46-49.

1121. Peterson, R. G. "Picture is a fact: Wittgenstein
and *The Naked Lunch*." *Twentieth-Century Literature* 12
(1966):78-86.

1122. Phillips, G. A. "Ludwig Wittgenstein. A philosophical theory of language acquisition and use." *Word. Journal
of the International Linguistic Association* (New York)
21 (1971):139-157.

1123. Pole, David. "Wittgenstein et la philosophie."
Archives de Philosophie 24 (1961):450-467.

1124. Popper, Karl. "The nature of philosophical problems
and their roots in science." *British Journal for the
Philosophy of Science* 3 (1952):124-156.

1125. Quinton, A. M. "Linguistic analysis." In *Philosophy
in the Mid-century.* Vol. 2. R. Klibansky, ed. Firenze:
La Nuova Italia Editrice, 1961, 146-202.

1126. Quinton, A. M. "Contemporary British philosophy."
In *A Critical History of Western Philosophy.* D. J. O'Connor,
ed. New York: Free Press, 1964, 530-556.

1127. Rabossi, Eduardo A. *Analisis filosófico, logica y
metafísica: Ensayos sobre la filosofía analítica y el
analisis filosófico "classico".* Caracas: Monte Avila,
1975. 135p.

1128. Radnitzky, Gerard. "Philosophie und Wissenschafts-
theorie zwischen Wittgenstein und Popper." *Conceptus*
11 (1977):249-282.

1129. Rankin, K. W. "Wittgenstein on meaning, understanding
and intenting." *American Philosophical Quarterly* 3 (1966):
1-13.

1130. Rankin, K. W. "The role of imagination, rule-
operations, and atmosphere in Wittgenstein's language-games."
Inquiry 10 (1967):279-291.

1131. Rhees, Rush. "Wittgenstein on language and ritual."
In *Essays on Wittgenstein in Honour of G. H. von Wright*
(Acta Philos. Fenn. 28 (1976)). Amsterdam: North-Holland,
1976, 450-484.

1132. Rhees, Rush. "Wittgenstein's builders." *Proceedings
of the Aristotelian Society* 60 (1959-60):171-186. Reprinted
in Fann. [See no. 23]

1133. Richman, R. J. "Something common." *Journal of
Philosophy* 59 (1962):821-830.

1134. Robinson, Guy. "Following and formalization."
Mind 73 (1964):46-63.

1135. Robinson, N. H. G. "After Wittgenstein." *Religious
Studies* 12 (1976):493-507.

1136. Rorty, Richard. "Wittgensteinian philosophy and
empirical psychology. *Philosophical Studies* (Dordrecht)
31 (1977):151-172.

1137. Rosen, Stanley. "Socrates' dream." *Theoria* 42
(1976):161-188.

1138. Rosenberg, Jay F. *Linguistic Representation*.
Boston: Reidel, 1974.

1139. Ross, Jacob J. "Rationality and common sense."
Philosophy 53 (1978):374-381.

1140. Rotenstreich, Nathan. "The thrust against language:
A critical comment on Wittgenstein's ethics." *Journal of
Value Inquiry* 2 (1968).

1141. Rotenstreich, Nathan. "Between persuasion and deeds."
In *Essays on Wittgenstein in Honour of G. H. von Wright*
(Acta Philos. Fenn. 28 (1976)). Amsterdam: North-Holland,
1976, 485-502.

1142. Rovatti, Pier Aldo. "La positività del paradosso in
Wittgenstein." *Aut Aut* (January 1968).

1143. Runes, D. D. "Ludwig Wittgenstein." In his
Pictorial History of Philosophy. New York: Philosophical
Library, 1959.

1144. Ryle, Gilbert. "Ludwig Wittgenstein." *Analysis*
12 (1951):1-9. Reprinted in Fann and in Copi and Beard
[See nos. 23 and 2014]. (Italian Trans. in *Rivista di
Filosofia* 43 (1952):186-193.

1145. Ryle, Gilbert. "The work of an influential but
little-known philosopher of science: Ludwig Wittgenstein."
Scientific American 197 (1957):251-259.

1146. Saisselin, R. G. "Language game in limbo concerning
a certain Ludwig Wittgenstein, written in ordinary language."
Queen's Quarterly (Canada) 69 (1963):607-615.

1147. Sanabria, J. Rubén. "Wittgenstein y la filosofia."
Humanitas. Anuario del Centro de Estudios Humanísticos
(México) (1975):23-44.

1148. Sánchez-Mazas, M. "La ciencia, el lenguaje y el
mundo según Wittgenstein." *Cuadernos Hispanoamericanos*
15 (1953):35-44; *Theoria* (Madrid) 2 (1954):127-130.

1149. Saran, A. K. "A Wittgensteinian sociology?"
Ethics 75 (1965):195-200.

1150. Schiavone, M. "Il pensiero filosofico di Ludwig
Wittgenstein alla luce del *Tractatus*." *Rivista di Filosofia
Neo-Scolastica* 47 (1955):225-252.

1151. Scrutton, Roger. *Art and Imagination: A Study in
the Philosophy of Mind.* New York: Barnes and Noble, 1974.

1152. Seligman, David B. "Wittgenstein on seeing aspects
and experiencing meanings." *Philosophy of Phenomenological
Research* 37 (1976-77):205-217.

1153. Senchuk, Dennis M. "Private objects: A study of
Wittgenstein's method." *Metaphilosophy* 7 (1976):217-240.

1154. Seung, T. K. *Cultural Thematics. The formation of
the Faustian Ethics.* New Haven: Yale Univ. Press, 1976,
xviii-283p. [Role of language in culture]

1155. Shalom, A. "Y a-t-il du nouveau dans la philosophie
anglaise?" *Etudes Philosophiques* 11 (1956):653-664.

1156. Shalom, A. "Wittgenstein, le langage et la philosophie." *Etudes Philosophiques* 13 (1958):486-494.

1157. Shibles, Warren. "L'originalité de Wittgenstein."
Etudes Philosophiques (1975):365-372.

1158. Shir, Jay. "Wittgenstein's aesthetics and the theory
of literature." *British Journal of Aesthetics* 18 (1978):
3-11.

1159. Shwayder, D. S. *Modes of Referring and the Problem
of Universals: An Essay in Metaphysics.* Berkeley: Univ.
of California Press, 1961.

1160. Smiley, P. O. "Importance of Wittgenstein."
The Tablet 203 (1954):116. [See Trethowan below, no. 1186]

1161. Smith, Barry. "Law and eschatology in Wittgenstein's
early thought." *Inquiry* 21 (1978):425-441.

1162. Sokolowski, Robert. "Ludwig Wittgenstein: Philosophy
as linguistic analysis." In *Twentieth-Century Thinkers.*
J. K. Ryan, ed. New York: Alba House, 1964, 175-204.

1163. Specht, Ernst Konrad. *Sprache und Sein. Untersuchungen zur sprachanalytischen Grundlegung der Ontologie.*
Berlin: Walter de Gruyter, 1967, viii-155p.

1164. Spurling, Laurie. *Phenomenology and the Social
World. The Philosophy of Merleau-Ponty and its Relevance
to the Social Sciences.* London: Routledge and Kegan Paul,
1977.

1165. Stebbing, Susan. "Logical positivism and analysis."
Proceedings of the British Academy 19 (1933):53-87.

1166. Stebbing, Susan. "Language and misleading questions."
Erkenntnis 8 (1939):1-6.

1167. Stegmüller, Wolfgang. "Eine Modelltheoretische
Präzirierund der Wittgensteinischen Bildtheorie." *Notre
Dame Journal of Formal Logic* 7 (1966):181-195.

1168. Stegmüller, Wolfgang. "Ludwig Wittgenstein als
Ontologe, Isomorphietheoretiker, Transzendentalphilosoph
und Konstruktivist." *Philosophische Rundschau* 13 (1965):
116-152.

1169. Stigen, A. "Interpretations of Wittgenstein."
Inquiry 5 (1962):167-175.

1170. Stocker, Michael A. G. "Memory and the private
language argument." *Philosophical Quarterly* 16 (1966):
47-53.

1171. Stolte, Dieter. "Logik ist die Hölle- Zu Wittgensteins
Schriften." *Der Monat* 14 (1961):66-70.

1172. Stolpe, S. "Ludwig Wittgensteins vag." *Credo* 36
(1955):110-114.

1173. Stoutland, Frederick. "The causation of behavior."
In *Essays on Wittgenstein in Honour of G. H. von Wright*
(Acta Philos. Fenn. 28 (1976)). Amsterdam: North-Holland,
1976, 286-325.

1174. Strasser, Stephan. "Ludwig Wittgenstein, in Problem
des 'Verstehens' in neuer sicht." In *Vérité et Vérifica-
tion. Wahrheit und Verifikation* (Phaenomenologich, 61).
The Hague: Nijhoff, 1974, 147-155.

1175. Stumpf, S. Enoch. "Analytic philosophy." In his
Socrates to Sartre. New York: McGraw-Hill, 1966, 437-452.

1176. Sullivan, J. P. "In defense of Wittgenstein."
Texas Quarterly 10 (1967):60-70.

1177. Swoyer, Chris. "Private languages and skepticism
[Wittgenstein]." *Southwestern Journal of Philosophy* 8
(1977):41-50. [Ramon M. Lemos, reply to "Private languages
and skepticism", 51-52]

1178. Taylor, Paul W. *Normative Discourse*. Englewood
Cliffs (New Jersey): Prentice-Hall, 1961.

1179. Tennessen, Herman. "Whereof one has been silent,
thereof one may have to speak." *Journal of Philosophy*
58 (1961):263-274.

1180. Tilgmann, B. R. "For the account showing that there is or is not a significant difference between the views of the earlier and the later Wittgenstein." *Review of Metaphysics* 16 (1962):380-383.

1181. Torretti, Roberto. "Las *Investigaciones* de Wittgenstein y la posibilidad de la filosofía." *Diálogos* 5 (1968): 35-60.

1182. Toulmin, Stephen. "Wittgenstein and psycholinguistics." Isenberg lecture delivered at Michigan State University, November 22, 1968.

1183. Toulmin, Stephen. "Ludwig Wittgenstein." *Encounter* 32 (1969):58-71.

1184. Toulmin, Stephen. "From logical positivism to conceptual history." In *The Legacy of Logical Positivism for the Philosophy of Science*. Stephen Barker and Peter Achinstein, eds. Baltimore: Johns Hopkins Univ. Press. [Relation between Hertz and Wittgenstein]

1185. Tranoy, K. "Contemporary philosophy: Analytic and continental." *Philosophy Today* 8 (1964):155-168.

1186. Trethowan, I. "Importance of Wittgenstein." *The Tablet* 203 (1954):140. [See Smiley, no. 1160]

1187. Trigg, Roger. *Reason and Commitment*. Cambridge at the Univ. Press, 1973. [Chapter 2: Wittgenstein and Religious Concepts, 28-43, 47-50, 53-55, 57-63, 94-99]

1188. Tuomela, Raimo. "Psychological concepts and functionalism." In *Essays on Wittgenstein in Honour of G. H. von Wright* (Acta Philos. Fenn. 28 (1976)). Amsterdam: North-Holland, 1976, 364-393.

1189. Urmson, J. O. "Facts and pictures of fact." In his *Philosophical Analysis*. Oxford Univ. Press, 1956, 54-93.

1190. Van de Vate, Dwight. "Other minds and the uses of language." *American Philosophical Quarterly* 3 (1966): 250-254.

1191. Van Peursen, Cornelis. *Phenomenology and Analytical Philosophy*. Duquesne Univ. Press, 1972. 190p.

1192. Visvader, John. "The use of paradox in Uroboric philosophies." *Philosophy East and West* 28 (1978):455-467.

1193. Voelke, André-Jean. "La fonction heuristique de la tradition en philosophie." *Studia Philosophica* 36 (1976): 15-24.

1194. von Morstein, Petra. "Erfahrung bei Ludwig Wittgenstein." *Archiv für Philosophie* 12 (1963):133-151.

1195. Vree, D. "Reflections on Wittgenstein, religion and politics." *Crhistian Scholar's Review* 3 (1973):113-133.

1196. Walsh, W. H. "Contemporary anti-metaphysics." In his *Metaphysics*. New York: Harcourt, Brace & World, 1963, 120-130.

1197. Walter, Allan B. "An Oxford dialogue on language and metaphysics." *Review of Metaphysics* 31 (1978):615-648.

1198. Warnock, G. J. "Wittgenstein." In his *English Philosophy since 1900*. Oxford Univ. Press, 1958, 62-93.

1199. Warnock, G. J. "The philosophy of Wittgenstein." In *Philosophy in the Mid-Century*. Vol. 2. R. Klibansky, ed. Firenze: La Nuova Italia Editrice, 1961, 203-207.

1200. Wasmuth, E. "Die Tür in Rüken: Hinweis auf Leben und Werk Wittgensteins." *Deutsche Rundschau* 80 (1954): 1018-1023.

1201. Weiler, Gershon. "The 'world' of actions and the 'world' of events." *Revue Internationale de Philosophie* 18 (1964):439-457.

1202. Wein, H. "Das sprachliche Bild. Gedanken zu Wittgensteins Früh- und Spätwerk." *Neue Zuericher Zeitung* no. 153 (1960).

1203. Wein, H. "Le monde du pensable et le langage. Quelques réflexions sur la critique linguistique Wittgensteinienne et sur ses conséquences." *Revue de Métaphysique et de Morale* 66 (1961):102-115.

1204. Weissman, David. "The existence of nonintrospectable mental states." In his *Dispositional Properties*. Carbondale: Southern Illinois Univ. Press, 1966, 119-158.

1205. Wellmer, A. "Empirico-analytical and critical social science." *Continuum* 8 (1970):12-26.

1206. White, Morton. "The uses of language: Ludwig Wittgenstein." In his *The Age of Analysis*. New York: A Mentor Book, 1955, 225-236.

1207. White, Roger. "Riddles and Anselm's riddle." *Aristotelian Society* 51 (1977):169-186.

1208. Wilson, Colin. "Wittgenstein and Whitehead." In his *Religion and the Rebel*. Boston: Houghton Mifflin, 1957, 290-322.

1209. Winch, Peter. "Rules: Wittgenstein's analysis," and "Some misunderstandings of Wittgenstein." In his *The Idea of a Social Science*. London: Routledge & Kegan Paul, 1958, 24-39.

1210. Winch, Peter. "Understanding a primitive society."
American Philosophical Quarterly 1 (1964):307-324.

1211. Wiplinger, Fridolin. "Ludwig Wittgenstein, Sprache
und Welt in seinem Denken." *Wort und Warheit* 16 (1961):
528-541.

1212. Wisdom, John. "Logical constructions (in five parts)."
Mind 40 (1931):188-216; 460-475; Ibid., 41 (1932):441-464;
42 (1933):43-66; 186-202.

1213. Wisdom, John. "Mace, Moore and Wittgenstein." In
C. A. Mace: A Symposium. Vida Carver, ed. London: Methuen
and Penguin Books, 1962. Reprinted in *Paradox and Discovery.*
Oxford: Basil Blackwell, 1966. Also reprinted in Fann.
[See no. 23]

1214. Wisdom, John. "A feature of Wittgenstein's technique."
Proceedings of the Aristotelian Society. Suppl. 35 (1961):
1-14. Reprinted in his *Paradox and Discovery.* Oxford:
Basil Blackwell, 1966. Also reprinted in Fann. [See no. 23]

1215. Wisdom, John O. "Esotericism." *Philosophy* 34 (1959):
338-354.

1216. Wolfe, Mays, and Brown, S. C., eds. *Linguistic
Analysis and Phenomenology.* Lewisburg (Pennsylvania):
Bucknell Univ. Press, 1971.

1217. Wolniewicz, Boguslaw. "Ludwig Wittgenstein."
Ruch Filozoficzy 22 (1963):8-17.

1218. Wolniewicz, Boguslaw. "Situations as the reference
of propositions." *Dialectics and Humanism* 5 (1978):171-
182.

1219. Wolter, Allan B. "The unspeakable philosophy of the
later Wittgenstein." *Proceedings of the American Catholic
Philosophical Association* 34 (1960):168-193.

1220. Wolter, Allan B. "An Oxford dialogue on language
and metaphysics." *Review of Metaphysics* 31 (1978):615-648.

1221. Wright, Edmond L. "Words and intentions."
Philosophy 52 (1977):45-62.

1222. Wuchterl, Kurt. "Die Hermeneutik und der operative
Aufbau der Philosophie. Dargestellt an der Philosophie
Wittgensteins." *Zeitschrift für Philosophische Forschung*
30 (1976):350-368.

1223. Zaslawsky, Denis. "Programme pour une philosophie
théorique objective." *Revue de Théologie et de Philosophie*
110 (1978):11-28.

1224. Zdarzil, Herbert. "Die Selbstaufhebung der
Philosophie. Persönlichkeit und Werk Ludwig Wittgensteins."
Hochland 53 (1960):107-115.

1225. Zemach, Eddy. "Wittgenstein's philosophy of the
mystical." *Review of Metaphysics* 18 (1964):39-57.
Reprinted in Copi and Beard. [See no. 14]

CHAPTER 5:
Entries Arranged
by Proper Names

ALLYACO, Petrus de

1226. Dumitriu, Anton. "Wittgenstein's solution of the
paradoxes and the conception of the scholastic logician
Petrus de Allyaco." *Journal of History of Philosophy*
2 (1974):227-237.

ANDERSON, A. R.

1227. Gasking, D. A. T. "Anderson and the *Tractatus*."
Australasian Journal of Philosophy 27 (1949):1-26.

ANSCOMBE, G. E. M.

1228. Stenius, Eric. "Miss Anscombe's retraction."
Analysis 27 (1967):86-96.

ANSELM

1229. White, Roger. "Riddles and Anselm's riddle."
Aristotelian Society 51 (1977):169-186.

APEL, Karl-Otto

1230. Roy, D. J. "Is 'philosophy' really possible? A
meditation on Heidegger and Wittgenstein with K.-O. Apel."
Revue de l'Université Laurentienne (Sudbury) 9 (1977):79-91.

1231. Toloken, Tucmas. "Über die Hermeneutik von Karl-Otto
Apel." *Ajatus* 33 (1971):280-286.

AQUINAS, Thomas

1232. Bearsley, Patrick J. "Aquinas the Wittgenstein on
the grounds of certainty." *Modern Schoolman* 51 (1973-74):301-
334.

1233. Bruening, William H. "Aquinas and Wittgenstein on God-talk." *Sophia* (Australia) 16 (1977):1-7.

1234. Ehrlich, Leonard H. "Mystery and mysticism in Wittgenstein, Aquinas, and Jaspers." (Abstract) *Journal of Philosophy* 64 (1967):745-746.

1235. Ehrlich, Leonard H. "Mystery and mysticism in Wittgenstein, Aquinas, and Jaspers." In *Akten XIV Kongress für Philosophie*, Wien, 1968. Wien: Herder, 651-659.

1236. Kenny, Anthony. "Aquinas and Wittgenstein." *Downside Review* 77 (1959):217-235. [See Williams below, no. 1240]

1237. Rotella, Oscar S. "Santo Tomás y Wittgenstein." *Revista de Filosofía* (México) 8 (1975):301-317.

1238. Rotella, Oscar S. "Santo Tomás y Wittgenstein." *Sapientia* 30 (1975):261-272.

1239. Rotella, Oscar S. "Santo Tomas y Wittgenstein." *Tommaso nel suo settimo centenario*. Atti del Congresso Internazionale (Roma-Napoli, 17-24 Aprile 1974), 6: L'essere. Napoli: Edizioni Domenicane Italiane, 1977, 665-676.

1240. Williams, C. J. F. "The marriage of Aquinas and Wittgenstein." *Downside Review* 78 (1960):203-212. [See Kenny above, no. 1236]

ARISTOTLE

1241. Ruf, Henry. "Wolniewicz on Wittgenstein and Aristotle." In *Boston Studies in the Philosophy of Science* 4: 218-225. Proceedings of the Boston Colloquium for the Philosophy of Science, 1966. Robert S. Cohen and M. W. Wartofsky, eds. (Synthese Library). Dordrecht-Boston: D. Reidel, 1969. New York: Humanities Press, 1969. [See Wolniewicz below, no. 1242]

1242. Wolniewicz, Boguslaw. "A parallelism between Wittgensteinian and Aristotelian ontologies." In *Boston Studies in the Philosophy of Science* 4 (1966):208-217. [See Ruf above, no. 1241]

1243. Zweig, Arnuld. "Theories of Real Definition: A Study of the Views of Aristotle, C. I. Lewis, and Wittgenstein." Ph.D. Dissertation, Stanford Univ., 1960, 194p. *Dissertation Abstracts* 21 (1960):212A.

AUGUSTINE

1244. Arrington, Robert L. "*Mechanism and Calculus*: Wittgenstein on Augustine's theory of ostension." In *Wittgenstein: Sources and Perspectives*. C. G. Luckhardt, ed. Ithaca (New York): Cornell Univ. Press, 1979, 303-338.

1245. Locher, W. "Die Vorstellung von der Sprache bei
Augustinus und Wittgenstein." *Hochland* 57 (1964-65):438-446.

1246. O'Reilley, P. "Constructor reconstructus: A
symposium on Wittgenstein's private language: 2. Wittgenstein, Augustine and the essence of language." *Philosophical
Studies* (Maynooth) 18 (1969):110-118.

1247. Suter, R. "Augustine on Time with some criticisms
from Wittgenstein." *Revue Internationale de Philosophie*
16 (1962):378-394.

1248. Suter, R. "El concepto del tiempo según San Agustín,
con algunos comentarios críticos de Wittgenstein." (Trad.
de Carmer M. Suter) *Convivium* no. 19-20 (1965):97-114.

AUNE, Bruce

1249. King-Farlow, John. "Postscript to Mr. Aune on a
Wittgensteinian dogma." *Philosophical Studies* 13 (1962):
62-63.

AUSTIN, J. L.

1250. Boss, Gilbert. "'I Promise': Les fonctions du langage
chez Hume et Austin." *Revue de Théologie et Philosophie* 110
(1978):29-48.

1251. Pears, David F. "Wittgenstein and Austin." In
British Analytical Philosophy, B. Williams and A. Montefiore,
eds. London: Routledge & Kegan Paul, 1966, 17-39.

AYER, A. J.

1252. Mathrani, G. N. "A comparative and critical study
of Wittgenstein's and Ayer's theories of meaning."
Philosophical Quarterly (India) 37 (1965):219-226.

BARFIELD, J.

1253. Mood, J. J. "Poetic languaging and primal thinking:
A study of Barfield, Wittgenstein, and Heidegger."
Encounter 26 (1965):417-433.

BECKETT, Samuel

1254. Morot-Sir, Edouard. "Pascal versus Wittgenstein,
with Samuel Beckett as the antiwitness." *Romance Notes*
15 (1973-74):201-206.

BERGSON, Henri

1255. Pariente, J.-C. "Bergson et Wittgenstein." *Revue
Internationale de Philosophie* 23 (1969):183-200. [Discussion:
J. Vuillemin, J.-C. Pariente, G. H. von Wright, M. Black,
G. G. Granger, B. F. McGuinness, J. Bouveresse, Ibid., 200-204]

BERKELEY, George

1256. Gibbens, Helen Paxton. "Berkeley and Wittgenstein.
Some Correlations." Ph.D. Dissertation, Univ. of Oklahoma,
1970, 169p. *Dissertation Abstracts* 31: 2437A.

1257. Tipton, Ian C. *Berkeley. The Philosophy of
Immaterialism.* London: Methuen, 1974. [Berkeley and
Wittgenstein on the treatment of meaning]

BETH

1258. Barth, E. M. "Het begrip 'tautologie' bij Wittgenstein
en Beth." *Algemeen Nederlands Tijdschrift voor Wijsbegeerte
en Psychologie* 60 (1968):89-100.

BRÉHIER, Emile

1259. Patri, Aimé. "Wittgenstein et Bréhier." *Paru*
(Monte Carlo) 10 (1955):140-144.

BROUWER, L. E.

1260. Richardson, John. *The Grammar of Justification. An
Interpretation of Wittgenstein's Philosophy of Language.*
New York: St. Martin's Press, 1976. 147p.

BURROUGHS, William

1261. Peterson, R. G. "Picture is a fact: Wittgenstein
and *The Naked Lunch.*" *20th Century Literature* 12 (1966):
78-86. [Compares the *Tractatus* to Burroughs' book]

CALIGARI

1262. Genova, J. "Wittgenstein and Caligari." *Philosophical
Forum* 4 (1972-73):186-198.

CANFIELD, J. V.

1263. Gudmunsen, Chris. "The 'empty mind' of Professor
Canfield." *Philosophy* 52 (1977):482-485.

CANTOR, Georg

1264. Bouveresse, J. "Le paradis de Cantor et le purgatoire
de Wittgenstein." *Critique* 33 (1977):316-351. [On Wittgenstein's *Lectures on the Foundations of Mathematics*]

CARNAP, Rudolf

1265. Lambros, Charles H. "Carnap's principle of tolerance
and physicalism." *Transactions of the Peirce Society*
10 (1974):17-33.

CARROLL, Lewis

1266. Pitcher, George. "Wittgenstein, nonsense, and Lewis
Carroll." *Massachusetts Review* 6 (1965):591-611.
[Reprinted in Fann, see no. 23]

CASSIRER, Ernst

1267. Rajan, R. Sandara. "Cassirer and Wittgenstein."
International Philosophical Quarterly 7 (1967):591-610.

1268. Raz, J. "Reflections on Wittgenstein's and Cassirer's
philosophies of language." *Iyyn* 16 (1965):121-122.

CAVELL, Stanley

1269. Hustwit, Ronald E. "Understanding a suggestion of
Professor Cavell's: Kierkegaard's religious stage as a
Wittgensteinian 'Form of Life'." *Philosophy Research
Archives* 4 (1978).

CHOMSKY, Noam

1270. Erde, Edmund L. "Philosophy and Science. Wittgenstein and Chomsky: An Examination of the Current Theory of
Innate Ideas." Ph.D. Dissertation, Univ. of Texas at Austin,
1970, 218p. *Dissertation Abstracts* 31: 1839A.

1271. McCauley, Leland M. "The Grammar of Social and
Scientific Discourse and its Educational Value. A Study
in Chomsky and Wittgenstein." Ph.D. Dissertation, Univ. of
Pittsburgh, 1975. *Dissertation Abstracts* 36 (1975):2160-
2161A.

1272. Oliver, G. "Depth grammar as a methodological concept
in philosophy." *International Philosophical Quarterly*
12 (1972):111-130.

1273. Waller, Bruce. "Chomsky, Wittgenstein, and the
behaviorist perspective on language." *Behaviorism* 5 (1977):
43-59.

DERRIDA, Jacques

1274. Altieri, Charles. "Wittgenstein on consciousness
and language: A challenge to Derridean literary theory."
MLN, 91 (1976):1397-1423.

1275. Grene, Marjorie. "Life, death, and language: some
thoughts on Wittgenstein and Derrida." *Partisan Review*
43 (1976):265-279.

DESCARTES, René

1276. Ameriks, Karlis Peter. "Cartesianism and Wittgenstein: The Legacy of Subjectivism in Contemporary Philosophy of Mind." Ph.D. Dissertation, Yale Univ., 1973. *Dissertation Abstracts* 34 (1973):2690A.

1277. Van de Pitte, F. P. "Reservations on a post-Wittgensteinian view of Descartes." *Philosophy and Phenomenological Research* 35 (1974):107-112.

DEWEY, John

1278. Vaugh, Scott R. "Pedagogical Experience and Theory of Meaning in Dewey and Wittgenstein." Ph.D. Dissertation, Michigan State Univ., 1976, 161p. *Dissertation Abstracts* 37 (1977):7608A.

FICKER, Ludwig von

1279. Janik, Allan. "Wittgenstein, Ficker and *Der Brenner*." In *Wittgenstein: Sources and Perspectives*. C. G. Luckhardt, ed. Ithaca (New York): Cornell Univ. Press, 1979, 161-189.

1280. Wittgenstein, Ludwig. "Letters to Ludwig von Ficker (Trans. by Bruce Gillette; edited by Allan Janik)." In *Wittgenstein: Sources and Perspectives*. C. G. Luckhardt, ed. Ithaca (New York): Cornell Univ. Press, 1979, 82-98.

FRAZER, James G.

1281. Bell, Richard H. "Understanding the fire-festivals and theories in religion." *Religious Studies* 14 (1978): 113-124.

1282. Bouveresse, Jacques. "Les causes, les raisons et les mythes." In *Wittgenstein: La rime et la raison. Science, éthique et esthétique*. Paris: Les Editions de Minuit, 1973, 205-234.

1283. Rudich, Norman and Stassen, Manfred. "Wittgenstein implied anthropology. Remarks on Wittgenstein's notes on Frazer." *History and Theory* 10 (1971):84-89.

1284. Wittgenstein, Ludwig. "Remarks on Frazer's *Golden Bough* (Trans. by John Beversluis)." In *Wittgenstein: Sources and Perspectives*. C. G. Luckhardt, ed. Ithaca (New York): Cornell Univ. Press, 1979, 61-81.

FREGE, Gottlieb

1285. Copi, Irving M. "Frege and Wittgenstein's *Tractatus*." *Philosophia* (Israel) 6 (1976):447-461.

1286. Geach, P. T. "Saying and showing in Frege and Wittgenstein." in *Essays on Wittgenstein in Honour of G. H. von Wright* (*Acta Philos. Fenn.* 28 (1976)). Amsterdam: North Holland, 1976, 54-70.

1287. Gustason, William. "Negation and Assertion in Frege and the *Tractatus*." Ph.D. Dissertation, Univ. of Michigan, 1968.

1288. Hacker, Peter. "Frege and the private language argument." *Idealist Studies* 2 (1972):265-287.

1289. Hacker, P. M. S. "Semantic holism: Frege and Wittgenstein." In *Wittgenstein: Sources and Perspectives*. C. G. Luckhardt, ed. Ithaca (New York): Cornell Univ. Press, 1979, 213-242.

1290. Hacker, P. M. S. "Frege and Wittgenstein on elucidations." *Mind* 74 (1975):601-609.

1291. Hawkins, Ben. "Note on a doctrine of Frege and Wittgenstein." *Mind* 75 (1966):583-585.

1292. Imbert, P. "L'heritage frégéen du *Tractatus*." *Revue Internationale de Philosophie* 23 (1969):205-222.

1293. Kluge, Eike-Henner W. "Functions and Things: An Essay in the Metaphysics of Frege and Wittgenstein." Ph.D. Dissertation, Univ. of Michigan, 1968, 380p. *Dissertation Abstracts* 29: 2753A.

1294. Koenne, W. "Die Beziehung Wittgensteins zu Frege im *Tractatus*." *Wissenschaft und Weltbild* 26 (1973):135-145.

1295. Savitt, Steven F. "Frege and Wittgenstein on Identity, Logic and Number." Brandeis Univ., 1972, 172p. *Dissertation Abstracts* 32: 7047A.

1296. Schwartz, Elisabeth. "Remarques sur 'l'espace des choses' de Wittgenstein et ses origines frégéennes." *Dialectica* 26 (1972):185-226.

1297. Solomon, Robert C. "Sens et essence: Frege et Wittgenstein." *Revue Internationale de Philosophie* 23 (1969).

1298. Stenius, Erik. "The sentence as a function of its constituents in Frege and in the *Tractatus*." In *Essays on Wittgenstein in Honour of G. H. von Wright* (*Acta Philos. Fenn.* 28 (1976)). Amsterdam: North Holland, 1976, 71-84.

1299. Walker, Jeremy. *A Study of Frege*. Ithaca (New York): Cornell Univ. Press, 1965.

FREUD, Sigmund

1300. Cioffi, F. "Wittgenstein's Freud." In *Studies in the Philosophy of Wittgenstein*. Peter Winch, ed. London: Routledge & Kegan Paul; New York: Humanities Press, 1969, 184-209.

1301. Geller, P. "Freud et Wittgenstein. Propos autour du symptome." *Annales de L'Université de Toulouse-Le Mirail* 9 (1973):75-81.

1302. Lazarowitz, Morris. *The Language of Philosophy. Freud and Wittgenstein*. In *Boston Studies in the Philosophy of Science* 60 (Synthese Library, 117). Boston-Dordrecht: D. Reidel, 1977, xvi-209p.

FUCHS, H.

1303. Thiselton, A. C. "Parables as language-event; some comments on Fuchs's hermeneutics in the light of linguistic philosophy." *Scottish Journal of Theology* 23 (1970):437-468.

GALILEO, Galilei

1304. Hill, David K. "Galileo and inertial motion." *Journal of the Western Virginia Philosophical Society* 9 (1975):5-9.

GELLNER, P.

1305. Coulson, J. "Philosophy and integrity." *Downside Review* 79 (1961):122-127.

GENTILE, G.

1306. Sainati, V. "Mitologia moralistica e filosofia della logica nel 'Sistema Di Logica' di G. Gentile." *Giornale di Metafisica* 31 (1976):247-290.

GOMBRICH, E. H.

1307. Lycan, William G. "Gombrich, Wittgenstein, and the duck-rabbit." *Journal of Aesthetics and Art Criticism* 30 (1971-72):229-237.

1308. Yoos, George E. "An Analysis of Three Studies of Pictorial Representation: M. C. Beardsley, E. H. Gombrich, and L. Wittgenstein." Ph.D. Dissertation, Univ. of Missouri-Columbia, 1971, 231p. *Dissertation Abstracts* 32: 3377A.

HEGEL, F. W.

1309. Lamb, David. "Hegel and Wittgenstein on language and sense-certainty." *Clio* 7 (1978):285-301.

1310. Strickler, Nina. "The Problem of the Absolute: A Study of Spinoza, Hegel and Wittgenstein." Ph.D. Dissertation, De Paul Univ., 1973. *Dissertation Abstracts* 34 (1973):3475A.

HEIDEGGER, Martin

1311. Apel, Karl-Otto. "Wittgenstein und Heidegger. Die Frage nach dem Sinn von Sein und der Sinnlosigkeitsverdacht gegen alle Metaphysik." *Philosophische Jahrbuch der Görre-Gesellschaft* 75 (1967-68):56-94. Reprinted in *Heidegger. Perspektiven zur Deutung seines Werks*. Otto Pöggeler, hersg. (Neue wissenschaftliche Bibliothek, 34, Philosophie). Köln, Berlin: Kiepenheuer und Witsch, 1969, 258-296. Spanish trans. de Barnabé Navarro, "Wittgenstein Heidegger: la pregunta por el sentido del ser y la sospecha de falta de sentido contra toda metafísica." *Diánoia* (México) 13 (1967):111-148.

1312. Becker, Oskar. "Heidegger und Wittgenstein." In *Heidegger: Perspektiven zur Deutung seines Werks*. Otto Pöggeler, ed. Cologne: Kiepenheuer und Witsch, 1969.

1313. Behl, L. "Wittgenstein and Heidegger." *Duns Scotus Philosophical Association Convention Report* 27 (1963):70-115.

1314. Bindeman, Steven. "The Role of Silence in the Philosophies of Martin Heidegger and Ludwig Wittgenstein." Ph.D. Dissertation, Duquesne Univ., 1978, 233p. *Dissertation Abstracts* 39 (1978):1631A.

1315. Chiodi, Pietro. "Essere e linguaggio in Heidegger e nel *Tractatus* di Wittgenstein." *Rivista di Filosofia* 46 (1955):170-191.

1316. Cristaldi, Mariano. "Nota sulla possibilità di un'ontologia del linguaggio in Wittgenstein e in Heidegger." *Teoresi* 22 (1967):47-86.

1317. Dufrenne, Mikel. "Wittgenstein et Heidegger." In *Jalons*. The Hague: Nijhoff, 1966, 188-207.

1318. Erickson, Stephen A. *Language and Being. An Analytic Phenomenology*. New Haven: Yale Univ. Press, 1970. [Ch. 2: Heidegger and Wittgenstein]

1319. Erickson, Stephen A. "Meaning and language [Heidegger and Wittgenstein]." *Man and World* 1 (1968):563-586.

1320. Fay, Thomas A. "Heidegger on Logic: An Encounter of his Thought with Wittgenstein." Ph.D. Dissertation, Fordham Univ., 1971, 350p. *Dissertation Abstracts* 32: 1012A.

1321. Fay, Thomas A. "Early Heidegger and Wittgenstein on world." *Philosophical Studies* (Maynooth) 21: 161-171.

1322. Fay, Thomas A. "Heidegger and Wittgenstein on the
question of ordinary language." *Philosophy Today* 23 (1979):
154-159.

1323. Goff, Robert Allen. "Wittgenstein's tools and
Heidegger's implements." *Man and World* 1 (1968):447-462.

1324. Harries, Karsten. "Wittgenstein and Heidegger: The
relationship of the philosopher to language." *The Journal
of Value Inquiry* 2 (1968):281-291.

1325. Heaton, J. M. "Saying and showing in Heidegger and
Wittgenstein." *Journal of the British Society for
Phenomenology* 3 (1972):42-45. [See McCormick below,
no. 1331]

1326. Hilmy, Sameer S. "Irrationalism in the Philosophies
of Heidegger and Wittgenstein." Master's Thesis, The
American Univ., 1976, 123p. *Masters Abstracts* 14 (1976):247.

1327. Horgby, I. "The double awareness in Heidegger and
Wittgenstein." *Inquiry* 2 (1959):235-264. [See Weil below,
no. 1341]

1328. Hottois, Gilbert. "Aspects du rapprochement par
K.-O. Apel de la philosophie de M. Heidegger et la
philosophie de L. Wittgenstein." *Revue Internationale de
Philosophie* 30 (1976):450-485.

1329. Luebbe, H. "Wittgenstein- ein Existentialist?"
Philosophisches Jahrbuch 69 (1962):311-324.

1330. Mandel, R. "Heidegger and Wittgenstein: A second
Kantian revolution." In *Heidegger and Modern Philosophy.
Critical Essays*. Michael Murray, ed. New Haven-London:
Yale Univ. Press, 1978, 259-270.

1331. McCormick, Peter. "Saying and showing in Heidegger
and Wittgenstein." *Journal of the British Society for
Phenomenology* 3 (1972):27-35. [See Heaton above, no. 1325]

----- Mood, J. J. [See Barfield above, no. 1253]

1332. Morrison, James C. "Heidegger's criticism of
Wittgenstein's conception of truth." *Man and World*
2 (1969):551-573.

1333. Morton, Michael. "The Phenomenon of Possibility:
Heidegger and Wittgenstein." Ph.D. Dissertation, Univ. of
Massachusetts-Amherst, 1977.

1334. Murray, Michael. "A note on Wittgenstein and
Heidegger [F. Waismann, "Notes on talks with Wittgenstein."]."
Philosophical Review 83 (1974):501-503.

1335. Oku, Masahiro. "Bittogenshutain to Haidegga."
Riso (Tokyo) 444 (1970):92-104.

1336. Rohatyn, Dennis Anthony. "A note on Heidegger and
Wittgenstein." *Philosophy Today* 15 (1971):69.

1337. Roy, D. J. "Is 'philosophy' really possible? A
meditation on Heidegger and Wittgenstein with K.-O. Apel."
Revue de l'Université Laurentienne (Sudbury) 9 (1977):79-91.

1338. Schaper, Eva. "Saying and showing in Heidegger and
Wittgenstein." *Journal of the British Society for
Phenomenology* 2 (1972):36-41.

1339. Sefler, George F. *Language and the World. A Method-
ological-structural Synthesis within the Writings of
Heidegger and Wittgenstein.* Atlantic Highlands (New Jersey):
Humanities Press, 1974, xxxiii-228p. [See review by Karsten
Harries, *The Philosophical Review* 85 (1976):422-426]

1340. Sefler, George F. "The Structure of Language and
its Relation to the World. A Methodological Study of the
Writings of Heidegger and Wittgenstein." Ph.D. Dissertation,
Georgetown Univ., 1970, 312p. *Dissertation Abstracts*
31: 2979A.

1341. Weil, G. M. "Esotericism and the double awareness."
Inquiry 3 (1960):61-72. [See I. Horgby above, no. 1327,
and Wisdom below, 1342]

1342. Wisdom, J. O. "Esotericism." *Philosophy* 34 (1959):
338-354.

HERACLITUS

1343. Shiner, Roger A. "Wittgenstein and Heraclitus: Two
river images." *Philosophy* 49 (1974):191-197.

HERTZ, H. R.

1344. Raphael, Leyla. "Wittgenstein et Hertz: pour une
lecture antipositiviste de Wittgenstein." Ph.D. Dissertation,
McGill Univ., 1978. *Dissertation Abstracts* 39 (1979):5556A.

1345. Toulmin, Stephen. "From logical positivism to conceptual history." In *The Legacy of Logical Positivism for
the Philosophy of Science.* Stephen Barker and Peter
Achinstein, eds. John Hopkins Univ. Press, 1970.

HICKS, John

1346. Keeling, L. Bryant and Morelli, Mario F. "Beyond
Wittgensteinian fideism: An examination of John Hicks'
analysis of religious faith." *International Journal for
Philosophy of Religion* 8 (1977):250-262.

HILBERT, D.

1347. Bacca, Juan David Garcia. "Sobre las relaciones
entre la logica esquematica de Wittgenstein y la logica
axiomatica de Hilbert." *Acta Científica Venezolana*
2 (1951):56-61, 103-105, 144-147.

HOLMER, Paul

1348. Sherry, P. "Learning how to be religious; the work
of Paul Holmer." *Theology* 77 (1974):81-90.

HUME, David

1349. Anscombe, G. E. M. "Hume and Julius Caesar."
Analysis 34 (1973):1-7.

1350. Boss, Gilbert. "'I Promise': Les fonctions du
langage chez Hume et Austin." *Revue de Théologie et
Philosophie* 110 (1978):29-48.

1351. Dauer, Francis. "The diagnosis of an argument."
Metaphilosophy 5 (1974):113-132.

1352. Hanfling, Oswald. "Hume and Wittgenstein." In
Impressions of Empiricism. Godfrey Vesey, ed. London:
Macmillan, 1972, 237p. *Royal Institute of Philosophy
Lectures* 9 (1974-75):47-65.

1353. Jones, P. "Strains in Hume and Wittgenstein." In
Hume: A Reevaluation. D. W. Livingstone and J. T. King.
New York: Fordham Univ. Press, 1976, 191-209.

1354. Richards, Glyn. "Conceptions of the self in Wittgenstein, Hume and Buddhism. An analysis and comparison."
The Monist 61 (1978):42-55.

HUSSERL, Edmund

1355. Copleston, Frederick C. "Wittgenstein frente a
Husserl." *Revista Portuguesa de Filosofía* 21 (1965):134-149.

1356. Daniel, Stephen H. "Wittgenstein on field and
stream." *Auslegung* 4 (1977):176-198.

1357. Dufrenne, Mikel. "Wittgenstein et Husserl." In
Jalons. The Hague: Martinus Nijhoff, 1966, 188-207.

1358. Hems, John M. "Husserl and/or Wittgenstein."
International Philosophical Quarterly 8 (1969):547-578.

1359. Hoche, Hans-Ulrich. "Phänomenologie und Sprachanalyse.
Bemerkungen zu Wittgenstein, Ryle und Husserl." In *Aufgaben
und Wege des Philosophieunterrichts*. Friedrich Borden, ed.
Neue Folge, Heft 4: Beiträge zu verschniedenen philosophischen Themen, 1972, 68p.

1360. Hollinger, Robert. "The role of aspect seeing in Wittgenstein's later thought." *Cultural Hermeneutics* 2(1974):229-241.

1361. Reeder, Harry Paul. "Public and Private Aspects of Language in Husserl and Wittgenstein." Ph.D. Dissertation, Univ. of Waterloo (Canada), 1977. *Dissertation Abstracts* 38 (1977):2852A.

1362. Ricoeur, Paul. "Husserl and Wittgenstein on language." In *Phenomenology and Existentialism*. Edward N. Lee and Maurice H. Mandelbaum, eds. Baltimore: Johns Hopkins Press, 1967, 207-217.

1363. Solomon, Robert C. "Husserl's private language." *Southwestern Journal of Philosophy* 5 (1974):203-208.

1364. Taylor, Earl. "*Lebenswelt* and *Lebensformen*: Husserl and Wittgenstein on the goal and method of philosophy." *Human Studies* 1 (1978):184-200.

1365. Van Peursen, Cornelis A. "E. Husserl and L. Wittgenstein." *Philosophy and Phenomenological Research* 20 (1959): 181-195.

1366. Weinzweig, Marjorie. "Phenomenology and ordinary language philosophy." *Metaphylosophy* 8 (1978):116-146. [Sec. 2: "grammar" vs. "eidetic" of Ed Husserl]

JAMES, William

1367. Fairbanks, M. "Wittgenstein and James." *New Scholasticism* 40 (1966):331-340.

1368. Wertz, Spencer K. "On Wittgenstein and James." *New Scholasticism* 46 (1972):446-448.

JOYCE, James

1369. White, D. A. "The labyrinth of language: Joyce and Wittgenstein." *James Joyce Quarterly* 12 (1975):294-304.

KAFKA, Franz

1370. Bramann, Jorn K. "Religious language in Wittgenstein and Kafka." *Diogenes* no. 90 (1975):26-35.

1371. Bramann, Jorn K. "Kafka and Wittgenstein on religious language." *Sophia* (Australia) 14 (1975):1-9.

KANT, Immanuel

1372. Bachmaier, P. *Wittgenstein und Kant. Versuch zum Begriff des Transzendentalen*. Frankfurt: Peter Lang, 1978. 213p.

1373. Carlo, W. E. "Wittgenstein, Kant and Professor
Strawson." In *Truth and the Historicity of Man*. George F.
McLean, ed. (Proceedings of the American Catholic Philo-
sophical Association, XLIII.) Washington: The Catholic
Univ. of America, 1969, 211-218.

1374. Dambska, Izydora. "Les idees kantiennes dans la
philosophie des máthematiques de Wittgenstein." *Organon*
11-13 (1976-77):249-260.

1375. Engel, S. Morris. "Wittgenstein and Kant."
Philosophy and Phenomenological Research 30 (1970):483-513.

1376. Fang, J. "Wittgenstein vs. Wittgenstein in a
philosophy of mathematics." In *Akten XIV Kongress für
Philosophie*, Vienna, 233-236. Reprinted in his *Kant-
Interpretation* 2, Verlag Ragensberg, 1969.

1377. Hartnack, J. "Kant and Wittgenstein." *Kant-Studien*
60 (1969):131-134.

1378. Heinrich, R. *Einbildung und Darstellung. Zum
Kantianismus des frühen Wittgenstein*. Kastellaun-Düsseldorf:
A. Henn Verlag, 1977. 74p.

1379. Montoya Sáenz, José. "Wittgenstein un filósofo
kantiano." In *Kant (1724-1974)*. (Aneles del Seminario de
Metafísica 9, 1974.) Madrid: Facultad de Filosofía y
Letras, Universidad Complutense de Madrid, 1974, 145-154.

1380. Rossvaer, Viggo. *Kant og Wittgenstein*. Oslo:
Universitet-forlaget, 1974, xii-471p.

1381. Schwyzer, Hubert. "Thought and reality: the metaphysics of Kant and Wittgenstein." *Philosophical Quarterly*
23 (1973):193-204.

KIERKEGAARD, Sören

1382. Bell, R. H. "Kierkegaard and Wittgenstein; two
strategies for understanding theology." *Illif Review*
31 (1974):21-34.

1383. Bell, R. H. and Hustwit, R. E., eds. *Essays on
Kierkegaard and Wittgenstein*. College of Wooster, 1978.

1384. Cavell, Stanley. "Existentialism and analytic
philosophy." *Daedalus* no. 93 (1964):946-974. [Sec. III
compares Wittgenstein with Kierkegaard]

1385. Gallagher, M. P. "Wittgenstein's admiration for
Kierkegaard." *The Month* 225 (1968):43-49.

1386. Hustwit, Ronald E. "Understanding a suggestion of
Professor Cavell's: Kierkegaard's religious stage as a
Wittgensteinian 'form of life'." *Philosophy Research Archives*
4 (1978).

1387. Johnson, R. H. *The Concept of Existence in the
'Concluding Unscientific Postscript'*. The Hague: Nijhoff,
1972.

1388. Quinn, Wylie S. "Kierkegaard and Wittgenstein: The
'Religious' as a 'Form of Life'." Ph.D. Dissertation,
Duke Univ., 1976, 222p. *Dissertation Abstracts* 37 (1977):
7804A.

KRAUS, Karl

1389. Kraft, Werner. "Ludwig Wittgenstein und Karl Kraus."
Die Neue Rundschau 72 (1961):812-844.

KUNG-SUN LUNG

1390. Rieman, Fred. "On linguistic skepticism in Wittgenstein and Kung-sun Lung." *Philos. E. W.* 27 (1977):183-
193.

LAING, R. D.

1391. Kreilkamp-Cudmore, Ann. "Language as Wittgenstein's
Way of Life." Ph.D. Dissertation, Boston Univ., 1973.
Dissertation Abstracts 33 (1973):6965A.

La VIA, Vincenzo

1392. Spagnolo, Salvatore. "Genesi e momenti della
'assoluto realismo' di Vincenzo La Via." *Teorisi* 30 (1975):
37-101.

LEWIS, C. I.

1393. Zweig, Arnulf. "Theories of Real Definition: A
Study of the Views of Aristotle, C. I. Lewis, and Wittgen-
stein." Ph.D. Dissertation, Stanford Univ., 1960, 194p.
Dissertation Abstracts 21 (1960):212A.

LIPPS, Hans

1394. Bräuer, Gottfrid. "Wege in die Sprache Wittgenstein
und Hans Lipps." *Bildung* (Stuttgart) 16 (1963):131-140.

LICHTENBERG, Georg

1395. Stern, J. P. *Comparing Wittgenstein and Lichtenberg
in his 'Lichtenberg: A Doctrine of Scattered Occasions'*.
Bloomington (Indiana): Indiana Univ. Press, 1959.

1396. von Wright, G. H. "Georg Lichtenberg als Philosoph."
Theoria 8 (1942):201-217.

LOCKE, Don

1397.   Thornton, M. T.   "Locke's criticism of Wittgenstein."
Philosophical Quarterly 19 (1969):266-271.

MACH, Ernst

1398.   Keyserling, A.   *Der Wiener Denkstil.   Mach, Carnap,
Wittgenstein.*   Graz, 1965.

1399.   Lübbe, Hermann.   *Bewusstsein in Geschichten.   Studien
zur Phänomenologie der Subjektivität: Mach, Husserl, Schapp,
Wittgenstein.*   (Rombach-Hochschulpaperback, 37.)   Freiburg:
Verlag Rombach, 1972.   174p.

MALCOLM, Norman

1400.   Mukheriji, S. R.   "Professor Malcolm on dreams."
Indian Philosophical Quarterly 5 (1978):575-585.

MANNHEIM, Karl

1401.   Bloor, David.   "Wittgenstein and Mannheim on the
sociology of mathematics." *Studies in the History of
Philosophy of Sciences* 4 (1973):173-191.

MARCEL, Gabriel

1402.   Mollaneda, R.   "Concrete Approach and Therapeutic
Activity: Marcel and Wittgensetin on Doing Philosophy."
Ph.D. Dissertation, Pontificia Universitatis Gregoriana
(Rome), 1975, 446p. *Dissertation Abstracts European* 37
(1976):1.

MARX, Karl

1403.   Manser, A. R.   *The End of Philosophy: Marx and
Wittgenstein* (Inaugural lecture).   Southampton: University,
1973. 14p.

MAUPERTUIS, Pierre-Louis

1404.   Kretzmann, Norman.   "Maupertuis, Wittgenstein, and
the origin of language." [Abstract] *Journal of Philosophy*
54 (1957):776.

MAUTHNER, Fritz

1405.   Bellino, Fr.   "Wittgenstein e Mauthner.   La filosofia
come *Sprachkritik*." *Raccolta di Studi e Ricerche* (Bari)
1 (1977):93-127.

1406.   Janik, Allan and Toulmin, Stephen E.   *Wittgenstein's
Vienna.*   New York: Simon & Schuster, 1973; London: George
Weidenfeld & Nicolson, 1973.

1407.   Leinfellner, Elisabeth.   "Zur nominalistischen
Begründung von Linguistik und Sprachphilosophie: F. Mauthner
und L. Wittgenstein."   *Studium Generale* 22 (1969):209-251.

1408.   Skerl, J.   "Fritz Mauthner's critique of language in
Samuel Beckett's *Watt*."   *Contemporary Literature* 15 (1974):
474-487.

1409.   Weiler, G.   "On Fritz Mauthner's critique of language."
Mind 67 (1958):80-87.

MEINONG, Alexius

1410.   Routley, Richard and Routley, Valerie.   "Rehabilitating
Meinong's theory of objects."   *Revue Internationale de
Philosophie* nos. 104-105 (1973), special issue on Meinong.

1411.   Ryle, Gilbert.   "'Anti-Gegenstandtheorie'."   *Revue
Internationale de Philosophie* nos. 104-105 (1973).

MELVILLE, Hermann

1412.   Taylor, Kent H.   "Wittgenstein and Melville: A Study
of the Character of 'Meaning'."   Ph.D. Dissertation, Univ.
of California at Santa Barbara, 1976, 222p.   *Dissertation
Abstracts* 38 (1977):793A.

MERLEAU-PONTY, Maurice

1413.   Epstein, Michele F.   "The common ground of Merleau-
Ponty's and Wittgenstein's philosophy of Man."   *Journal of
the History of Philosophy* 13 (1975):221-234.

1414.   Kemp, Peter.   "The linguistic philosophy of
Merleau-Ponty."   In *Danish Yearbook of Philosophy* 4 (1967).
Copenhagen: Munksgaard, 1968.

1415.   Kwant, Remy C.   "Merleau-Ponty en Wittgenstein II."
Tijdschrift voor Filosofie 32 (1970):3-28.   [Résumé:
Merleau-Ponty et Wittgenstein II, 29]

1416.   Lawhead, William Fisher.   "Wittgenstein and Merleau-
Ponty on Language and Critical Reflection."   Ph.D. Dissertation, Univ. of Texas at Austin, 1978.

1417.   Marsh, James L.   "The triumph of ambiguity: Merleau-
Ponty and Wittgenstein."   *Philosophy Today* 19 (1975):243-255.

MOORE, G. E.

1418.   Brunius, Teddy.   *G. E. Moore's Analyses of Beauty.
An Impasse and a Way Out.*   Uppsala: Univ. of Uppsala, 1964.
78p.

1419. Gargani, A. G. "linguaggio e società in G. E. Moore
e nell'ultimo Wittgenstein." *Giornale Critico della
Filosofia Italiana* 44 (1965):98-118.

1420. Hoagland, Sarah L. "The Status of Common Sense,
G. E. Moore and L. Wittgenstein: A Comparative Study."
Ph.D. Dissertation, Univ. of Cincinnati, 1975. *Dissertation
Abstracts* 36 (1975):2256-2257A.

1421. Hottois, Georges. "Philosophie du sens commun et
dissolution de la philosophie." *Logique et Analyse* 17
(1974):253-275.

1422. Hudson, W. D. "Wittgenstein on fundamental propositions." *Southwestern Journal of Philosophy* 7 (1977):7-22.

1423. Levi, Albert W. "G. E. Moore and Ludwig Wittgenstein."
In his *Philosophy and Modern World*. Bloomington (Indiana):
Indiana Univ. Press, 1959, 436-481.

1424. Lewy, C. "*Mind* under G. E. Moore (1921-1947)."
Mind 85 (1976):37-46.

1425. Linville, Kent. "Wittgenstein on 'Moore's paradox'."
In *Wittgenstein: Sources and Perspectives*. C. G. Luckhardt,
ed. Ithaca (New York): Cornell Univ. Press, 1979, 286-302.

1426. Malcolm, Norman. "Moore and Wittgenstein on the
sense of *I Know*." In *Essays on Wittgenstein in Honour of
G. H. von Wright (Acta Philos. Fenn., 28 (1976))*. Amsterdam:
North-Holland, 1976, 215-240.

1427. Moore, G. E. *Commonplace Book, 1919-1953*. Casimir,
ed. New York: Macmillan, 1962.

1428. Mundle, C. W. K. "The rôles of G. E. Moore and
Wittgenstein compared." In *A Critique of Linguistic
Philosophy*. Oxford: Clarendon Press, 1976, 153-165.

MUSIL, Robert

1429. Nyiri, J. C. "Zwei geistige Leitsterne: Musil und
Wittgenstein." *Literatur und Kritik* 1/3 (1977):167-179.

1430. Nyiri, J. C. "Musil und Wittgenstein: Ihr Bild vom
Menschen." *Conceptus* 11 (1977):306-314.

NIETZSCHE, Friedrich

1431. Heller, Erich. "Wittgenstein and Nietzsche." In
An Artist's Journey into the Interior and Other Essays.
New York: Random House, 1965, 201-226.

1432. Schacht, Richard. "Philosophy as linguistic analysis:
A Nietzschean critique." *Philosophical Studies* 25 (1974):
153-171.

1433. Wallace, Kyle. "Nietzsche's and Wittgenstein's
perspectivism." *Southwestern Journal of Philosophy*
4 (1973):101-107.

PASCAL, Blaise

1434. Morot-Sir, Edouard. "Pascal versus Wittgenstein,
with Samuel Beckett as the antiwitness." *Romance Notes*
15 (1973-74):201-206.

PEARS, D. F.

1435. Villanueva, Enrique. "Prof. Pears sobre Wittgenstein."
Crítica 6 (1972):131-138.

PEIRCE, C. S.

1436. Fairbanks, Mathew J. "C. S. Peirce and logical
atomism." *New Scholasticism* 38 (1964):178-188.

1437. Rorty, R. "Pragmatism, categories, and language."
Philosophical Review 70 (1961):197-223.

PHILLIPS, D. Z.

1438. Klinefelter, D. S. "D. Z. Phillips as philosopher
of religion." *Journal of the American Academy of Religion*
42 (1974):307-325.

PLATO

1439. Bondeson, William B. "Plato and the foundation of
logic and language." *Southwestern Journal of Philosophy*
6 (1975):29-49.

1440. Centore, F. F. "Atomism and Plato's *Theatetus*."
Philosophical Forum (Boston) 5 (1974):475-485.

1441. Rosen, Stanley. "Return to the origin: Reflections
on Plato and contemporary philosophy." *International
Philosophical Quarterly* 16 (1976):151-177.

POLANYI, Michael

1442. Daley, C. B. "Polanyi and Wittgenstein." In
Intellect and Hope: Essays in the Thought of Michael Polanyi.
Thomas Langford and William Poteat, eds. Durham (North
Carolina): Duke Univ. Press, 1968, 136-168.

POPPER, Karl

1443. Bartley, W. W., III. "Theory of language and philos-
ophy of science as instruments of educational reform:
Wittgenstein and Popper as Austrian schoolteachers." In
*Methodological and Historical Essays in the Natural and
Social Sciences*. Robert S. Cohen and Marx W. Watofsky, eds.

(Synthese Library, 60, Boston Studies in the Philosophy of Science, 14) Dordrecht-Boston: D. Reidel, 1974, 307-337.

1444. Masat Lucchetta, Paola. "Popper interprete di Wittgenstein." *Sapienza* 30 (1977):300-327.

1445. Radnitzky, Gerard. "Philosophie und Wissenschafts-theorie zwischen Wittgenstein und Popper." *Conceptus* 11 (1977):249-282.

1446. Rodrigues, Joad Resina. "Science, méthodologie et philosophie chez K. Popper." *Revue Philosophique de Louvain* 68 (1972):240-274.

QUINE, W. V. O.

1447. Gettner, Alan F. "Analytic Truth in the Philosophies of Quine and the Later Wittgenstein." Ph.D. Dissertation, Columbia Univ., 1971, 244p. *Dissertation Abstracts* 32:3209A.

1448. Marconi, Diego. "Quine e le logiche devianti." *Filosofia* (Rome) 25 (1974):37-60; Ibid., 25 (1974):135-152.

1449. Womack, James A. "Quine and Wittgenstein on Reference." Ph.D. Dissertation, New York Univ., 1976, 259p. *Dissertation Abstracts* 37 (1977):5891A.

RICOEUR, Paul

1450. Ihde, Don. *Hermeneutic Phenomenology*. New York: New York Univ. Press, 1971.

RILKE, Rainer Maria

1451. Ficker, Ludwig. "Rilke und der unbekannte Freund." *Der Brenner* 18 (1954):234-248.

RUSSELL, Bertrand

1452. Clark, Ronald W. *The Life of Bertrand Russell.* New York: Knopf, 1976, 766p.

1453. Devant, James B. "Wittgenstein on Russell's theory of types." *Notre Dame Journal of Formal Logic* 16 (1975): 102-108.

1454. Feys, R. "Le raisonnement en termes de faits dans la logistique ressellienne." *Revue Néo-Scholastique de Philosophie* 29 (1927):393-421; Ibid., 30 (1928):154-192, 257-274.

1455. Frayn, Michael. "Russell and Wittgenstein." *Commentary* 43 (1967):68-75.

1456. Iglesias, M. Teresa. "Russell's introduction to Wittgenstein's *Tractatus*." *Russell*. 1977, 21-38.

1457.   Leblanc, Hugues.   "That *Principia Mathematica*, first
edition, has a predicative interpretation after all."
Journal of Philosophical Logic 4 (1975):67-70.

1458.   Leyvraz, J. P.   "Bertrand Russell et l'impact de
Wittgenstein."   *Revue Internationale de Philosophie* 26
(1972):461-482.

1459.   McGuinness, Brian.   "Bertrand Russell's and Ludwig
Wittgenstein's 'Notes on Logic'."   *Revue Internationale
de Philosophie* 26 (1972):444-460.

1460.   Muehlmann, Robert.   "Russell and Wittgenstein on
identity."   *Philosophical Quarterly* 19 (1969):221-230.

1461.   Norman, Jack.   "Russell and *Tractatus* 3.1432."
Analysis 29 (1967):190-192.

1462.   Mijuskovic, Ben.   "The simplicity argument in Wittgenstein and Russell."   *Critica* 8 (1976):85-103.

1463.   Pears, D. F.   "Logical atomism: Russell and Wittgenstein."   In *The Revolution in Philosophy*.   A. J. Ayer et al.,
eds.   44-55.

1464.   Pears, David.   "The relation between Wittgenstein's
picture theory of propositions and Russell's theories of
judgment."   In *Wittgenstein: Sources and Perspectives*.
C. G. Luckhardt, ed.   Ithaca (New York): Cornell Univ.
Press, 1979, 190-212.

1465.   Russell, Bertrand.   "Russell & Wittgenstein. Selec-
tions from his *My Philosophical Development*. *Encounter*
(January 1959):8-9.

1466.   Russell, Bertrand.   *My Philosophical Development*.
New York: Simon & Schuster, 1959.

1467.   Ryle, Gilbert.   "Bertrand Russell (1872-1970)."
Revue Internationale de Philosophie 26 (1972):436-443.

RUSSIA

1468.   Moran, John.   "Wittgenstein and Russia."   *New Left
Review* 73 (1972):85-96.

RYLE, Gilbert

1469.   Bouwsma, O. K.   "A difference between Ryle and
Wittgenstein."   *Rice University Studies* 58 (1972):77-87.

-----   Hoche, Hans-Ulrich.   [See no. 1359]

1469a.   Warnock, Mary.   "Gilbert Ryle's editorship."
Mind 85 (1976):47-56.

SARTRE, Jean-Paul

1470. Sprengard, K. A. "Neue Möglichkeiten der Ethik.
Kant, Wittgenstein, Sartre." In *Bewusst Sein*. Gerhard
Funke zu eigen. Herausgegeben von A. J. Bucher et al.
Bonn: Bouvier Verlag Herbert Grundmann, 1975, 290-308.

SAUSSURE, Ferdinand de

1471. Mandelbaum, Maurice. "Language and chess, de Saussure's analogy." *Philosophical Review* 77 (1968):356-357.

1472. Verburg, P. A. "Het Schaakspel-Model bij F. de Saussure en bij L. Wittgenstein." *Wijsgerig Perspectief of
Maatschappij en Wetenschap* (Amsterdam) 1 (1960-61):227-234.

SCHOPENHAUER, Arthur

1473. Engel, S. Morris. "Schopenhauer's impact on Wittgenstein." *Journal of the History of Philosophy* 7 (1969):
285-302.

1474. Gardiner, Patrick. "Schopenhauer and Wittgenstein."
In his *Schopenhauer*. London: Penguin Books, 1963, 275-282.

1475. Griffiths, A. Phillips. "Wittgenstein, Schopenhauer,
and ethics." In *Understanding Wittgenstein*. Godfrey, ed.
(Royal Institute of Philosophy Lectures 7, 1972-73)
London: Macmillan, 1974; New York: St. Martin's Press, 1974,
96-116.

1476. Griffiths, A. Phillips. "Wittgenstein and the four-
fold root of sufficient reason." *Aristotelian Society*
50 (Suppl. 1976):1-20.

1477. Janik, Allan. "Schopenhauer and the early Wittgenstein." *Philosophical Studies* (Maynooth) 15 (1966):76-95.

SELLARS, R. W.

1478. Giegel, Hans Joachim. *Die Logik der seelischen
Ereignisse*. Zu Theorien von L. Wittgenstein und W. Sellars.
Frankfurt am Main: Suhrkamp, 1969.

SEXTUS EMPIRICUS

1479. Penick, John J. "Wittgenstein on Sensory Pyrrhonism."
Ph.D. Dissertation, Univ. of North Carolina at Chapel Hill,
1975. *Dissertation Abstracts* 36 (1975):3773A.

1480. Watson, Richard A. "Sextus and Wittgenstein."
Southern Journal of Philosophy 7 (1969):229-238.

SKINNER, B. F.

1481.   Begelman, D. A.   "Wittgenstein."   *Behaviorism*
4 (1976):201-207.

1482.   Day, W. F.   "On certain similarities between the
philosophical investigations of Ludwig Wittgenstein and the
operationism of B. F. Skinner."   *Journal of Experimental
Analysis of Behavior* 12 (1969):489-506.

SOCRATES

1483.   Craft, Jimmy L.   "Some Remarks on Socrates and
Wittgenstein."   Ph.D. Dissertation, Univ. of Texas at
Austin, 1977, 195p.   *Dissertation Abstracts* 38 (1977):2843A.

1484.   Kaufmann, Walter.   "'Wittgenstein' and 'Wittgenstein
and Socrates'."   In his *Critique of Religion and Philosophy.*
New York: Harper & Row, 1958, 52-59.

1485.   Rosen, Stanley.   "Socrates' dream."   *Theoria* 42
(1976):161-188.

STENIUS, Erik

1486.   Bunting, I. A.   "Some difficulties in Stenius'
account of the independence of atomic states of affairs."
Australasian Journal of Philosophy 43 (1965):368-375.

1487.   Shwayder, D. S.   "Critical notice of Stenius."
Mind 72 (1963):275-289.   Reprinted in *Essays on Wittgenstein's
'Tractatus'.*   Copi and Beard, eds.   New York: Macmillan,
1966; London: Routledge & Kegan Paul, 1966.

STRAWSON, P. F.

1488.   Glouberman, M.   "Strawson's hidden realism."   *Journal
of Critical Analysis* 5 (1975):135-145.

1489.   Reinhardt, L. R.   "Wittgenstein and Strawson on other
minds."   In *Studies in the Philosophy of Wittgenstein.*
Peter Winch, ed.   London: Routledge & Kegan Paul; New York:
Humanities Press, 1969, 152-165.

1490.   Sievert, Donald E.   "Austin, Wittgenstein and
Strawson on Mind."   Ph.D. Dissertation, Univ. of Iowa,
1967, 141p.   *Dissertation Abstracts* 28: 3229A.

1491.   Stubbs, Anne C.   "Strawson and skepticism."
Philosophic Studies (Maynooth) 21 (1972):111-136.

TOLSTOY, Leo

1492.   Magnanini, D.   "Tolstoj e Wittgenstein come 'imatatori
di Cristo'."   *Sapienza* 32 (1979):89-100.

TILLICH, Paul

1493. Hartshorne, Charles.   "A logic of ultimate contrasts:
Wittgenstein and Tillich: Reflection on metaphysics and
language." In *Creative Synthesis and Philosophical Method*.
London: S. C. M. Press, 1970.

VESEY, Godfrey

1494. Benjamin, M. "Vesey on volition. The 'second
mistake' [Wittgenstein]. *Michigan Academian*. *Michigan
Academy of Science, Art and Letters* (Ann Arbor) 6 (1974):
377-387.

VICO, Giambatista

1495. Riverso, Emanuele. "Vico and Wittgenstein." In
Giambattista Vico's Science of Humanity. Giorgio Taglia-
cozzo, ed. Baltimore: Johns Hopkins Univ. Press, 1976,
263-273.

VIENNA

1496. Bouveresse, Jacques. "Les derniers jours de
l'humanité." *Critique* 31 (1975):753-805.

von WRIGHT, G. H.

1497. Battistella, Ernesto H. "Interpretación del atomismo
logico del *Tractatus* mediante la logica modal relativa de
von Wright." *Revista Venezola de Filosofía* (1976):7-18.

1498. Martin, Rex. "The problem of the 'tie' in von Wright's
schema of practical inference. A Wittgensteinian solution."
In *Essays on Wittgenstein in Honour of G. H. von Wright*
(*Acta Philos. Fenn.* 28 (1976)). Amsterdam: North-Holland,
1976, 326-363.

WAISMANN, Friedrich

1499. Baker, Gordon P. "*Verehrung und Verkehrung*:
Waismann and Wittgenstein." In *Wittgenstein: Sources and
Perspectives*. C. G. Luckhardt, ed. Ithaca (New York):
Cornell Univ. Press, 1979, 243-285.

WHITEHEAD, Alfred N.

1500. Burke, T. E. "Theological originality [Whitehead
and Wittgenstein]." *Religious Studies* 12 (1976):1-20.

1501. Frick, I. E. "Whitehead and 'ordinary language'
philosophers." *Indian Journal of Philosophy* 4 (1964):69-84.

1502. Martin, Margaret J. "The Views of Whitehead and
Wittgenstein." Ph.D. Dissertation, Southern Illinois at
Carbondale, 1978, 163p. *Dissertation Abstracts* 39 (1978):922A.

1503. Wilson, Colin. "Wittgenstein and Whitehead." In his
Religion and the Rebel. Boston: Houghton Mifflin, 1957,
290-322.

WINCH, P.

1504. Almond, P. C. "Winch and Wittgenstein." *Religious
Studies* 12 (1976):473-482.

WINTERS, Yvor

1505. Davis, D. "Limits. An essay on Yvor Winters and
Ludwig Wittgenstein." *Poetry Nation* (Manchester) 4 (1977):
21-25.

YEATS, William Butler

1506. Spiess, Richard F. "Observations concerning Yeats'
'Last Poems' and Wittgenstein's *Tractatus Logico-philo-
sophicus*." *Revue des Langues Vivantes - Tijdschrift voor
Levende Talen* 43 (1976):82-86.

CHAPTER 6:
Entries Arranged
by Subjects

Absurd

1507. Engel, S. Morris. "Wittgenstein and the feeling of
the absurd." *Journal of Existentialism* 6 (1966).

Absolute

1508. Strickler, Nina. "The Problem of the Absolute: A
Study of Spinoza, Hegel and Wittgenstein." Ph.D. Dissertation, De Paul Univ., 1973. *Dissertation Abstracts* 34
(1973):3475A.

Act - Action

1509. Brodbeck, May. "Significato e azione." *Rivista di
Filosofia* 54 (1963):267-293.

1510. Geach, Peter T. "Wittgenstein's alleged rejection
of mental acts." In his *Mental Acts*. London: Routledge
& Kegan Paul, 1957, 2-4.

1511. McCann, Hugh. "Volition and basic action."
Philosophical Review 83 (1974):451-473.

1512. Moore, Harold F. "Explanation and understanding:
Recent models for interpreting action." *International
Philosophical Quarterly* 13 (1973):419-434.

1513. Weiler, G. "The 'world' of actions and the 'world' of events." *Revue Internationale de Philosophie* 18 (1964): 439-457.

1514. Weitz, Morris. "The concept of human action." *Philosophic Exchanges* 1 (1972):201-237.

1515. Winch, Peter. "Trying and attempting." *Aristotelian Society* 45 (1971):209-227.

1516. Ziriff, G. E. "Where is the agent of behavior?" *Behaviorism* 3 (1975):1-21.

Aesthetic (and Art)

1517. Aldrich, Virgil C. "Art and the human form." *Journal of Aesthetics and Art Criticism* 29 (1971):295-302.

1518. Alvim Júnior, Fausto. "Wittgenstein. Sôbre a explicação estética e a explicação cientifica causal." *Crítica* 5 (1971):21-55 [Resumen, 56-58; Abstract, 59].

1519. Barrett, C. "Les leçons de Wittgenstein sur l'esthétique." *Archives de Philosophie* 28 (1965):5-22.

1520. Barrett, C., Paton, Margaret, and Blocker, Harry. "Wittgenstein and problems of objectivity in aesthetics" (A symposium). *British Journal of Aesthetics* 7 (1967): 158-174.

1521. Bell, Julian. "An epistle on the subject of the ethical and aesthetic beliefs of Herr Ludwig Wittgenstein." In *Whips and Scorpions: Specimens of Modern Satiric Verse, 1914-1931.* London: Wishart, 1932, 21-30. Reprinted in *Essays on Wittgenstein's* Tractatus. I. M. Copi and R. W. Beard, eds. New York: Macmillan; London: Routledge & Kegan Paul, 1966, 67-74.

1522. Blocker, H. E. "An Examination of Problems Involved in the Ascription of Emotive Features to Works of Art." Ph.D. Dissertation, Univ. of California at Berkeley, 1966.

1523. Bouveresse, Jacques. *Wittgenstein, la rime et la raison. Science, éthique, et esthétique* (Coll. Critique). Paris: Les Editions de Minuit, 1973. 239p.

   book reviews:
   A. Kenny, *Archives de Philosophie* 37 (1974):343-345;
   G. Penco, *Proteus* 4 (1973):206-210.

1524. Brunius, Teddy. *G. E. Moore's Analyses of Beauty. An Impasse and a Way Out.* Uppsala: Univ. of Uppsala, 1964. 78p.

1525. Cioffi, Frank. "Aesthetic explanation and aesthetic
perplexity." In *Essays on Wittgenstein in Honour of G. H.
von Wright*(Acta Philos. Fenn. 28 (1976)). Amsterdam:
North-Holland, 1976, 417-449.

1526. Coleman, Francis J. "A critical examination of
Wittgenstein's aesthetics." *American Philosophical
Quarterly* 5 (1968):257-266.

1527. Dickie, George. *Aesthetics: An Introduction*.
Indianapolis: Pegasus, 1971.

1528. Diffey, T. J. "Existentialism and the definition
of 'art'." *British Journal of Aesthetics* 13 (1973):103-119.

1529. Dorfles, Gillo. "Appunti per un'estetica Wittgensteiniana." *Rivista di Estetica* 12 (1967):134-150.

1530. Frongia, Guido. "Ludwig Wittgenstein: etica,
estetica, psicoanalisis e religione." *Giornale Critica
della Filosofia Italiana* 50 (1971):120-130.

1531. Gallie, W. B. "Art and politics: Part I."
Aristotelian Society 46 (1972):103-124.

1532. Genova, A. C. "Death as a terminus ad quem."
Philosophical Forum (Boston) 4 (1972-73):186-198.
[Aesthetic purpose for the *Tractatus*]

1533. Khatchadourian, Haig. *The Concept of Art*. New York:
New York Univ. Press, 1971.

1534. Korsmeyer, Carolyn. "Wittgenstein and the ontological
problem of art." *Journal of Aesthetics Education* 11 (1977):
45-57.

1535. Kuspit, Donald B. "The art of reductionism."
Main Currents 29 (1972):21-27.

1536. Levin, David M. "More aspects to the concept of
aesthetic aspects." *Journal of Philosophy* 65 (1968):483-
489.

1537. Lewis, P. B. "Wittgenstein on words and music."
British Journal of Aesthetics 17 (1977):111-121.

1538. Lycan, William G. "Gombrich, Wittgenstein, and the
duck-rabbit." *Journal of Aesthetics and Art Criticism*
30 (1971-72):229-237.

1539. Mace, G. A. "On the directedness of aesthetic
responses [Wittgenstein and problems of objectivity in
aesthetics]." *British Journal of Aesthetics* 8 (1968):155-
160. [See Barrett above, no. 1519]

1540. Mandelbaum, Maurice. "'Family resemblances' and generalization concerning the arts." *American Philosophical Quarterly* 2 (1965):219-228.

1541. Masuhari, Takashi. "Was lobt sich in Bezug auf ästhetischen Wert Ausdrucken und was Nicht. Zur Ästhetik Wittgensteins." *Conceptus* 11 (1977):315-326.

1542. Mercier, André. "L'oggettività della scienza e trasponibile nell'arte e nella morale?" *Filosofia* (Italia) 23 (1972):355-378.

1543. Martland, T. R. "On 'The limits of my language mean the limits of my world'." *Review of Metaphysics* 29 (1975): 19-26.

1544. Osborne, Harold, ed. *Aesthetics*. Oxford: Univ. Press, 1972.

1545. Osborne, Harold. "Wittgenstein on aesthetics." *British Journal of Aesthetics* 6 (1966):385-390.

1546. Rader, M. M. "Games and definitions: Excerpt from *Philosophical Investigations*." In his *A Modern Book of Esthetics*, 3d ed. New York: Holt, Rinehart & Winston, 1960, 195-199.

1547. Scalafani, Richard J. "'Art', Wittgenstein, and open-textured concepts." *Journal of Aesthetics and Art Criticism* 29 (1970-71):333-341.

1548. Shiner, Roger A. "Wittgenstein on the beautiful, the good and the tremendous." *British Journal of Aesthetics* 14 (1974):258-271.

1549. Shir, Jay. "Wittgenstein's aesthetics and the theory of literature." *British Journal of Aesthetics* 18 (1978): 3-11.

1550. Snoeyenbos, Milton H. "On the possibility of theoretical aesthetics." *Metaphilosophy* 9 (1978):108-121.

1551. Tanner, Michael. "Wittgenstein and aesthetics." *Oxford Review* (Michaelmas) (1966):14-24.

1552. Tilghman, B. R. "Wittgenstein, games, and art." *Journal of Aesthetics and Art Criticism* 31 (1972-73):517-524.

1553. Tilghman, B. R. "The literary work of art." In *Language and Aesthetics. Contributions to the Philosophy of Art*, B. R. Tilghman, ed. Lawrence (Kansas): Univ. Press of Kansas, 1973.

1554. Todd, George F. "Expression without feeling." *Journal of Aesthetics and Art Criticism* 30 (1972):477-488.

1555. Van Haecht, Louis. "L'esthétique analytique."
Revue Philosophique de Louvain 68 (1972):11-30.

1556. Weitz, Morris. "Wittgenstein's aesthetics." In
*Language and Aesthetics. Contributions to the Philosophy
of Art*, Ben R. Tilghman, ed. Lawrence (Kansas): Univ.
Press of Kansas, 1973, 71-89.

1557. Wollheim, Richard. *Art and its Objects, an Introduction to Aesthetics*. New York: Harper & Row, 1968.

1558. Wollheim, Richard. "Wittgenstein on art." *New
Statesman* 72 (1966):367-368.

Anagogic

1559. Lemoine, Roy Emanuel. *The Anagogic Theory of
Wittgenstein's* Tractatus (Janua linguarum, Series Minor,
214). The Hague-Paris: Mouton, 1975. 215p.

Analogy

1560. Chapman, Thomas. "Analogy." *The Thomist* 39 (1975):
127-141.

1561. Levin, Michael E. "When is it five o'clock on the
sun?" *Southern Journal of Philosophy* 12 (1974):65-70.

1562. Meiland, J. W. "Analogy, verification and other
minds." *Mind* 75 (1966):564-568.

Anthropology

[See also: Frazer, Section 5]

1564. Garulli, Enrico. "Ludwig Wittgenstein e l'antro-
pologia." In *Il Problema Filosofico dell'antropologia*.
Atti del XXXI Convegno del Centro di Studi filosofici tra
Professori Universitari, Gallarte, 1976. Brescia:
Morcelliana, 1977, 257-264.

1565. Rudich, Norman, and Stassen, Manfred. "Wittgenstein's
implied anthropology. Remarks on Wittgenstein's *Notes on
Frazer*." *History and Theory* 10 (1971):84-89.

Aporetik (a priori)

1566. Bensch, Rudolf. *Ludwig Wittgenstein. Die apriorischen und mathematischen Sätze in seinem Spätwerk* (Abhanlungen zur Philosophie, Psychologie und Pädagogik, 79). Bonn: Bouvier Verlag, 1973. 164p.

1567. Specht, Ernst Konrad. "Wittgenstein und das Problem der Aporetik." *Kantstudien* 57 (1966):309-322.

1568. Specht, Ernst Konrad. "Wittgenstein und das Problem des 'a priori'." *Revue Internationale de Philosophie* 23 (1969):167-178. [Discussion: M. Black, E. K. Specht, J. Vuillemin, Rousseau, A. R. Raggio, J. Bouveresse, 178-182]

Architecture (of Wittgenstein)

1569. Leitner, Bernhard. *The Architecture of Ludwig Wittgenstein.* A documentation compiled by Bernhard Leitner, with excerpts from the family recollections by Hermine Wittgenstein. English text ed. by Dennis Young. Published for the Press of the Nova Scotia College of Art and Design [English and German text, 2d tp in German]. London: Studio International Publications, 1973. 127p.

1570. Masunari, Takashi. "An architectural work of Ludwig Wittgenstein: On its characteristics and *raison d'etre*." *Bigaku* 27 (1976):54. [In Japanese]

Aspect Seeing

1571. Hester, M. B. "Metaphor and aspect seeing." *Journal of Aesthetics and Art Criticism* 25 (1966):205-212.

1572. Hollinger, Robert. "The role of aspect seeing in Wittgenstein's later thought." *Cultural Hermeneutics* 2 (1974):229-241.

1573. Seligman, David B. "Wittgenstein on seeing aspects and experiencing meanings." *Philosophy and Phenomenological Research* 37 (1976):205-217.

Atheism

[See also: God, Religion, Theology]

1574. Strolz, Walter. "Das Problem bei Freud, Wittgenstein, Bloch." In *Atheismus*, Ludwig Klin, hrsg. München, 1970, 23-35.

Attente

1575. Leyvraz, Jean-Pierre. "La notion d'attente chez
Wittgenstein." *Studia Philosophica* 32 (1972):141-161.

Behavior

[See also: Chomsky]

1576. Stoutland, Frederick. "The causation of behavior."
In *Essays on Wittgenstein in Honour of G. H. von Wright*
(Acta Philos. Fenn. 28 (1976)). Amsterdam: North-Holland,
1976, 286-325.

Behaviorism

[See also: Action, Chomsky, Skinner]

1577. Begelman, D. A. "Wittgenstein." *Behaviorism* 4
(1976):201-207.

1578. Germana, Joseph. "Wittgenstein: Wittgenstein."
Behaviorism 5 (1977):61-62.

1579. Holborow, L. C. "Behaviorism and the private
language argument." In *The Private Language Argument*,
O. R. Jones, ed. London: Macmillan; New York: St. Martin's
Press, 1971.

1580. Holborow, L. C. "Wittgenstein's kind of behaviorism?"
Philosophical Quarterly 17 (1967):345-357.

1581. Johnson, Charles W. "On Wittgenstein." *Behaviorism*
5 (1977):39-42.

1582. Mundle, C. W. K. "Behaviourism and the private
language argument." In *The Private Language Argument*,
O. R. Jones, ed. London: Macmillan; New York: St. Martin's
Press, 1971.

1583. Mundle, C. W. K. "Private language and Wittgenstein's
kind of Behaviorism." *Philosophical Quarterly* 16 (1966):
35-46.

Being

1584. Price, Jeffrey Thomas. "Language and Being in
Wittgenstein's *Philosophical Investigations*." Ph.D.
Dissertation, Pennsylvania State Univ., 1969, 141p.
Dissertation Abstracts 31: 1845A.

Belief

1585. High, Dallas M. "Belief, falsification, and Wittgenstein." *International Journal of Philosophy of Religion*
3 (1972):240-250.

1586. Radford, Colin. "Religious belief and contradiction."
Philosophy 50 (1975):437-444.

Bibliography

1587. Fann, K. T. "Bibliography." In his *Wittgenstein's
Conception of Philosophy*, 112-171. [See no. 24]

1588. Fann, K. T. "A Wittgenstein bibliography: Writings
by and about him." *International Philosophical Quarterly*
7 (1967):311-319.

1589. Fann, K. T. "Supplement to the Wittgenstein bibliography." *Revue Internationale de Philosophie* 23 (1969):
363-370.

1590. Vera, Francisco. "Bibliografia." *Teorema*, 1972,
153-168. [Issue devoted to Wittgenstein]

Body

1591. Hartnack, Justus. "Me and my body." In *Essays on
Wittgenstein in Honour of G. H. von Wright* (Acta Philos.
Fenn. 28 (1976)). Amsterdam: North-Holland, 1976, 241-249.

Buddhism

[See also: Zen]

1592. Gudmunsen, Chris. *Wittgenstein and Buddhism* (Barnes
and Noble book). New York: Harper & Row, 1977. 128p.

1593. Gudmunsen, Chris. "On the Mahāyāna and Wittgenstein."
Religion. Journal of Religion and Religions (London) 4
(1974):96-103.

1594. Kalansuriya, A. D. P. "Wittgenstein, meaning-model
and Buddhism." *Indian Philosophical Quarterly* 4 (1977):
381-391.

1595. Kalupahana, David J. "The notion of suffering in
early Buddhism compared with some reflections of early
Wittgenstein." *Philosophy East & West* 27 (1977):423-431.

1596. Richards, Glyn. "Conceptions of the self in
Wittgenstein, Hume, and Buddhism: An analysis and comparison." *The Monist* 61 (1978):42-55.

'Can'

1597. Teichman, Jenny. "Wittgenstein on 'Can'." *Analysis*
34 (1977):381-391.

Cartesian

[See also: Doubt, Privacy]

1598. Chandra, Suresh. "Wittgenstein's technique and the
Cartesian doubt." *Philosophical Quarterly* (India) 33
(1960-61).

1599. Kenny, Anthony. "Cartesian privacy." In *Wittgenstein: The* Philosophical Investigations (A collection of
critical essays). New York: Doubleday, Anchor Books, 1966,
353-370.

1600. Morick, Harold. "Cartesian privilege and the
strictly mental." *Philosophy and Phenomenological Research*
31 (1971):546-551.

1601. Solomon, Robert C. "Wittgenstein and Cartesian
privacy." *Philosophy Today* 16 (1972):163-179.

Cartesianism

1602. Ameriks, Karlis Peter. "Cartesianism and Wittgenstein: The Legacy of Subjectivism in Contemporary Philosophy
of Mind." Ph.D. Dissertation, Yale Univ., 1973. *Dissertation Abstracts* 34 (1973):2690A.

Case

1603. Cook, Monte. "Wittgenstein's appeal to particular
cases." *Modern Schoolman* 54 (1976):55-66.

Certainty

1604. Ayer, A. J. "Wittgenstein on certainty." In *Understanding Wittgenstein* (Royal Institute of Philosophy lectures,
Vol. 7, 1972-73). Godfrey Vesey, ed. London: Macmillan,
1974, 226-245.

1605. Beardsley, Patrick J. "Aquinas and Wittgenstein on the grounds of certainty." *Modern Schoolman* 51 (1974):301-334.

1606. Black, Carolyn. "Taking." *Theoria* 40 (1974):60-75.

1607. Bogen, James. "Wittgenstein and skepticism." *Philosophical Review* 83 (1974):364-373.

1608. Derksen, A. A. "Review of *Über Gewissheit*. Hrsg. von G. E. M. Anscombe." *Bijdragen* 31 (1970):196-199.

1609. Finch, Henry Leroy. "Wittgenstein's last word: Ordinary certainty." *International Philosophical Quarterly* 15 (1975):383-395.

1610. Gill, Jerry H. "Saying and showing: Radical themes in Wittgenstein's *On Certainty*." *Religious Studies* 10 (1974):279-290.

1611. Palmer, A. "Review of Wittgenstein, *On Certainty*." *Mind* 81 (1972):453-457.

1612. von Wright, H. G. "Wittgenstein on certainty." In *Problems in the Theory of Knowledge*, G. H. von Wright, ed. The Hague: Martinus Nijhoff, 1972, 47-60. [B. F. McGuinness, "Comments on Professor von Wright's 'Wittgenstein on certainty." Ibid., 61-65]

1613. White, A. R. "Review of Wittgenstein, *On Certainty*." *Philosophical Books* 11 (1970):30-32.

1614. Zimmerman, Jürg. "Zu Wittgenstein *Über Gewissheit* Versuch eines Überblicks (1974-54)." *Studia Philosophica* 36 (1976):226-239.

Colour Incompatibility

1615. Arbini, R. "Frederick Ferré on colour incompatibility." *Mind* 72 (1963):586-590. [See Ferré below, no. 1616]

1616. Ferré, Frederick. "Colour incompatibility and language games." *Mind* 70 (1961):90-94. [See Swiggart below, no. 1617]

1617. Swiggart, P. "The incompatibility of colours." *Mind* 72 (1963):133-136. [See Ferré above, no. 1616]

Communication

1618.   Johnstone, H. W.   "Rhetoric and communication in
philosophy."   In *Contemporary Philosophic Thought*, Vol. 3.
H. E. Kiefer, ed.   New York: State Univ. of New York Press,
1970, 351-364.

1619.   Deaño, Alfredo.   "Filosofía, lenguaje y comunicacion."
Convivium 37 (1971):23-54.

Common Sense

1620.   Hoagland, Sarah Lucia.   "The Status of Common Sense:
G. E. Moore and L. Wittgenstein: A Comparative Study."
Ph.D. Dissertation, Univ. of Cincinnati, 1975.   *Dissertation
Abstracts* 36 (1975):2256-2257A.

1621.   Preti, G.   "Realismo ontologico e senso comune."
Rivista Critica di Storia della Filosofia 8 (1953):533-544.

Concept

1622.   Keyt, David.   "Wittgenstein, the Vienna Circle, and
precise concepts."   In *Proceedings of the XIV International
Congress of Philosophy*, Vol. 2.   Vienna: Herder, 1968, 237-
246.

Connection

1623.   Hunter, John.   "Wittgenstein on describing and
making connections."   *Philosophical Quarterly* 26 (1976):
243-250.

Continuity (of Wittgenstein's thought)

1624.   Dunlop, Lowell A.   "Sense, Nonsense and Senseless-
ness.   An Essay in the Continuity of the Thought of Wittgenstein."   Ph.D. Dissertation, Marquette Univ., 1972.
Dissertation Abstracts 33 (1973):4774-4775A.

Contradiction

1625.   Arrington, Robert L.   "Wittgenstein on contradiction."
Southern Journal of Philosophy 7 (1969):37-44.

Conventionalism

1626. Antonelli, María Teresa. "A propósito del último Wittgenstein: Observaciones sobre el convencionalismo (Version de Joaquín Jimeno Casalduero)." *Crisis* 3 (1956): 473-484.

Correctness

1627. Rosenberg, Jay F. "The concept of linguistic correctness." *Philosophical Studies* 30 (1976):171-184.

Correspondence Hypothesis

1628. Goldberg, Bruce. "The correspondence hypothesis." *Philosophical Review* 77 (1968):438-454.

Criterion

1629. Ager, Tryg A. "Inner states and outer criteria." *Philosophical Forum* (Boston) 4 (1973):475-499.

1630. Albritton, R. "On Wittgenstein's use of the term 'criterion'." *Journal of Philosophy* 56 (1959):845-857. Reprinted in *Wittgenstein: The* Philosophical Investigations (A collection of critical essays), George Pitcher, ed. New York: Doubleday, Anchor Books, 1966, 231-250.

1631. Baker, G. "Criteria: A new foundation for semantics." *Ratio* 16 (1974):156-189.

1632. Bertman, Martin A. "Criterion and defining criterion [Wittgenstein]." *Philosophical Studies* (Ireland) 24 (1976): 118-130.

1633. Bertman, Martin A. "Criterion and defining criterion in Wittgenstein." *International Logic Review* 8 (1977): 170-181.

1634. Birnbacher, Dieter. *Die Logik der Kriterien. Analysen z. Spätphilosophie Wittgensteins.* Hamburg: Meiner, 1974, iv-155p.

1635. Canfield, John V. "Criteria and rules of language." *Philosophical Review* 83 (1974):70-87.

1636. Canfield, John V. "Criteria and method." *Metaphilosophy* 5 (1974):298-315.

1637.   Clegg, Jerry S.   "Symptoms."   *Analysis* 32 (1972):
90-98.

1638.   Cohen, Trevor E.   "Criteria and the Problem of Other
Minds in Wittgenstein's Later Philosophy."   Ph.D. Disser-
tation, Univ. of New South Wales (Australia), 1975.
Dissertation Abstracts 36 (1976):6143A.

1639.   Garver, Newton.   "Wittgenstein on criteria."   In
Knowledge and Experience, C. D. Rollins, ed.   Pittsburgh:
Univ. of Pittsburgh, 1962, 55-71.   [A symposium with
comments by Ginet, Siegler and Ziff, 55-87]

1640.   Garver, Newton.   "Grammar and Criteria."   Ph.D.
Dissertation, Cornell Univ., 1965.

1641.   Ginet, Carl.   "Comments."   [To N. Garver above, see
no. 1639]   In *Knowledge and Experience*, C. D. Rollins, ed.
Pittsburgh: Univ. of Pittsburgh, 1962, 72-76.

1642.   Klawonn, Erich.   "Criteria and private language."
Danish Yearbook of Philosophy 3 (1966):29-54.

1643.   Koethe, John L.   "The role of criteria in Wittgenstein's later philosophy."   *Canadian Journal of Philosophy*
7 (1977):601-622.

1644.   Lewis, Harry A.   "Criteria, Theory and Knowledge of
Other Minds."   Ph.D. Dissertation, Stanford Univ., 1967.

1645.   Long, Thomas A.   "Wittgenstein.   Criteria and Private
Experience."   Ph.D. Dissertation, Univ. of Cincinnati,
1965, 161p.   *Dissertation Abstracts* 26: 4004A.

1646.   Long, Thomas A.   "Two conceptions of Wittgenstein's
criteria."   *Philosophical Quarterly* 39 (1966):81-97.

1647.   Lycan, W. Gregory.   "Noninductive evidence: Recent
work on Wittgenstein's 'Criteria'."   *American Philosophical
Quarterly* 8 (1971):109-125.

1648.   Rajan, R. Sandara.   "Wittgenstein's conception of
criterion."   *The Journal of the Indian Academy of Philosophy*
6 (1967):45-58.

1649.   Ricketts, Thomas G.   "Wittgenstein's conception of
'criterion'."   *The Undergraduate Journal of Philosophy*
1 (1969):30-38.

1650.   Scriven, Michael.   "The logic of ceiteria."   *Journal
of Philosophy* 56 (1959):857-868.

1651.   Siegler, F. A.   "Comments."   [To N. Garver above,
see no. 1639]   In *Knowledge and Experience*, C. D. Rollins,
ed.   Pittsburgh: Univ. of Pittsburgh, 1962,77-80.

1652. Thompson, Janna L. "About criteria." *Ratio* 13
(1973):30-43.

1653. Todd, D. D. "A note on 'criteria'." *The Journal
of Critical Analysis* 3 (1972):198-207.

1654. Wellman, C. "Wittgenstein's conception of a
criterion." *Philosophical Review* 71 (1962):433-447.

1655. Wellman, C. "Wittgenstein's conception of a
criterion." In *Wittgenstein and the Problem of Other
Minds*, Harold Morick, ed. New York: McGraw-Hill, 1967,
154-169.

1656. Wolgast, E. H. "Wittgenstein and criteria." *Inquiry*
7 (1964):348-366.

1657. Ziff, Paul. "Comments." [To N. Garver above, see
no. 1639] In *Knowledge and Experience*, C. D. Rollins, ed.
Pittsburgh: Univ. of Pittsburgh, 1962, 81-85.

Cyclical Comparatives

1658. Packard, Dennis Jay. "A note on Wittgenstein and
cyclical comparatives." *Analysis* 36 (1975):37-40.

Death

1659. Bruening, William H. "Wittgenstein's view of death."
Philosophical Studies (Ireland) 25 (1977):48-68.

1660. Johnstone, Henry W. "On Wittgenstein on death."
*Proceedings of the Seventh Inter-American Congress of
Philosophy*. Quebec: Les Presses Universitaires Laval,
1967, 66-71.

1661. Shibles, Warren. *Death: An Interdisciplinary
Analysis*. Whitewater (Wisconsin): Language Press, 1974.

1662. Smart, Ninian. "Wittgenstein, death and the last
judgment." In *Philosophers and Religious Truth*, 2d revised
ed. London-New York: St. Martin's Press, 1969.

1663. Van Evra, James W. "On death as a limit." *Analysis*
31 (1971):170-176.

1664. Wyschogrod, Edith. "Death and some philosophies of
language." *Philosophy Today* 22 (1978):255-265.

Definition

1665. Forgie, J. William. "Wittgenstein on naming and ostensive definition." *Studi Internazionali di Filosofia* 8 (1976):13-26.

1666. Hacker, P. M. S. "Wittgenstein on ostensive definition." *Inquiry* 18 (1975):267-287.

1667. Steinvorth, U. "Wittgensteins transzendentale Untersuchung der ostensiven Definition (zur Kritik der bisherigen Identifizierung von Gebrauch und Rolle bei Wittgenstein)." *Kantstudien* 60 (1969):495-505.

1668. Zweig, Arnulf. "Theories of Real Definition: A Study of the Views of Aristotle, C. I. Lewis and Wittgenstein." Ph.D. Dissertation, Stanford Univ., 1960, 194p. *Dissertation Abstracts* 21 (1960):212A.

Depth Structure

1669. Chatterjee, A. K. "Depth structures in recent philosophies of language." *Indian Philosophical Quarterly* 4 (1976):63-74.

Description

1670. Premo, Blanche Lillie Kolar. "Wittgenstein's Notion of Description: From Logic to Grammar." Ph.D. Dissertation, Marquette Univ., 1974. *Dissertation Abstracts* 36 (1975):351-352A.

Dreams and Dreaming

1671. Chappell, V. C. "The concept of dreaming." In *Philosophical Essays on Dreaming*, C. E. M. Dunlop, ed. Ithaca (New York): Cornell Univ. Press, 1977, 280-308.

1672. Chihara, C. S. "What dreams are made on." In *Philosophical Essays on Dreaming*, C. E. M. Dunlop, ed. Ithaca (New York): Cornell Univ. Press, 1977, 251-264.

1673. Curley, E. M. "Dreaming and conceptual revision." In *Philosophical Essays on Dreaming*, C. E. M. Dunlop, ed. Ithaca (New York): Cornell Univ. Press, 1977, 317-346.

1674. Malcolm, Norman. "The concept of dreaming." In *Wittgenstein and the Problem of Other Minds*, Harold Morick, ed. New York: McGraw-Hill, 1967, 215-227.

1675. Price, J. T. "Dream recollection and Wittgenstein's language." *Dialogue* 13 (1974):35-41.

1676. Putnam, Hilary. "Dreaming and 'depth-grammar'." In *Analytical Philosophy*, R. J. Butler, ed. Oxford: Basil Blackwell, 1962, 211-235.

Education - Teaching

1677. Allmaker, Ali Martin. "'Wholeness' in the Philosophy of the Later Wittgenstein and its Applicability to the Philosophy of Education." Ph.D. Dissertation, State Univ. of New York at Albany, 1972. *Dissertation Abstracts* 33 (1972):2603A.

1678. Bartley, W. W., III. "Theory of language and philosophy of science as instruments of educational reform: Wittgenstein and Popper as Austrian schoolteachers." In *Methodological and Historical Essays in the Natural and Social Sciences*, Robert S. Cohen and Marx W. Watofsky, eds. (Synthese Library, 60, Boston Studies in the Philosophy of Science, 14). Dordrecht-Boston: D. Reidel, 1974, 307-337.

1679. Green, Joe L. "Wittgenstein's influence on philosophy of education." *Educational Studies* 8 (1977): 1-20.

1680. Kuppfer, H. "Pädagogische Möglichkeiten in der Philosophie Ludwig Wittgensteins." *Pädagogische Rundschau* 23 (1969):857-868.

1681. McBride, Frank Abbott. "The Later Wittgenstein's Conception of Teaching." Ph.D. Dissertation, Michigan State Univ., 1972. *Dissertation Abstracts* 33 (1972):2428A.

1682. Prange, K. "Können, Üben, Wissen. Zur Problematik des Lernens in der Sprachphilosophie Ludwig Wittgensteins." *Pädagogische Rundschau* 26 (1972):707-734.

Egocentric Predicament

1683. Wellman, C. "Wittgenstein and the egocentric predicament." *Mind* 68 (1959):223-233.

Elucidation

1684. Hacker, P. M. S. "Frege and Wittgenstein on elucidations." *Mind* 84 (1975):601-609.

Emotion

1685. Sachs, David. "Wittgenstein on emotion." In *Essays on Wittgenstein in Honour of G. H. von Wright* (Acta Philos. Fenn. 28 (1976)). Amsterdam: North-Holland, 1976, 250-285.

Empirical Realists

1686. Dauer, Francis W. "Empirical realists and Wittgensteinians." *Journal of Philosophy* 69 (1972):128-147.

Empiricism

1687. Huber, Carlos E. "Der Englische Empirismus als Bewusstseinsphilosophie: Seine Eigenart und das Problem der Geltung von Bewusstseinhalten in ihm." *Gregorianum* 58 (1977):641-674.

Entitlement Question

1688. Cherry, Chr. "Professor Schwyzer's entitlement question." *Philosophical Quarterly* 24 (1974):261-264. [H. Schwyzer, "Thought and reality: The metaphysics of Kant and Wittgenstein." *Philosophical Quarterly* 23 (1973): 193-206]

Erklärung

1689. Fujimoto, Takashi. "The notion of *Erklärung*." In *Ludwig Wittgenstein. Philosophy and Language.* Muirhead Library of Philosophy. London: George Allen & Unwin; New York: Humanities Press, 1972, 222-232.

Error

1690. James, Dominique. "Le probleme de l'erreur dans les *Investigations Philosophiques* de Ludwig Wittgenstein." *Studia Philosophica* 34 (1974):25-56.

Essence and Essentialism

1691. Beal, M. W. "Essentialism and closed concepts." *Ratio* 16 (1974):190-205.

1692. Cohen, Mendel. "Wittgenstein's anti-essentialism."
Australasian Journal of Philosophy 46 (1968):210-224.

----- Diffey, T. J. [See no. 1528]

1693. Hochberg, H. "Facts, possibilities and essences in
the *Tractatus*." In *Essays on Wittgenstein*, E. D. Klemke,
ed. Urbana: Univ. of Illinois Press, 1971, 485-533.

1694. Lenk, Hans. "Was the philosophy of the later Wittgenstein essentialistic?" [Summary] In *Akten XIV International
Kongress für Philosophie*, Vol. 6. Vienna: Herder, 1968,
384-386.

1695. Lenk, Hans. "War der späte Wittgenstein ein Essen-
tialist?" *Man and World* 3 (1970):16-25.

1696. Schwyzer, Hubert. "Essence without universals."
Canadian Journal of Philosophy (September 1974):51-68.

Ethics

1697. Beehler, Rodger. *Moral Life*. Oxford: Blackwell,
1978.

----- Bell, Julian. [See no. 1521]

----- Bouveresse, Jacques. [See no. 1523]

1698. Britton, Karl W. "Philosophische Ethik der Gegen-
wart in England [übers von j Schoolmeier]." *Zeitschrift
für Evangelische Ethik* 6 (1962):101-115.

1699. Cavalier, Robert. "Wittgenstein, Ethics and the
Will." Ph.D. Dissertation, Duquesne Univ., 1978.
Dissertation Abstracts 39 (1978):1632A.

1700. Daly, G. B. "Logical positivism, metaphysics and
ethics, I: Ludwig Wittgenstein." *Irish Theological
Quarterly* 23 (1956):111-150.

1701. Davies, C. A. "Morality and ignorance." *Philosophy*
50 (1975):283-293.

1702. Engel, S. Morris. "Reason, morals and philosophic
irony." *The Personalist* 45 (1964):533-555.

----- Frongia, Guido. [See no. 1530]

1703. Griffith, A. P. "Wittgenstein, Schopenhauer, and
ethics." In *Understanding Wittgenstein* (Royal Institute
of Philosophy lectures, Vol. 7, 1972-73). Godfrey Vesey,
ed. London: Macmillan, 1974, 96-116.

1704. Giacomini, Ugo. "Appunti sull'etica di Wittgenstein."
Aut Aut (Gennaio) (1966):72-80.

1705. Hargrove, Eugene Carroll. "Wittgenstein and Ethics."
Ph.D. Dissertation, Univ. of Missouri at Columbia, 1974.
Dissertation Abstracts 36 (1975):1578A.

1706. Klemke, E. D. "Wittgenstein's lecture on Ethics."
Journal of Value Inquiry 9 (1975):118-127.

1707. Lecaldano, Eugenio. *Le analisi del linguaggio morale,
"Buono" e "dovere" nella filosofia inglese dal 1903 al 1965.*
Roma: Edizioni dell'Ateneo, 1969. 283p.

1708. Levi, Albert W. "The biographical sources of
Wittgenstein's ethics." *Telos* (Winter 1978-79):63-76.

1709. Leyvraz, Jean-Pierre. "Le problème moral chez
Wittgenstein." *Revue de Théologie et de Philosophie*
(1975):280-290.

1710. Machan, T. R. "Wittgenstein and meta-ethics."
Journal of Thought 8 (1973):252-259.

1711. Magnus, Bernd. "Nihilism, reason, and 'the good'."
Review of Metaphysics 25 (1971):292-310.

1712. Mayberry, Thomas C. "On 'why should I be moral'."
Canadian Journal of Philosophy 8 (1978):361-373.

1713. Pitcher, George. "Wittgenstein and ethics." In
Ludwig Wittgenstein. Philosophy and Language, A. Ambrose
and M. Lazerowitz, eds. Muirhead Library of Philosophy.
London: George Allen & Unwin; New York: Humanities Press,
1972, 120-139.

1714. Redpath, Theodore. "Wittgenstein and ethics." In
Pitcher, 95-119. [See no. 76]

1715. Rhees, Rush. "Some developments in Wittgenstein's
view of ethics." *Philosophical Review* 74 (1965):17-26.

1716. Rhees, Rush. *Without Answers* (Studies in ethics
and the philosophy of religion). London: Routledge & Kegan
Paul; New York: Schocken Books, 1969.

> book reviews:
> P. T. Geach, *Journal of Philosophy* 68 (1971):530-532;
> R. W. Newell, *Philosophical Books* 11 (1970):25-27.

1717. Rothenstreich, Nathan. "The thrust against language:
A critical comment on Wittgenstein's ethics." *The Journal
of Value Inquiry* 2 (1968).

1718. Sprengard, K. A. "Neue Möglichkeiten der Ethik:
Kant--Wittgenstein--Sartre." In *Bewusst Sein*. Gerhard
Funke zu eigen. A. J. Bucher, et al., hrsg. Bonn:
Bouvier Verlag Herbert Grundmann, 1975, 290-308.

1719. Studhalter, Kurt. *Ethik, Religion und Lebensform
bei Ludwig Wittgenstein* (Veröffentlichungen der Universität
Innsbruck, 82). Innsbruck: Universität Innsbruck, 1973.
78p.

1720. Walker, Jeremy. "Wittgenstein's earlier ethics."
American Philosophical Quarterly 5 (1968):219-232.

Excluded Middle

1721. McDonough, Richard M. "Wittgenstein and the Law of
the Excluded Middle." Ph.D. Dissertation, Cornell Univ.,
1975. *Dissertation Abstracts* 36 (1976):7475A.

Existentialism

        [See also: Section 5: Items Arranged by
                    Proper Names: Kierkegaard,
                    Heidegger, Jaspers, Merleau-Ponty]

1722. Cavell, Stanley. "Existentialism and analytic
philosophy." *Daedalus* 93 (1964):946-974. [Section 3
compares Wittgenstein with Kierkegaard]

----- Engel, S. Morris. [See no. 1507]

1723. Engel, S. Morris. "Wittgenstein, existentialism and
the history of philosophy." In *Deutung und Bedeutung*.
(Studies in German and comparative literature).
B. Schludermann, ed. Paris: Mouton, 1973, 228-247.

1724. Lübbe, Hermann. "Wittgenstein--ein Existentialist?"
Philosophische Jahrbuch 69 (1962):311-324.

Experience

1725. Bouveresse, Jacques. *Le mythe de l'interiorité.
Expérience, signification et langage privé chez Wittgenstein*
(Critique). Paris: Les Editions de Minuit, 1976, xiv-802p.

1726. Kulkarni, N. G. "Wittgenstein's theory of experience."
Journal of the Philosophical Association (India) 11 (1968):
27-35.

1727. Malcolm, Norman. "The privacy of experience." In
Epistemology: New Essays in the Theory of Knowledge, Avrum
Strool, ed. New York: Harper & Row, 1967, 129-158.

1728. Rhees, Rush. "Wittgenstein's notes for lectures on
private experience and sense data." *Philosophical Review*
77 (1968):271-274.

1729. Stenius, Erik. "Linguistic structure and the
structure of experience." *Theoria* 20 (1954):153-174.

1730. von Morstein, Petra. "Erfährung bei Ludwig Wittgenstein." *Archiv für Philosophie* 12 (1963):133-151.

Explanation

1731. Cherry, Christopher. "Explanation and explanation
by hypothesis." *Synthèse* 33 (1976):315-339.

1732. Gruender, D. "Wittgenstein on explanation and
description." *Journal of Philosophy* 59 (1962):523-530.

1733. Harris, Charles Edwin, Jr. "Wittgenstein's
Criticism of Ostensive Explanation." Ph. D. Dissertation,
Vanderbilt Univ., 1964, 218p. *Dissertation Abstracts*
25: 5332A.

Expression

1734. Finn, David R. "Expression." *Mind* 84 (1975):192-
209.

Fact

----- Hochberg, H. [See no. 1693]

1735. Lucas, J. R. "On not worshipping facts." *Philosophical Quarterly* 8 (1958):144-156.

1736. Miller, David. "The uniqueness of atomic facts
in Wittgenstein's *Tractatus*." *Philosophical Review* 86
(1977):520-544.

1737. O'Brien, George D. "Meaning and Fact: A Study in
the Philosophy of Wittgenstein." Ph.D. Dissertation,
Univ. of Chicago, 1961.

1738. Urmson, J. O. "Facts and pictures of facts." In
his *Philosophical Analysis*. Oxford Univ. Press, 1956,
54-93.

1739. Wolniewicz, Bogulsaw. "The notion of fact as a modal operator." *Teorema*, 1972, 59-66.

Family Resemblance

[See also: Universals]

1740. Bambrough, R. "Universals and family resemblances." *Proceedings of the Aristotelian Society* 61 (1960-61):207-222. Reprinted in *Wittgenstein. The* Philosophical Investigations (A collection of critical essays), George Pitcher, ed. Garden City (New York): Doubleday, Anchor Books, 1966, 186-204. Also reprinted in *The Problem of Universals*, C. Landesman, ed. New York: Basic Books, 1971, 119-130.

1741. Coder, David. "Family resemblances and paradigm cases." *Dialogue* 6 (1967):355-366.

1742. Griffin, Nicholas. "Wittgenstein, universals and family resemblances." *Canadian Journal of Philosophy* 3 (1974):635-651.

1743. Gupta, R. K. "Wittgenstein's theory of 'family resemblances' in his *Philosophical Investigations* (Secs. 65-80)." *Philosophia Naturalis* 12 (1970):282-286.

1744. Hazard, Paul Alfred. "A problem with Wittgenstein's 'family resemblance'." *Laval Théologique et Philosophique* 31 (1975):265-291.

1745. Hollinger, Robert. "Natural kinds, family resemblances." *The Personalist* 55 (1974):323-333.

1746. Huby, Pamela M. "Family resemblance." *Philosophical Quarterly* 18 (1968):66-67. [Concerning L. Pompa's paper on Wittgenstein's concept of family resemblance. See no. 1752]

1747. Khatchadourian, Haig. "Common names and family resemblances." *Philosophy and Phenomenological Research* 18 (1958):341-358. Reprinted in *Wittgenstein: The* Philosophical Investigations (A collection of critical essays), George Pitcher, ed. Garden City (New York): Doubleday, Anchor Books, 1966, 205-230.

1748. Llewelyn, J. E. "Family resemblance." *Philosophical Quarterly* 18 (1968):344-346. [Criticism of Pompa, see below, nos. 1752 and 1753]

1749. Lyon, Ardon. "Family resemblance, vagueness, and change in meaning." *Theoria* 34 (1968):66-75. [See H. Wennerberg below, no. 1760]

1750. Manser, A. R. "Games and family resemblances." *Philosophy* 42 (1967):210-225.

1751. Moutafakis, J. "Of family resemblances and aesthetic discourse." *The Philosophical Forum* (Boston) 7 (1975):71-89.

1752. Pompa, L. "Family resemblance." *Philosophical Quarterly* 17 (1967):63-69. [See Huby above, no. 1746]

1753. Pompa, L. "Family resemblance: A reply." *Philosophical Quarterly* 18 (1968):347-353. [A reply to Huby and Llewelyn, see nos. 1746 and 1748]

1754. Rolston, Howard Lee. "Wittgenstein's Concept of Family Resemblance." Ph.D. Dissertation, Harvard Univ., 1972. 276p.

1755. Raggio, Andrés R. "'Family resemblance predicates', modalités et réductionisme." *Revue Internationale de Philosophie* 23: 339-355. [Discussion: G.-G. Granger, E. K. Specht, A. R. Raggio, M. Black, J. Vuillemin, Molino, 356-362]

1756. Schwyzer, Hubert. "Whether the theory of family resemblances solves the problem of universals." *Philosophical Quarterly* 23 (1973):193-206.

1757. Simon, Michael A. "When is resemblance a family resemblance?" *Mind* 78 (1969):408-416.

1758. Simon, Michael A. "Games, essences and family resemblances." In *Akten XIV International Kongress für Philosophie*, Vol. 3. Wien: Herder, 1968, 476-481.

1759. Thorp, J. W. "Whether the theory of family resemblances solves the problem of universals." *Mind* 8 (1972):567-570. [See Schwyzer above, no. 1756]

1760. Wennerberg, Hjalmar. "The concept of family resemblances in Wittgenstein's later philosophy." *Theoria* 33 (1967):107-132. [See Lyon above, no. 1749]

Fantasy

1761. Broyles, James E. "An observation on Wittgenstein's use of fantasy." *Metaphilosophy* 5 (1974):291-297.

Fideism

[See also: Belief, Certainty]

1762. Hudson, W. Donald. *Wittgensteinian Fideism* (New studies in the philosophy of religion). Garden City (New York): Doubleday, Anchor Books, 1970.

1763. Hudson, W. Donald. "On two points against Wittgensteinian fideism." *Philosophy* 43 (1968):269-273. [See Kai Nielsen below, no. 1765]

1764. Nielsen, Kai. "Wittgensteinian fideism." *Philosophy* 42 (1967):191-209.

1765. Nielsen, Kai. "Wittgensteinian fideism again: A reply to Hudson." *Philosophy* 44 (1969):63-65. [See Hudson above, no. 1763]

Finitism

1766. Ambrose, Alice. "Finitism and the limits of empiricism." *Mind* 46 (1937):379-385. A revised version reprinted in her *Essays in Analysis*.

1767. Bouveresse, Jacques. "Sur le 'finitisme' de Wittgenstein." In *La parole malheureuse. De l'alchimie linguistique à la grammaire philosophique*. Paris: Les Editions de Minuit, 1971, ch. 4.

1768. Bell, David A. "Wittgenstein's Notion of Form of Life in the *Philosophical Investigations*." Ph.D. Dissertation, Univ. of North Carolina, 1977. *Dissertation Abstracts* 38 (1977):838A.

1769. French, Peter A. "Wittgenstein's limits of the world." *Midwest Studies in Philosophy* 1 (1976):114-124. [See Shibles and Shekleton below, nos. 1773, 1774]

1770. Goff, Robert. "Aphorism as *Lebensform* in Wittgenstein's *Philosophical Investigations*." In *New Essays in Phenomenology. Studies in the Philosophy of Experience*. Ed. with an introduction by James M. Edie. Chicago: Quadrangle Books, 1969, 58-71.

1771. Hunter, J. F. M. "'Forms of life' in Wittgenstein's *Philosophical Investigations*." In *Essays on Wittgenstein*, E. D. Klemke, Ed. Urbana: Univ. of Illinois Press, 1971, 273-297.

1772. Lee, Myung-Hyun. "The Later Wittgenstein's Reflection on Meaning, Language and Forms of Life." Ph.D. Dissertation, Brown Univ., 1974. *Dissertation Abstracts* 35 (1975):7351A.

1773. Shekleton, James. "Rules and *Lebensformen*." *Midwest Studies in Philosophy* 1 (1976):125-132. [See French above, no. 1769]

1774. Shibles, Warren. "Comments on 'Wittgenstein's limits of the world'." *Midwest Studies in Philosophy* 1 (1976): 132-134. [See French above, no. 1769]

1775. Sutherland, Stewart R. "On the idea of a form of life." *Religious Studies* 11 (1975):293-306.

----- Studhalter, Kurt. [See no. 1719]

1776. Zabeeh, F. "On language games and forms of life." In *Essays on Wittgenstein*, E. D. Klemke, ed. Urbana: Univ. of Illinois Press, 1971, 328-373.

Games

1777. Cherry, Christopher. "Games and the world." *Philosophy* 51 (1976):57-61.

1778. Cherry, Christopher. "Games and language." *Mind* 84 (1975):528-547.

----- Manser, A. R. [See no. 1750]

1779. Midgley, Mary. "The game game." *Philosophy* 49 (1974):231-253.

God

1780. Bambrough, Renford. *Reason, Truth and God*. London: Methuen, 1969.

1781. Bell, Richard H. "Theology as grammar: Is God an object of understanding?" *Religious Studies* 11 (1975): 307-317.

1782. Bildhauer, William M. "The Reality of God: An Investigation of the Adequacy of Wittgenstein's Fideism." Ph.D. Dissertation, Univ. of Arizona, 1972. *Dissertation Abstracts* 33 (1973):6394-6395A.

1783. Bruening, William H. "Aquinas and Wittgenstein on God-talk." *Sophia* (Australia) 16 (1977):1-7.

1784. Cell, Edward. *Language, Existence, God. Interpretations of Moore, Russell, Ayer, Wittgenstein, Wisdom, Oxford Philosophy, and Tillich*. Nashville (Tennessee): Abingdon Press, 1971. 400p.

1785. Durrant, Michael. *The Logical Status of "God"*.
London: Macmillan, 1972.

1786. Gastwirth, Paul. "Concepts of God." *Religious Studies* 8 (1972):147-152.

1787. Gill, Jerry H. "Wittgenstein and religious language."
Theology Today 21 (1964):59-72.

1788. Gill, Jerry H. "God-talk: Getting on with it. A review of current literature." *Southern Journal of Philosophy* 6 (1968):115-124.

1789. Keightley, A. W. *Wittgenstein, Grammar and God*.
London: Epworth Press, 1976. 176p.

1790. Nielsen, Kai. "God and forms of life." *Indian Philosophical Review* (1969).

1791. Northrop, F. S. C. "Language, mysticism and God."
In his *Man, Nature and God*. New York: Simon & Schuster, 1962, 238-245.

Good

1792. Wellman, Carl. "The meaning of *good*." In *Essays on Wittgenstein in Honour of G. H. von Wright* (Acta Philos.
Fenn. 28 (1976)). Amsterdam: North-Holland, 1976, 394-416.

Grammar - Grammatical

1793. Bouveresse, Jacques. "La notion de 'grammaire' chez le second Wittgenstein." *Revue Internationale de Philosophie* 23 (1969):319-335. [Discussion: B. F. McGuinness, J. Bouveresse, G.-G. Granger, M. Black, A. R. Raggio, 336-338]

1794. Hallie, Philip P. "Wittgenstein's grammatical-empirical distinction." *Journal of Philosophy* 60 (1963): 565-578.

1795. Halloran, S. M. "Wittgensteinian grammar."
The Personalist 51 (1970):212-221.

1796. Hunter, J. F. M. "Some grammatical states."
Philosophy 52 (1977):155-166.

1797. Johnson, Ralph H. "Wittgenstein: Philosophy and grammar." In *Philosophy and Christian Theology*, George F. McLean, ed. Washington (D.C.): The Catholic Univ. of America, 1970, 99-107.

1798.   Klein, J. T.   "Philosophy and depth grammar: An
interpretation of Wittgenstein."   *ETC* 33 (1976):253-262.

1799.   Lang, Martin. *Wittgensteins philosophische Grammatik.*
Entstehung und Perspektiven der Strategie eines radikalen
Aufklärers.   's-Gravenhage: Nijhoff, 1971, iv-160p.

1800.   Steinman, Daine C.   "The Role of the Notion of Grammar
in Wittgenstein's Later Work."   Ph.D. Dissertation, Univ.
of Minnesota, 1977, 232p. *Dissertation Abstracts* 38 (1977):
3565A.

Hermeneutics

1801.   Premo, Blanche L.   "The early Wittgenstein and
hermeneutics." *Philosophy Today* 16 (1972):43-65.

1802.   Wuchterl, Kurt.   "Die Hermeneutik und der operative
Aufbau der Philosophie.   Dargestellt an der Philosophie
Wittgensteins." *Zeitschrift für Philosophische Forschung*
30 (1976):350-368.

1803.   Zimmermann, Jörg. *Wittgensteins sprachphilosophische*
Hermeneutik (Philosophische Abhandlungen, 46).   Frankfurt
am Main: V. Klostermann, 1975, viii-318p.

History

1804.   Kellner, Hans D.   "Time out: The discontinuity of
historical consciousness." *History and Theory* 14 (1975):
275-296.

1805.   Legrand, Michel.   "Langage ordinaire, historicité et
science." *Revue Philosophique de Louvain* 72 (1974):539-
552.

1806.   Lübbe, Hermann.   "'Sprachspiele' und 'Geschichten'."
Kantstudien 52 (1960-61):220-242.

"I"

1807.   Gill, Jerry H.   "Wittgenstein on the use of 'I'."
Southern Journal of Philosophy 5 (1967):26-35.

1808.   Klein, J. Theodore.   "Wittgenstein's analysis of the
use of 'I' in the *Philosophical Investigations*." *Modern*
Schoolman 51 (1973):47-53.

1809.   Zemach, Eddy M.   "The reference of 'I'." *Philo-*
sophical Studies 23 (1972):68-75.

Idealism

1810. Anscombe, G. E. M. "The question of linguistic idealism." In *Essays on Wittgenstein in Honour of G. H. von Wright* (Acta Philos. Fenn. 28 (1976)). Amsterdam: North-Holland, 1976, 188-215.

1811. Springer, William C. "The 'idealism' in Wittgenstein." *Proceedings of the New Mexico-West Texas Philosophical Society* (April 1972):44-48.

1812. Williams, B. "Wittgenstein and idealism." In *Understanding Wittgenstein* (Royal Institute of Philosophy lectures, Vol. 7, 1972-73). Godfrey Vesey, ed. London: Macmillan; New York: St. Martin's Press, 1974, 76-95.

Identity

1813. Borowski, E. J. "Identity and personal identity." *Mind* 85 (1976):481-502.

1814. Garver, Newton. "Criteria of personal identity." *Journal of Philosophy* 61 (1964):779-784.

1815. Muehlmann, Robert. "Russell and Wittgenstein on identity." *Philosophical Quarterly* 19 (1969):221-230.

1816. Savitt, Steven F. "Frege and Wittgenstein on Identity, Logic and Number." Ph.D. Dissertation, Brandeis Univ., 1972, 172p. *Dissertation Abstracts* 32: 7047A.

1817. Spisani, Franco. "The concept of identity in Wittgenstein." *Systematics* 10 (1972-73):119-121.

1818. Spisani, Franco. "Il concetto di identità in Wittgenstein." *Teorema*, 1972, 113-115.

1819. Spisani, Franco. "El concepto de 'identitad' in Wittgenstein." Trad. del Italiano: Antonio Ibarguengoitia. *Revista de Filosofía México* 6 (1973):275-279.

1820. Spisani, Franco. "Il concetto di identità in Wittgenstein." *Sophia* 41 (1973):90-92.

1821. Waismann, Friedrich. "Über den Begriff der Identität." *Erkenntnis* 6 (1936):56-64.

1822. White, Roger. "Wittgenstein on identity." *Proceedings of the Aristotelian Society* 78 (1977-78):157-174.

Image

1823. Aldrich, V. C. "Images as things and things as images." *Mind* 64 (1955):261-263.

1824. Aldrich, V. C. "Image-mongering and image-management." *Philosophy and Phenomenological Research* 23 (1962): 51-61.

1825. Warnock, Mary. "The nature of the mental image. Phenomenology, Sartre and Wittgenstein." In *Imagination*. Berkeley-Los Angeles: Univ. of California Press, 1976, 131-195.

Imagination

1826. Dilman, Ilham. "Imagination." *Proceedings of the Aristotelian Society, Supplement* 41 (1967):19-36. [See Ishiguro below, no. 1828]

1827. Dilman, Ilham. "Imagination." *Analysis* 28 (1968): 90-97. [See no. 1828]

1828. Ishiguro, Hidé. "Imagination." *Proceedings of the Aristotelian Society, Supplement* 41 (1967):37-56. [A reply to Dilman, see no. 1827]

1829. Strawson, P. F. "Imagination and perception." In *Freedom and Resentment, and other Essays*. London: Methuen; New York: Barnes and Noble, 1974, 45-65.

1830. von Morstein, Petra. "Imagine." *Mind* 83 (1974): 228-243.

Immortality

1831. Anderson, Leland Tyson. "Wittgenstein and the Logical Possibility of Immortality." Ph.D. Dissertation, Temple Univ., 1972. *Dissertation Abstracts* 33 (1972):356A.

Incorrigibility

1832. Sheridan, Gregory. "The electroencephalogram argument against incorrigibility." *American Philosophical Quarterly* 6 (1969):62-70.

1833. Suárez, Alfonso García. "Conocimiento, incorregibilidad y sensaciones." *Teorema*, 1974, 67-80.

Induction

1834. Aimonetto, Italo. "L'induzione matematica o
ragionamento ricorsivo." *Filosofia* (Italy) 24 (1974):153-
176.

1835. Dilman, Ilham. *Induction and Deduction. A Study in
Wittgenstein.* Oxford: Basil Blackwell & Mott, 1973, 225p;
New York: Harper & Row, 1973.

> book reviews:
> J. Bogen, *Dialogue* 13 (1974):198-201;
> J. Burnham, *Australasian Journal of Philosophy* 51
>   (1973):265-267;
> P. T. Mackenzie, *Canadian Journal of Philosophy* 5
>   (1975):309-321;
> T. E. Wilkerson, *Mind* 84 (1975):297-299.

Inference

1836. Rhees, R. "Questions on logical inference." In
Understanding Wittgenstein (Royal Institute of Philosophy
lectures, Vol. 7, 1972-73). Godfrey Vesey, ed. London:
Macmillan; New York: St. Martin's Press, 1974, 30-48.

Infinity

1837. Griffith, William B. "Problems about Infinity.
Wittgenstein's Contributions." Ph.D. Dissertation, Yale
Univ., 1963. 144p.

Influence (of and on Wittgenstein)

1838. Kaplan, Bernard. "Some considerations of influences
on Wittgenstein." *Idealistic Studies* 1 (1971):73-88.

1839. Nelson, J. O. "The influence of the later Wittgen-
stein on American philosophy." In *Aspect of Contemporary
American Philosophy*, Franklin H. Donnell, ed. Wurzburg-
Wien: Physica Verlag, 1965, 50-60.

Innate Ideas

1840. Erde, Edmund L. "Philosophy and Science. Wittgenstein and Chomsky: An Examination of the Current Theory
of Innate Ideas." Ph.D. Dissertation, Univ. of Texas at
Austin, 1970, 218p. *Dissertation Abstracts* 31: 1839A.

Inner Processes

1841. Hunter, J. F. M.   "Wittgenstein on inner processes
and outward criteria." *Canadian Journal of Philosophy*
7 (1977):805-817.

Inner States

1842. Rembert, Andrew.   "Wittgenstein on learning the
names of inner states." *Philosophy Review* 84 (1975):
236-248.

Instinct

1843. La Fave, Sandra. "The Conception of Instinct."
Ph.D. Dissertation, Claremont Graduate School, 1979, 366p.
Dissertation Abstracts 39 (1979):6811A.

Intending, Intention, Intentionality

1844. Gustafson, D. "Expressions of intentions." *Mind*
83 (1974):321-340.

1845. Rankin, K. W. "Wittgenstein on meaning, understanding, and intending." *American Philosophical Quarterly*
3 (1966):1-13.

1846. Rosenberg, Jay. "Intentionality and self in the
Tractatus." *Noûs* 2 (1968):341-358.

1847. Wright, Edmond L. "Words and intentions."
Philosophy 52 (1977):45-62.

Intuitionism

1848. Fogelin, Robert J. "Wittgenstein and intuitionism."
American Philosophical Quarterly 5 (1968):267-274.

Isomorphism

1849. Engel, S. Morris. "Isomorphism and linguistic waste."
Mind 74 (1965):28-45.

1850. Storer, Thomas. "Linguistic isomorphisms." *Philosophy of Science* 19 (1952):77-85.

Italian Interpretation of Wittgenstein

1851. Belohradsky, Vaclav. *Interpretazioni italiane de
Wittgenstein* (Studi sul pensiero filosofico e religioso
dei secoli XIX e XX, 21). Milano: Marzorati, 1972. 326p.

  book review:
  D. Rambaudi, *Giornale di Metafisica* 27 (1972):605-607.

Judgment

1852. Morawetz, Thomas H. "Wittgenstein and synthetic
a priori judgments." *Philosophy* 49 (1974):429-434.

1853. Pears, David. "The relation between Wittgenstein's
picture theory of propositions and Russell's theories of
judgment." In *Wittgenstein: Sources and Perspectives*,
C. G. Luckhardt, ed. Ithaca (New York): Cornell Univ.
Press, 1979, 190-212.

1854. Stock, G. "Wittgenstein on Russell's theory of
judgment." In *Understanding Wittgenstein* (Royal Institute
of Philosophy lectures, Vol. 7, 1972-73). Godfrey Vesey,
ed. London: Macmillan; New York: St. Martin's Press, 1974,
62-75.

Justice

1855. Kent, Edward. "Justice as respect for person."
Southern Journal of Philosophy 6 (1968):70-77.

Knowledge

1856. Albritton, K. "Knowledge and doubt." Isenberg
lecture delivered at Michigan State Univ., November 8, 1968.

1857. Aune, Bruce. "Knowing and merely thinking."
Philosophical Studies 12 (1960):53-58.

1858. Aune, Bruce. "Does knowledge have an indubitable
foundation?" In his *Knowledge, Mind, and Nature.*
New York: Random House, 1967, 31-62.

1859. Cooper, C. "Wittgenstein's theory of knowledge."
In *Understanding Wittgenstein*, Godfrey Vesey, ed. London:
Macmillan; New York: St. Martin's Press, 1974, 246-284.

1860. Cappelleti, V. "La struttura del conoscere secondo
L. Wittgenstein." *La Nuova Critica* 7-8 (1958-59):47-77.

1861. Chastaing, Maxime. "Wittgenstein et les problèmes de la connaissance d'autrui." *Revue Philosophique de la France et de l'Etranger* 85 (1960):297-312.

1862. Gallacher, Hugh P. "Wittgenstein over kennis." *Kennis Methode* 2 (1978):18-29.

1863. Gruender, D. "Language, society, and knowledge." *Antioch Review* 28 (1968):187-212.

1864. Haller, Rudolf. "Concerning the so-called 'Munchhausen trilemma'." *Ratio* 16 (1974):125-140. [Propositional knowledge]

1865. King-Farlow, John, and Jones, Prudence. "Deux traditions épistémologiques." *Dialogue* 14 (1975):464-473.

1866. Morawetz, Thomas. *Wittgenstein and Knowledge.* Univ. of Massachusetts Press, 1978. 159p.

1867. Sellars, Wilfrid. "Being and being known." *Proceedings of the American Catholic Philosophical Association* 34 (1960):28-49.

1868. Shiner, Roger A. "Wittgenstein and the foundations of knowledge." *Proceedings of the Aristotelian Society* 78 (1977-78):103-124.

1869. Stawinski, Arthur W. "Wittgenstein and the Perceptual Foundations of Knowledge." Ph.D. Dissertation, Northwestern Univ., 1973. *Dissertation Abstracts* 34 (1974):4345A.

1870. Stroll, Avrum, ed. *Epistemology: New Essays in the Theory of Knowledge.* New York: Harper & Row, 1967.

1871. War, Andrew. "The way things are." *Ratio* 15 (1973): 74-83.

Language

1872. Albrecht, Erhard. "Zur Kritik der Auffassungen Ludwig Wittgensteins über das Verhältnis von Sprache, Logik, und Erkenntnistheorie." *Deutsche Zeitschrift für Philosophie* 16 (1968):813-829.

1873. Anthony, Clifford H. "Language as a Mirror of the World in Wittgenstein's *Tractatus*." Ph.D. Dissertation, Univ. of Western Ontario (Canada), 1973. *Dissertation Abstracts* 35 (1974):508A.

1874. Antonelli, Maria Teresa. "Linguagem e ulterioridade em Wittgenstein." *Revista Portuguesa de Filosofia* 22 (1966):28-48.

1875. Arrington, Robert L. "The logic of our language."
Tulane Studies in Philosophy 16 (1967):1-17.

1876. Ayer, A. J. "Can there be a private language?"
Proceedings of the Aristotelian Society, Supplement
28 (1954):63-76. Reprinted in Ayer's *The Concept of a
Person.* New York: St. Martin's Press, 1963. Also reprinted
in *Wittgenstein and the Problem of Other Minds*, Harold
Morick, ed. New York: McGraw-Hill, 1967, 82-96. And in
Wittgenstein: The Philosophical Investigations (A collec-
tion of critical essays). George Pitcher, ed. Garden City
(New York): Doubleday, Anchor Books, 1966, 251-266.

1877. Ayer, A. J. "Could language be invented by a
Robinson Crusoe?" In *The Private Language Argument*,
O. R. Jones, ed. London: Macmillan; New York: St. Martin's
Press, 1971, 50-61.

1878. Filho, Balthazar Barbosa. "Nota sobre o conceito
de jogo-de-linguagem nas *Investigações* de Wittgenstein."
ITA Humanidades (Saõ José dos Campos) 9 (1973):75-104.

1878a. Bellino, Fr. "Wittgenstein e Mauthner. La
filosofia come *Sprachkritik.*" *Raccolta di Studi e Ricerche*
(Bari) 1 (1977):93-127.

1879. Benarab, G. "Die operativ-pragmatische Basis der
Sprachphilosophie Ludwig Wittgensteins. Eine Studie zur
Kontinuität Sprachphilosophie Wittgensteins." Ph.D.
Dissertation, Univ. of Hamburg, BRD, 1973, 309p. *Disser-
tation Abstracts European* 37 (Spring 1977):3.

1880. Berggren, Douglas. "Language games and symbolic
forms." [Abstract] *Journal of Philosophy* 58 (1961):708-
709.

1881. Bernstein, R. J. "Wittgenstein's three languages."
Review of Metaphysics 15 (1961):278-298. Reprinted in
Copi and Beard [see no. 14].

1882. Bertrán, Miguel Angel. "Wittgenstein o la naturaleza
colectiva del lenguaje." *Teorema*, 1972, 101-112.

1883. Binkley, Timothy G. "Wittgenstein's Language."
Ph.D. Dissertation, Univ. of Texas at Austin, 1970, 294p.
Dissertation Abstracts 31 (1971):3591A.

1884. Binkley, Timothy G. *Wittgenstein's Language.*
The Hague: Martinus Nijhoff, 1973. 227p.

1885. Black, Max. "Wittgenstein's views about language."
Iyyun 17 (1966):61-64.

1886. Black, Max. "Some problems connected with language."
Proceedings of the Aristotelian Society 39 (1938-39):43-68.
Reprinted as "Wittgenstein's *Tractatus*" in his *Language
and Philosophy*. Ithaca (New York): Cornell Univ. Press,
1944. Also reprinted in Copi and Beard, *Essays on Wittgenstein's* Tractatus. New York: Macmillan; London: Routledge
& Kegan Paul, 1966, 95-114.

1887. Blasco, José-Luis. "Wittgenstein: Filosofía del
lenguaje." *Convivium* (1971):55-66.

1888. Blasco, José-Luis. "El lenguaje ordinario en el
Tractatus." *Teorema*, 1972, 101-112.

1888a. Boer, Stephen E. "Language Games. An Interpretation and Critique of the Later Wittgenstein's Philosophy
of Language." Ph.D. Dissertation, Univ. of Michigan, 1973.
Dissertation Abstracts 34 (1973):1961A.

1889. Bogen, James B. "Aspects of the Development of
Wittgenstein's Philosophy of Language." Ph.D. Dissertation,
Univ. of California at Berkeley, 1968, 474p. *Dissertation
Abstracts* 29: 1248A.

1890. Bogen, James B. *Wittgenstein's Philosophy of
Language. Some Aspects of its Development*. London:
Routledge & Kegan Paul, 1972, xii-244p; New York: Humanities
Press, 1972.

1891. Borgman, Albert. *The Philosophy of Language.
Historical Foundations and Contemporary Issues*. The Hague:
Martinus Nijhoff, 1974.

1892. Bortolaso, Giovanni. "Ludwig Wittgenstein:
linguaggio e metafisica." *Civiltà Cattolica* 120 (1969):
142-149.

1893. Bortolaso, G. "L'analisi del linguaggio secondo L.
Wittgenstein." *Civiltà Cattolica* 109 (1958):268-276.

1894. Bortolaso, G. "Analisi del linguaggio e filosofia."
Civiltà Cattolica 109 (1958):597-605.

1895. Bortolaso, G. "Logica e analisi del linguaggio
secondo L. Wittgenstein." *Civiltà Cattolica* 109 (1958):
495-503.

1896. Brennan, Joseph G. "The philosophy of language."
In *The Meaning of Philosophy*, 2d ed. New York: Harper &
Row, 1968.

1897. Bruner, Jerome S. "From communication to language--
A psychological perspective." *Cognition* 3 (1974-75):255-
287.

1898. Burr, R. "Wittgenstein's later language philosophy and some issues in philosophy of mysticism." *International Journal of Philosophy of Religion* 7 (1976):261-287.

1899. Canfield, John V. "A model *Tractatus* language." *Philosophical Forum* 4 (1972-73):199-217.

1900. Canfield, John V. "Anthropological science fiction and logical necessity." *Canadian Journal of Philosophy* 4 (1975):467-479. [On Stroud, "Wittgenstein's anthropological view of language"]

1901. Carlson, John W. "Wittgenstein on Language and Philosophical Understanding: A Study of Continuity in his Thought." Ph.D. Dissertation, Univ. of Notre Dame, 1970, 285p. *Dissertation Abstracts* 31: 4834A.

1902. Carney, James D. "The private language argument." *Southern Journal of Philosophy* 9 (1971):353-359.

1903. Carney, James D. "Is Wittgenstein impaled on Miss Hervey's dilemma?" *Philosophy* 38 (1963):167-170. [See H. Hervey, "The problem of the model language-game"]

1904. Carney, James B. "Private language: The logic of Wittgenstein's argument." *Mind* 69 (1960):560-565.

1905. Castañeda, Hector-Neri. "The private-language argument." A symposium with comments by Chappell and Thompson. In *Knowledge and Experience*, C. D. Rollins, ed. Pittsburgh: Univ. of Pittsburgh, 1962, 88-125.

1906. Castañeda, Hector-Neri. "The private language argument as a reductio ad absurdum." In *The Private Language Argument*, O. R. Jones, ed. London: Macmillan; New York: St. Martin's Press, 1971, 133-154, 173-182. Also in *Essays on Wittgenstein*, E. D. Klemke, ed. Urbana: Univ. of Illinois Press, 1971, 214-239.

1907. Chappell, V. C. "The private language argument." In *The Private Language Argument*, O. R. Jones, ed. London: Macmillan; New York: St. Martin's Press, 1971, 155-168. [See Jones and Castañeda, nos. 52 and 1906]

1908. Chiodi, Pietro. "Essere e linguaggio in Heidegger e nel *Tractatus* di Wittgenstein." *Rivista di Filosofia* 46 (1955):170-191.

1909. Cherry, Christopher. "Games and language." *Mind* 84 (1975):528-547.

1910. Clegg, J. S. "Wittgenstein on verification and private language." *Canadian Journal of Philosophy* Suppl. 1 (1974):205-213.

1911. Cloeren, Hermann J. "The neglected analytical heritage." *Journal of the History of Ideas* 36 (1975):513-529.

1912. Cook, John W. "Solipsism and language." In *Ludwig Wittgenstein. Philosophy and Language*, A. Ambrose and M. Lazerowitz, eds. London: George Allen & Unwin; New York: Humanities Press, 1972, 37-72.

1913. Cooke, Vincent M. "Wittgenstein's Use of the Private Language Discussion." Ph.D. Dissertation, Univ. of Wisconsin, 1971, 117p. *Dissertation Abstracts* 32: 3363A.

1914. Cooke, Vincent M. "Wittgenstein's use of the private language discussion." *International Philosophical Quarterly* 14 (1974):25-49.

1915. Cox, Charles H. "Wittgenstein's concept of language and its implications for metaphysics and theology." *Religious Humanism* 9 (1975):79-83.

1916. Cristaldi, M. "Nota sull possibilità di un'ontologia del linguaggio in Wittgenstein e in Heidegger." *Teoresi* 23 (1967):147-186.

1917. De Dijn, Herman. "De taalspelen van Wittgenstein." *Tijdschrift voor Filosofie* 39 (1977):656-663.

1918. Divatia, S. H. "Language and philosophy." *Darshana International* 4 (1964):78-84.

1919. Dipre, Gilio L. "The Language Games of Wittgenstein: A Prolegomenon to a Metaphysics of Being." Ph.D. Dissertation, Saint Bonaventure Univ., 1968. *Dissertation Abstracts* 30 (1969):5479A.

1920. Dwyer, Peter J. "Thomistic first principles and Wittgenstein's philosophy of language." *Philosophical Studies* (Maynooth) 16 (1967):7-29.

1921. Engel, S. Morris. *Wittgenstein's Doctrine of the Tyranny of Language*. The Hague: Nijhoff, 1971.

1922. Engel, S. Morris. "Thought and language." *Dialogue* 3 (1964):160-170.

1923. Erickson, Stephen A. "Meaning and language." *Man and World* 1 (1968):563-586.

1924. Fairbanks, Mathew J. "Language-games and sensationalism." *Modern Schoolman* 40 (1963):275-281.

1925. Fisher, Mark. "Reason, emotion, and love." *Inquiry* 20 (1977):189-203.

1926.   Fitzgerald, Gisela.   "The Language of Private
Sensations: Russell in Light of Wittgenstein's Private
Language Remarks."   Ph.D. Dissertation, Purdue Univ., 1973.
Dissertation Abstracts 35 (1974):513-514A.

1927.   Follesdal, Dagfinn.   "Comments on Stenius, 'Mood
and language-game'."   *Synthèse* 17 (1967):275-280.
[See Stenius below, no. 2046]

1928.   Fodor, Jerry A., and Katz, Jerrold.   "The availability
of what we say."   *Philosophical Review* 72 (1963):57-71.

1929.   Friedman, H. R.   "The ontic status of linguistic
entities."   *Foundations of Language* 13 (1975):73-94.

1930.   Funke, Gerhard.   "Einheitssprache, Sprachspiel und
Sprachauslegung bei Wittgenstein."   *Zeitschrift für
Philosophische Forschung* 22 (1968):1-30, 216-247.

1931.   Gahringer, R. E.   "Can games explain language?"
Journal of Philosophy 56 (1959):661-667.

1932.   Garelli, Jacques.   "Wittgenstein et l'analyse du
language."   *Les Temps Modernes* 18 (1963):2268-2278.

1933.   Gargani, A. G.   "Linguaggio e società in Moore e
nell'ultimo Wittgenstein."   *Giornale Critico della Filosofia
Italiana* 44 (1965):98-118.

1934.   Gargani, A. G.   *Linguaggio ed esperienza in Ludwig
Wittgenstein* (Istituto di Filosofia dell'Università di
Pisa).   Pisa: Università degli Studi, 1965.   58p.

1935.   Gargani, A. G.   *Linguaggio ed esperienza in Ludwig
Wittgenstein*.   Firenze: F. Le Monnier, 1966, xii-504p.

1936.   Garver, Newton.   "Private language and private
sensations."   In *The Private Language Argument*, O. R. Jones,
ed.   London: Macmillan; New York: St. Martin's Press, 1971,
95-102.   [See Castañeda above, no. 1906]

1937.   Garver, Newton.   "Wittgenstein on private language."
In E. D. Klemke [see no. 57], 187-196.   [See Castañeda
above, no. 1905]

1938.   Garver, Newton.   "Wittgenstein on private language."
Philosophy and Phenomenological Research 20 (1960):389-396.

1939.   Gert, Bernard.   "Wittgenstein and private language."
[Abstract] *Journal of Philosophy* 61 (1964):700.

1940.   Giacomini, Ugo.   "Il problema del linguaggio nella
seconda ricerca filosofica di Wittgenstein."   *Aut Aut*
69 (1962):238-244.

1941. Gill, Jerry H. "Wittgenstein and religious language."
Theology Today 21 (1964):59-72.

1942. Gosselin, M. "Enkele beschouwingen naar aanleiding
van 'Language as hermeneutic in the later Wittgenstein'."
[see F. Kerr below, no. 1976] *Tijdschrift voor Filosofie*
28 (1966):72-81. [Summary: A few considerations in
connection with "Language as hermeneutic in the later
Wittgenstein," 82-83]   [See F. Kerr, "Reply to M. Gosselin,"
no. 1977]

1943. Gram, M. S. "Privacy and language." In E. D. Klemke
[see no. 57], 298-327.

1944. Grandy, Richard E. "The private language argument."
Mind 85 (1976):246-250.

1945. Granger, Giles-G. "Wittgenstein et la métalangue."
Revue Internationale de Philosophie 23 (1969):223-233.
[Discussion: G. H. von Wright, A. R. Raggio, G.-G. Granger,
M. Black, E. K. Specht, 234-236]

1946. Greenlee, Douglas. "Why language is not an instru-
ment." *Dialogue* 9 (1970):380-388.

1947. Gregory, T. S. "Mere words? Wittgenstein and the
care of language." *The Tablet* 203 (April 10, 1954):343-345.

1948. Gruender, C. David. "Language, society, and
knowledge." *Antioch Review* 28 (1968):187-212.

1949. Gumpel, Liselotte. "The essence of 'reality' as a
construct of language." *Foundations of Language* 11 (1974):
167-185.

1950. Hadot, Pierre. "Réflexions sur les limites du
langage: à propos du *Tractatus Logico-Philosophicus* de
Wittgenstein." *Revue de Métaphysique et de Morale* 67
(1959):469-484.

1951. Hadot, Pierre. "Wittgenstein, philosophe du langage."
Part 1, *Critique* 15 (1959):866-881; Part 2, 972-983.

1952. Hadot, Pierre. "Jeux de langage et philosophie."
Revue de Métaphysique et de Morale 67 (1962):330-343.

1953. Hallett, Garth. "The theoretical content of
language." *Gregorianum* 54 (1973):307-336.

1954. Hallett, Garth. "Is there a picture theory of
language in the *Tractatus*?" *The Heythrop Journal* 14 (1973):
317-321.

1955. Hamburg, Carl. "Whereof one cannot speak."
Journal of Philosophy 50 (1953):662-664.

1956.   Hardin, C. L.   "Wittgenstein on private language."
Journal of Philosophy 56 (1959):513-528.   Reprinted in
E. D. Klemke.   [See no. 57]

1957.   Hardwick, Charles S.   "Language Learning and Language
Games in Wittgenstein's Later Work."   Ph.D. Dissertation,
Univ. of Texas at Austin, 1967, 217p.   *Dissertation
Abstracts* 28: 1849A.

1958.   Hardwick, Charles S.   *Language Learning in Wittgenstein's Later Philosophy* (Janua linguarum, Series Minor,
104).   The Hague: Mouton, 1971.   152p.

1959.   Hawkins, D. J. B.   "Wittgenstein and the cult of
language."   Aquinas Paper, no. 27.   London: Blackfriars
Publications, 1956.   Reprinted in his *Crucial Problems of
Modern Philosophy*.   South Bend (Indiana): Univ. of Notre
Dame Press, 1962, 66-79.

1960.   Henze, Donald F., and Saunders, John T.   *The Private-
Language Problem: A Philosophical Dialogue*.   New York:
Random House, 1967.

1961.   Hervey, Helen.   "The private language problem."
Philosophical Quarterly 7 (1957):63-79.

1962.   Hervey, Helen.   "The problem of the model language
game in Wittgenstein's later philosophy."   *Philosophy* 36
(1961):333-351.

1963.   Hervey, Helen.   "A reply to Dr. Carney's challenge."
Philosophy 38 (1963):170-174.

1964.   Hervey, Helen.   "Private language and private
sensations."   In O. R. Jones, 76-95 [see no. 52].

1965.   Hertzberg, Lars.   "On the factual dependence of the
language-game."   In *Essays on Wittgenstein in Honour of
G. H. von Wright* (Acta Philos. Fenn. 28 (1976)).   Amsterdam:
North-Holland, 1976, 126-153.

1966.   Hicks, J. R.   "Language Games and Inner Experience."
Ph.D. Dissertation, Univ. College, London, 1961.

1967.   High, Dallas M.   *Language, Persons, and Belief.
Studies in Wittgenstein's Philosophical Investigations
and Religious Uses of Language*.   New York: Oxford Univ.
Press, 1967.

1968.   Hinst, Peter.   "Die früh- und Spätphilosophie L.
Wittgensteins."   *Philosophische Rundschau* 15 (1968):51-66.

1969.   Hintikka, Jaakko.   "Language-games."   *Dialectica*
31 (1977):225-245.   [Summary, Zusammenfassung, 225;
Résumé, 226]

1970. Hintikka, Jaakko. "Language-games." In *Essays on Wittgenstein in Honour of G. H. von Wright* (Acta Philos. Fenn. 28 (1976)). Amsterdam: North-Holland, 1976, 105-125.

1971. Hottois, Gilbert. *La philosophie du langage de Ludwig Wittgenstein*. Préface de J. Bouveresse. Bruxelles: Editions de l'Université de Bruxelles, 1976. 220p.

1972. Hudson, W. D. "Language-games and presuppositions." *Philosophy* 53 (1978):94-99.

1973. Hunter, J. F. M. "Wittgenstein's theory of linguistic self-sufficiency." *Dialogue* 6 (1967):367-378.

1974. Jones, O. R., ed. *The Private Language Argument*. London: Macmillan; New York: St. Martin's Press, 1971. 284p.

1975. Kambartel, Friedrich. "Formales und inhaltliches Sprechen (Frege, Hilbert, Wittgenstein)." In *Das Problem der Sprache*. Akten deutscher Kongress für Philosophie, Heidelberg, 1966. H.-G. Gadamer, hrsg. München: Wilhelm Fink Verlag, 1967, 293-312.

1976. Kerr, F. "Language as hermeneutic in the later Wittgenstein." *Tijdschrift voor Filosofie* 27 (1965):491-520. [See Gosselin above, no. 1942]

1977. Kerr, F. "Reply to Gosselin." *Tijdschrift voor Filosofie* 28 (1966):84-89.

1978. Keyt, David. "Wittgenstein's picture theory of language." *Philosophical Review* 73 (1964):493-511. Reprinted in Copi and Beard [see no. 14].

1979. King-Farlow, John. "*Constructor Reconstructus*: A symposium on Wittgenstein's primitive languages: I. Wittgenstein's primitive languages." *Philosophical Studies* (Maynooth) 18 (1969):100-110. [See O'Reilley below, no. 2013]

1980. Knüfermann, Bernhard. *Theorien Wittgensteins in der Bildsprache* (Reihe A, 1). München: Willing, 1967. 140p.

1981. Kozy, John, Jr. "A new look at linguistic analysis." *Southern Journal of Philosophy* 5 (1967):155-159.

1982. Kreilkamp-Cudmore, Ann. "Language as Wittgenstein's Way of Life." Ph.D. Dissertation, Boston Univ. Graduate School, 1973. *Dissertation Abstracts* 33 (1973):6965A.

1983. Kretzmann, Norman. "Maupertuis, Wittgenstein and the origin of language." [Abstract] *Journal of Philosophy* 54 (1957):776.

1984. Kultgen, J. H. "Can there be a public language?"
[Abstract] *Journal of Philosophy* 63 (1966):582-583.

1985. Kultgen, J. H. "Can there be a public language?"
Southern Journal of Philosophy 6 (1968):31-44.

1986. Kuntz, P. G. "Order in language, phenomena and
reality: Notes on linguistic analysis, phenomenology and
metaphysics." *The Monist* 49 (1965):107-136.

1987. Lawhead, William Fisher. "Wittgenstein and Merleau-
Ponty on Language and Critical Reflection." Ph.D. Dissertation, Univ. of Texas at Austin, 1978.

1988. Lazerowitz, M. *The Language of Philosophy*. Freud
and Wittgenstein. Boston: Reidel, 1977.

1989. Lazerowitz, Morris. "Necessity and language." In
Ludwig Wittgenstein. Philosophy and Language, A. Ambrose
and M. Lazerowitz, eds. London: George Allen & Unwin;
New York: Humanities Press, 1972, 233-270.

1990. Lenk, H. "Zu Wittgensteins Theorie der Sprachspiele."
Kantstudien 58 (1967):458-480.

1991. Levinson, Stephen C. "Activity types and language."
Pragmatics, Microfiche 3, D1 (May 1958).

1992. Linsky, Leonard. "Wittgenstein on language and some
problems of philosophy." *Journal of Philosophy* 54 (1957):
285-293.

1993. Linsky, Leonard. "Wittgenstein, le langage et
quelques problèmes de philosophie." *Langages* (Paris)
(1966):85-95.

1994. Llewelyn, J. E. "On not speaking the same language."
Australasian Journal of Philosophy 40 (1962):35-48, 127-145.

1995. Locher, A. "Die Vorstellung von der Sprache bei
Augustinus und Wittgenstein." *Hochland* 57 (1964-65):438-
446.

1996. Locke, Don. "The private language argument." In
his *Myself and Others*. Oxford Univ. Press, 1968, 72-109.

1997. Lucier, P. "Le statut du langage religieux dans
la philosophie de Ludwig Wittgenstein." *Studies in
Religion* (Toronto) 3 (1973):14-28.

1998. Lugton, Robert C. "Ludwig Wittgenstein: The logic
of language." *ETC* 22 (1965):165-192.

1999. Lütterfelds, Wilhelm. "Die Dialektik 'Sinnvoller
Sprache' in Wittgensteins *Tractatus Logico-Philosophicus*."
Zeitschrift für Philosophische Forschung 28 (1974):562-584.

2000. MacCormac, Earl R.   "Wittgenstein's imagination."
Southern Journal of Philosophy 10 (1972):453-461.

2001. Mackenzie, Nollaig.   "Basic sentences and objectivity:
A private language argument." *Dialogue* 12 (1973):217-232.

2002. Mandelbaum, Maurice.   "Language and chess:
De Saussure's Analogy." *Philosphical Review* 77 (1968):
356-357.

2003. Martland, T. R.   "On 'The limits of my language mean
the limits of my world'." *Review of Metaphysics* 29
(1975-76):19-26.

2004. Martínez Díez, Felícisimo.   "El pensamiento de
L. Wittgenstein sobre el lenguaje religioso y ético."
Studium 15 (1975):463-490.

2005. Maurer, A. A.   "Language and metaphysics." In
Recent Philosophy, Hegel to Present, E. Gilson, ed.
New York: Random House, 1966, 520-549.

2006. McNulty, T. Michael.   "Reflections on religious
language." *New Scholasticism* 49 (1975):127-139.

2007. Mojtabai, A. G.   "Linguistic analysis and religious
language." *Philosophy Today* 2 (1967):60-71.

2008. Mood, J. J.   "Poetic languaging and primal thinking;
a study of Barfield, Wittgenstein, and Heidegger."
Encounter 26 (1965):417-433.

2009. Mundle, C. W. K.   "Private language and Wittgenstein's
kind of behaviorism." *Philosophical Quarterly* 16 (1966):
35-46.

2010. Mundle, C. W. K.   *A Critique of Linguistic Philosophy.*
Part 2: Ludwig Wittgenstein, the instigator of the
revolution in philosophy. Oxford: Clarendon Press, 1976.

2011. Nails, Debra.   "On Wittgenstein: The language-game
and linguistics." *Auslegung* 3 (1976):132-155.

2012. Nielsen, H. A.   "Wittgenstein on language."
Philosophical Studies (Maynooth) 8 (1958):115-121.

2013. O'Reilley Eastman, W.   "*Constructor Reconstructus,*
II. Wittgenstein and the essence of language [a symposium]."
Philosophical Studies (Maynooth) 18 (1969). [See King-Farlow
above, no. 1977]

2014. Parret, Herman.   "Indépendance et interdépendance
de la forme et de la fonction du langage." *Revue Philosophique de Louvain* 73 (1975):56-78.

2015. Payer, Peter. "Wittgensteins Sprachphilosophische Grundmetaphern." *Conceptus* 11 (1977):283-288.

2016. Perkins, Moreland. "Two arguments against a private language." *Journal of Philosophy* 62 (1965):443-458. Reprinted in *Wittgenstein and the Problem of Other Minds*, Harold Morick, ed. New York: McGraw-Hill, 1967, 97-118.

2017. Pradhan, R. C. "Truth and language: A Wittgensteinian analysis." *Indian Philosophical Quarterly* 6 (1978): 29-39.

2018. Price, Jeffrey T. *Language and Being in Wittgenstein's* Philosophical Investigations. The Hague-Paris: Mouton, 1973.

2019. Puligandla, R. "The problem of private language." *Philosophical Quarterly* (India) 39 (1966):1-18.

2020. Pushadham, P. "The 'Language Game' of Praising in Prayers." Ph.D. Dissertation, Pontificia Universitatis Gregoriana, 1975, 232p. *Dissertation Abstracts European* 37 (1977):479.

2021. Rankin, K. W. "The role of imagination, rule-operations, and atmosphere in Wittgenstein's language-games." *Inquiry* 10 (1967):279-291.

2022. Rappaport, Steven. "Aune's Wittgenstein on the empiricist thesis." *Philosophical Studies* 24 (1973):258-262.

2023. Reeder, H. "Public and Private Aspects of Language in Husserl and Wittgenstein." Ph.D. Dissertation, Univ. of Waterloo (Canada), 1977.

2024. Rembert, Andrew. "Wittgenstein on learning the names of inner states." *Philosophical Review* 84 (1975):236-248.

2025. Rhees, Rush. "Wittgenstein on language and ritual." In *Essays on Wittgenstein in Honour of G. H. von Wright* (Acta Philos. Fenn. 28 (1976)). Amsterdam: North-Holland, 1976, 450-484.

2026. Rhees, Rush. "Can there be a private language?" *Proceedings of the Aristotelian Society, Supplement* 28 (1954):77-94. Reprinted in *Philosophy and Ordinary Language*, C. Caton, ed. Urbana: Univ. of Illinois Press, 1964. Also in *Wittgenstein. The* Philosophical Investigations, G. Pitcher, ed. Garden City (New York): Doubleday, Anchor Books, 1966, 267-285.

2027. Rhees, Rush. "Wittgenstein's builders." *Proceedings of the Aristotelian Society* 60 (1959-60):171-186. Reprinted in *Wittgenstein: The Man and his Philosophy*, K. T. Fann, ed. New York: Dell, 1967, 251-264.

2028. Richardson, John T. E. *The Grammar of Justification. An Interpretation of Wittgenstein's Philosophy of Language.* London: Chatto & Windus. Published for Sussex Univ. Press, 1976. 147p.

2029. Riverso, Emanuele. "L'analisi del linguaggio come metodo d'indagine filosofica." *Rassegna di Scienze Filosofiche* 16 (1963):23-66.

2030. Rosenberg, Jay F. "What's happening in philosophy of language today--A metaphysician's eye view." *American Philosophical Quarterly* 9 (1972):101-106.

2031. Rosenberg, Jay F. "Wittgenstein's theory of language as picture." *American Philosophical Quarterly* 5 (1968):18-30.

2032. Saisselin, R. G. "Language game in limbo concerning a certain Ludwig Wittgenstein, written in ordinary language." *Queen's Quarterly* (Canada) 69 (1963):607-615.

2033. Sánchez-Mazas, Miguel. "La ciencia, el lenguaje y el mundo ségun Wittgenstein." *Theoria* (Madrid) 2 (1954): 127-130.

2034. Schwyzer, H. R. G. "The Acquisition of Concepts and the Use of Language." Ph.D. Dissertation, Univ. of California at Berkeley, 1968.

2035. Schwyzer, H. R. G. "Wittgenstein's picture theory of language." *Inquiry* 5 (1962):46-64. Reprinted in Copi and Beard [see no. 14]. [See Stenius below, no. 2045]

2036. Sefler, George F. *Language and World. A Methodo-logical-structural Synthesis within the Writings of Heidegger and Wittgenstein.* Atlantic Highlands (New Jersey): Humanities Press, 1974.

2037. Sefler, G. F. "The Structure of Language and its Relation to the World. A Methodological Study of the Writings of M. Heidegger and L. Wittgenstein." [See Dissertations]

2038. Sellars, Wilfrid. "Some reflections on language games." *Philosophy of Science* 21 (1954):204-228.

2039. Shalom, A. "Wittgenstein, le langage et la philos-ophie." *Les Études Philosophiques* 13 (1958):486-494.

2040. Shalom, A. "L. Wittgenstein, du langage comme image au langage comme outil." *Langages* (Paris) (1966):96-107.

2041. Shapere, D. "Philosophy and the analysis of language." *Inquiry* 3 (1960):29-48.

2042. Shirley, Edward S. "Castañeda on the private-
language argument. A refutation of a refutation."
Southwestern Journal of Philosophy 4 (1973):133-138.

2043. Smart, Harold. "Language-games." *Philosophical
Quarterly* 7 (1957):224-235.

2044. Smerud, Warren D. "Can There Be a Private Language?
A Review of Some principal Arguments." Ph.D. Dissertation,
Univ. of Washington, 1967.

2045. Stenius, Erik. "Wittgenstein's picture theory of
language: A reply to Mr. H. R. G. Schwyzer." *Inquiry*
6 (1963):184-195. Reprinted in Copi and Beard [see no. 14].
[See Schwyzer above, no. 2035]

2046. Stenius, Erik. "Mood and language game." *Synthèse*
17 (1967):254-274. [See Follesdal above, no. 1927]

2047. Stern, Kenneth. "Private language and skepticism."
Journal of Philosophy 60 (1965):745-759.

2048. Struhl, Karsten J. "Language games and forms of
life." *Journal of Critical Analysis* 2 (1970):25-30.

2049. Suárez, Alfonso García. "Es el lenguaje del *Tractatus* un lenguaje privado?" *Teorema*, 1972, 117-119.

2050. Swoyer, Chris. "Private languages and skepticism
[Wittgenstein]." *Southwestern Journal of Philosophy*
8 (1977):41-50. [Ramon M. Lemos, "Reply to 'Private
languages and skepticism', 51-52]

2051. Tanburn, N. P. "Private language again." *Mind*
72 (1963):88-102.

2052. Taylor, Earl. "Lebenswelt and Lebensformen:
Husserl and Wittgenstein on the goal and method of philosophy." *Human Studies* 1 (1978):184-200.

2053. Taylor, P. W. "Wittgenstein's conception of
language." In his *Normative Discourse*. Englewood Cliffs
(New Jersey): Prentice-Hall, 1961, 263-279.

2054. Thomson, J. J. "Private languages." *American
Philosophical Quarterly* 1 (1964):20-31. Reprinted in
The Philosophy of Mind, S. Hampshire, ed. New York:
Harper & Row, 1966. Also in O. R. Jones, 168-173 [see no.
1974].

2055. Thyssen, Johannes. "Sprachregelung und Sprachspiel."
Zeitschrift für Philosophische Forschung 20 (1966):3-22.

2056. Todd, William. "Private languages." *Philosophical
Quarterly* 12 (1962):206-217.

2057. Verburg, P. A. "Het optimum de taal bij Wittgenstein."
Philosophia Reformata 26 (1961):161-172.

2058. Wein, H. "Le monde du pensable et le langage.
Quelques réflexions sur la critique linguistique Wittgensteinienne et sur ses conséquences." *Revue de Métaphysique
et de Morale* 66 (1961):102-115.

2059. Whelan, John M. "Private Language Reexamined."
Ph.D. Dissertation, Univ. of Texas at Austin, 1976.

2060. White, D. A. "The labyrinth of language: Joyce
and Wittgenstein." *James Joyce Quarterly* 12 (1975):294-304.

2061. Wiplinger, Fridolin. "Ludwig Wittgenstein, Sprache
und Welt in seinem Denken." *Wort und Wahrheit* 16 (1961):
528-541.

2062. Wisdom, John. "Wittgenstein on private language."
In *Ludwig Wittgenstein. Philosophy and Language*, A. Ambrose
and M. Lazerowitz, eds., 26-36.

2063. Zeichenko, G. A. "Analysis of natural language and
present-day positivism." *Voprosy Filosofii* (1964):99-108.
[In Russian]

Law

2064. Kemmerling, A. "Regel und Geltung im Lichte der
Analyse Wittgensteins." *Rechtstheorie* (Berlin) 6 (1975):
104-131.

2065. Smith, Barry. "Law and eschatology in Wittgenstein's
early thought." *Inquiry* 21 (1978):425-441.

Linguistics

2066. Brown, Cecil H. *Wittgensteinian Linguistics*.
The Hague: Mouton, 1974.

2067. Nails, Debra. "On Wittgenstein: The language-game
and linquisitcs." *Auslegung* 3 (1976):132-155.

Literary Criticism

2068. Abrams, M. H. "A note on Wittgenstein and literary
criticism. *ELH* 41 (1974):541-551.

Literary Theory

2069. Altieri, C. "Wittgenstein. Consciousness and
language. A challenge to Derridean literary theory."
Modern Language Notes (Baltimore) 91 (1976):1397-1423.

Literature

2071. Reichert, John. *Making Sense of Literature.*
Chicago: Univ. of Chicago Press, 1978. 222p. [Draws
importantly upon the implications for aesthetics that have
been drawn (by Aldrich, Clark, and others) from Wittgenstein's treatment of "seeing" and "seeing as".]

2072. Shir, Jay. "Wittgenstein's aesthetics and the
theory of literature." *British Journal of Aesthetics*
18 (1978):3-11.

2073. Stern, Joseph Peter. "Vom Nutzen der Wittgensteinischen Philosophie für das Studium der Literatur."
Deutsche Viertelj. Lit. Geistesg. 50 (1976):557-574.

Logic

2074. Battistella, Ernesto H. "Interpretación del
Atomismo Lógico del *Tractatus* mediante la lógica modal
relativa de von Wright." *Revista Venezola de Filosofia*
(1976):7-18.

2075. Büchler, Lucien. "La logique étICO-relativistique
en face des paradoxes." *Revue de Métaphysique et de
Morale* 70 (1965):243-246.

2076. Cassirer, Eva. "On logical structure." *Proceedings
of the Aristotelian Society* 64 (1963-64):177-199.

2077. Chadwick, J. A. "Logical constants." *Mind* 36
(1927):1-11.

2078. Chihara, C. "Wittgenstein and logical compulsion."
Analysis 21 (1961):136-140. Reprinted in G. Pitcher [see
no. 76].

2079. Cowan, J. L. "Wittgenstein's philosophy of logic."
Philosophical Review 70 (1961):362-375. Reprinted in
K. T. Fann [see no. 23].

2080. Dilman, Ilham. "Wittgenstein, philosophy and logic."
Analysis 31 (1970-71):33-42.

2081. Dumitriu, Anton. "Wittgenstein's solution of the
paradoxes and the conception of the scholastic logician
Petrus de Allyaco." *Journal of the History of Philosophy*
12 (1974):227-237.

2082. Fay, Thomas A. "Heidegger on Logic: An Encounter
of his Thought with Wittgenstein." Ph.D. Dissertation,
Fordham Univ., 1971, 350p. *Dissertation Abstracts* 32: 1012A.

2083. Freundlich, R. "Logik und Mystik." *Zeitschrift
für Philosophische Forschung* 7 (1953):554-570.

2084. Hintikka, Jaakko. "Are logical truths analytic?"
Philosophical Review 74(1965):178-203.

2085. Hintikka, Jaakko. "Identity, variables and
impredicative definitions." *Journal of Symbolic Logic*
21 (1957):225-245.

2086. Kneale, William. "Truths of logic." *Proceedings
of the Aristotelian Society* 46 (1945-46):207-234.

2087. Kreisel, G. "'Der unheilvolle Einbruch der Logik in
die Mathematik'." In *Essays on Wittgenstein in Honour of
G. H. von Wright* (Acta Philos. Fenn. 28 (1976)). Amsterdam:
North-Holland, 1976, 166-187.

2088. Kutschera, Franz von. "Gebrauch und Bedeutung
exemplarish eingefuehrter Praedikate." *Philosophisches
Jahrbuch* 77 (1970):355-377.

2089. Levinson, A. B. "Wittgenstein and logical laws."
Philosophical Quarterly 14 (1964):345-354. Reprinted in
K. T. Fann.

2090. Levinson, A. B. "Wittgenstein and logical necessity."
Inquiry 6 (1964):367-373.

2091. Mondadori, Fabrizio. "Wittgenstein sui fondamenti
della necessità logica." *Rivista Critica di Storia della
Filosofia* 26 (1971):57-78.

2092. Mouloud, Noël. "La logique et les 'jeux du
langage'. Quelques suggestions de Wittgenstein pour une
philosophie des signes." In *Les Signes et leur Interpré-
tation*. Paris: Gallimard, 1971, 31-50.

2093. Palmer, H. "The other logical constant." *Mind*
68 (1958):50-59.

2094. Slater, B. H. "Wittgenstein's later logic."
Philosophy 54 (1979):199-210.

2094a. Welding, S. O. "Logic as based on truth-value
relations." *Revue Internationale de Philosophie* 30
(1976):151-166.

2095. Wisdom, John. "Logical constructions." *Mind* 40 (1931):188-216, 460-475; 41 (1932):441-464; 42 (1933): 43-66, 186-202. Some parts reprinted in Copi and Beard.

Logical Atomism

2095a. Bergmann, Gustav. "The revolt against logical atomism." In *Essays on Bertrand Russell*, E. D. Klemke, ed. Urbana: Univ. of Illinois Press, 1970.

2096. Griffin, James. *Wittgenstein's Logical Atomism*. (Oxford classical and philosophical monographs). Oxford: Clarendon Press; New York: Oxford Univ. Press, 1964.

2097. Pears, D. F. "Logical atomism: Russell and Wittgenstein." In *The Revolution in Philosophy*, A. J. Ayer, ed., 44-55.

2098. Shoemaker, S. "Logical atomism and language." *Analysis* 20 (1960):49-52.

2099. White, Alan. "Logical atomism: Russell and Wittgenstein." In *G. E. Moore. A Critical Exposition*. Oxford: Basil Blackwell, 1958, 201-208.

2100. Canfield, John V. "Anthropological science fiction and logical necessity." *Canadian Journal of Philosophy* 4 (1974-75):467-479. [See Stroud below, no. 2101]

2101. Stroud, B. "Wittgenstein and logical necessity." *Philosophical Review* 74 (1965):504-518. Reprinted in E. D. Klemke and G. Pitcher [see nos. 57 and 76]. [See Canfield above, 2100]

Logical Space

2102. Gale, Richard M. "Could logical space be empty?" In *Essays on Wittgenstein in Honour of G. H. von Wright* (Acta Philos. Fenn. 28 (1976)). Amsterdam: North-Holland, 1976, 85-104.

2103. Pinkerton, R. J. "Logical space in the *Tractatus*." *Indian Philosophical Quarterly* 2 (1974):9-29.

2104. Zemach, Eddy. "Material and logical space in Wittgenstein's *Tractatus*." *Methodos* 16 (1964):127-140.

Logical Positivism

2105. Black, Max. "Relation between logical positivism and the Cambridge School of analysis." *Erkenntnis* 8 (1939-40):24-35.

2106. Blumberg, A. E., and Feigl, H. "Logical positivism: A new movement in European philosophy." *Journal of Philosophy* 28 (1931):281-296.

2107. Broad, C. D. "Wittgenstein and the Vienna Circle." *Mind* 71 (1962):251.

2108. Gert, Bernard. "Wittgenstein and logical positivism." [Abstract] *Journal of Philosophy* 57 (1961):707.

2109. Ganguly, S. *Logical Positivism as a Theory of Meaning.* Calcutta: Allied Pub., 1967.

2110. McGill, V. F. "An evaluation of logical positivism." *Science and Society* 1 (1936-37):45-80.

2111. Stebbing, Susan. "Logical positivism and analysis." *Proceedings of the British Academy* 19 (1933):53-87.

2112. Toulmin, Stephen. "From logical positivism to conceptual history." In *The Legacy of Logical Positivism for the Philosophy of Science,* S. Barker and P. Achinstein, eds. Baltimore: Johns Hopkins Univ. Press, 1970.

2113. Weinberg, J. R. *An Examination of Logical Positivism.* London: Routledge & Kegan Paul, 1936. Paperback ed., New Jersey: Littlefield, Adams & Co., 1960.

Mahayana

2114. Gudmunsen, C. "On the Mahayana and Wittgenstein." *Religion. Journal of Religion and Religions* (London) 4 (1974):96-103.

Man

2115. Cox, Charles H. "Wittgenstein's picture of man." *Religious Humanism* 8 (1974):186-188.

2116. Epstein, Michele F. "The common ground of Merleau-Ponty's and Wittgenstein's philosophy of man." *Journal of the History of Philosophy* 13 (1975):221-234.

Marxism

2117. Benton, Ted. "Winch, Wittgenstein and Marxism."
Radical Philosophy 13 (1976). [See no. 894]

2118. Cornforth, Maurice. *Marxism and Linguistic Philosophy.*
London: Lawrence & Wishart; New York: International
Publishers, 1965.

Materialism

2119. Hunter, J. F. M. "Wittgenstein and materialism."
Mind 86 (1977):514-531.

2120. Laycock, H. "Ordinary language and materialism."
Philosophy 42 (1967):363-367.

Mathematics

2121. Ambrose, Alice. "Mathematical generality." In
Ludwig Wittgenstein. Philosophy and Language, A. Ambrose
and M. Lazerowitz, eds., 287-318. [See no. 1]

2122. Ambrose, Alice. "Proof and the theorem proved."
Mind 68 (1959):435-445. Reprinted in her *Essays in
Analysis*. [See no. 2; see also Castañeda below, no. 2132]

2123. Ambrose, Alice. "Proof and theorem proved."
[Abstract] *Journal of Philosophy* 55 (1958):901-902.

2124. Ambrose, Alice. "Wittgenstein on some questions
in foundations of mathematics." *Journal of Philosophy*
52 (1955):197-213. Reprinted in *Essays in Analysis* [see
no. 2]. Also reprinted in Fann [see no. 23].

2125. Ambrose, Alice. "Finitism in mathematics." *Mind*
44 (1935):186-203, 317-340.

2126. Anderson, A. R. "Mathematics and the 'language
game'." *Review of Metaphysics* 11 (1958):446-458. Reprinted
in *Philosophy of Mathematics*, P. Benacerraf and H. Putnam,
eds. [See below]

2127. Benacerraf, Paul, and Putnam, Hilary. "Wittgenstein."
In their *Philosophy of Mathematics*. Englewood Cliffs
(New Jersey): Prentice-Hall, 1965, 25-38.

2128. Black, Max. "Verificationism and Wittgenstein's
reflections on mathematics." *Revue Internationale de
Philosophie* 23 (1969):284-294. [Discussion: 295-298]

2129. Black, Max. "Wittgenstein: An (unauthorized) report of some of his views on pure mathematics, which constitute, by implications and explicitly, a thorough repudiation of the logistic thesis." In his *The Nature of Mathematics*. London, 1933, 129-134.

2130. Bouveresse, Jacques. "Philosophie des mathematiques et therapeutique d'une maladie philosophique: Wittgenstein et la critique de l'apparence ontologique dans les mathematiques." *Cahiers pour l'Analyse* no. 10 (1969). Reprinted in his *La parole malheureuse*. Paris: Les Editions de Minuit, 1971.

2131. Campanale, D. "Il problema dei fondamenti della matematica nella critica di Wittgenstein." *Rassegna di Scienze Filosofiche* 12 (1959):18-41.

2132. Castañeda, Hector-Neri. "On mathematical proofs and meaning." *Mind* 70 (1961):385-390. [Criticizes Ambrose above, see no. 2122]

2133. Chihara, Charles. "Mathematical discovery and concept formation." *Philosophical Review* 72 (1963):17-34. Reprinted in Pitcher [see no. 76].

2134. Cotroneo, G. "Un tentativo di storia di Wittgenstein sui fondamenti della matematica." *Giornale Critico della Filosofia Italiana* 44 (1965).

2135. Dambska, I. "Les idées de Wittgenstein sur la non-contradiction et sur le caractère des propositions mathematiques." In *Akten XIV International Kongress für Philosophie*, Vol. 6. Wien: Herder, 1971, 20-207.

2136. Dambska, Izydora. "Les idées kantiennes dans la philosophie des mathematiques de Wittgenstein." *Organon* 11-13 (1976-77):249-260.

2137. Dummett, M. "Wittgenstein's philosophy of mathematics." *Philosophical Review* 68 (1959):324-348. Reprinted in Pitcher [see no. 76]. Also reprinted in Benacerraf and Putnam [see no. 2127].

2138. Dummett, Michael. "Wittgenstein's philosophy of mathematics." Reprinted in his *Truth and Other Enigmas*. Cambridge (Massachusetts): Harvard Univ. Press, 1978, 166-185.

2139. Egidi, Rosaria. "Due tesi di Wittgenstein sui fondamenti della matematica." *Giornale Critico della Filosofia Italiana* 44 (1965):527-538.

2140. Goodstein, R. L. "Wittgenstein's philosophy of mathematics." In *Ludwig Wittgenstein. Philosophy and Language*, A. Ambrose and M. Lazerowitz, eds., 271-286.

2141. Gross, David. "Wittgenstein's Criticism of Platonism
in Mathematics." Ph.D. Dissertation, Univ. of Iowa, 1978.
Dissertation Abstracts 39 (1978):3631-3632A.

2142. Hart, Wilbur D. "Wittgenstein: Philosophy, Logic
and Mathematics." Ph.D. Dissertation, Harvard Univ., 1969.
232p.

2143. Harward, Donald W. "Wittgenstein and the character
of mathematical propositions." *International Logical
Review* 3 (1972):246-251.

2144. Henry, Granville C., Jr. "Aspects of the influence
of mathematics on contemporary philosophy." *Philosophia
Mathematica* 3 (1966):17-37. [A section on Wittgenstein]

2145. Huff, Douglas. "Wittgenstein and mathematical
foundations." *Dianoia* 10 (1974):56-65.

2146. Kambartel, Friedrich. "Philosophische Perspektiven
der Diskussion um die Grundlagen der Mathematik. Zu Verlauf
und Knosequenzen eines Kapitels der Philosophiegeschichte."
Archiv für Geschichte der Philosophie 45 (1963):157-193.
[Wittgenstein, 183ff]

2147. Kielkopf, Charles Francis. "An Examination of
Wittgenstein's *Remarks on the Foundations of Mathematics*."
Ph.D. Dissertation, Univ. of Minnesota, 1962, 195p.
Dissertation Abstracts 24: 329A.

2148. Kielkopf, Charles Francis. *Strict Finitism. An
Examination of Wittgenstein's* Remarks on the Foundations
of Mathematics (Studies in Philosophy, 15). The Hague:
Mouton, 1970. 192p.

2149. Klenk, Virginia H. "Wittgenstein's Philosophy of
Mathematics." Ph.D. Dissertation, Univ. of Pittsburgh,
1972. *Dissertation Abstracts* 33 (1973):4477A.

2150. Klenk, Virginia H. *Wittgenstein's Philosophy of
Mathematics*. The Hague: Nijhoff, 1976, vii-126p.

2151. Kreisel, G. "'Der unheilvolle Einbruch der Logik
in die Mathematik'." In *Essays on Wittgenstein in Honour
of G. H. von Wright* (Acta Philos. Fenn. 28 (1976)).
Amsterdam: North-Holland, 166-187.

2152. Levin, Michael Eric. "Wittgenstein's Philosophy
of Mathematics." Ph.D. Dissertation, Columbia Univ., 1969,
526p. *Dissertation Abstracts* 30: 4494A.

2153. Molitor, Arnulf. "Bemerkungen zu Ludwig Wittgensteins posthumer Philosophie der Mathematik." *Salsburger
Jahrbuch Philosophie* 10-11 (1966-67):35-63.

2154. Plochmann, G. K. "Mathematics in Wittgenstein's
Tractatus." *Philosophia Mathematica* 2 (1965):1-12.

2155. Shwayder, D. S. "Wittgenstein on mathematics."
In *Studies in the Philosophy of Wittgenstein*, Peter Winch,
ed. London: Routledge & Kegan Paul; New York: Humanities
Press, 1969, 66-116.

2156. Steiner, Mark. *Mathematical knowledge*. Ithaca
(New York): Cornell Univ. Press, 1975.

2157. Thibodeau, Eugene F. "An Interpretation of Wittgen-
stein's Later (1929-1951) Philosophy of Mathematics."
Ph.D. Dissertation, New York Univ., 1973. *Dissertation
Abstracts* 34 (1973):826A.

2157a. Wrigley, Michael. "Wittgenstein's philosophy of
mathematics." *Philosophical Quarterly* 27 (1977):50-59.

Meaning

2158. Berlinski, David. "The Well-tempered Wittgenstein:
A Study of the Picture Theory of Meaning." Ph.D. Dissertation, Princeton Univ., 1967. *Dissertation Abstracts*
29: 4045A.

2158a. Bhat, P. R. "Referential theory of meaning and
later Wittgenstein." *Darshana International* (Moradabad)
17 (1977):30-33.

2159. Butchvarov, P. "Meaning-as-use and meaning-as-
correspondence." *Philosophy* 35 (1960):314-325.

2160. Campbell, William B. "Wittgenstein's Picture Theory
of Meaning." Ph.D. Dissertation, Washington Univ., 1973.
Dissertation Abstracts 34 (1974):6038A.

2161. Canfield, John V. "A model *Tractatus* language."
The Philosophical Forum (Boston) 4 (1972-73):199-217.

2162. Daitz, E. "The picture theory of meaning." *Mind*
62 (1953):184-201. Reprinted in *Essays in Conceptual
Analysis*, A. Flew, ed. London: Macmillan, 1964.

2163. Erickson, Stephen A. "Meaning and language
[Heidegger and Wittgenstein]." *Man and World* 1 (1968):
563-586.

2164. Gibbs, B. R. "Wittgenstein and the Problem of
Meaning." Master's Thesis, Univ. of Canterbury (New
Zealand), 1961.

2165. Gray, Bennison. "The problem of meaning in linguistic
philosophy." *Logique et Analyse* 15 (1972):609-627.

2166. Grünfeld, Joseph. "Context and meaning in Wittgenstein." *Science de l'Esprit* 22 (1970):379-397.

2167. Haight, David. "The source of linguistic meaning."
Philosophy and Phenomenological Research 37 (1976):239-247.

2168. Hallett, Garth. "Did Wittgenstein really *define*
'meaning'?" *The Heythrop Journal* 11 (1970):294-298.

2169. Hallett, Garth. "Wittgenstein and the 'contrast
theory of meaning'." *Gregorianum* 51 (1970):679-710.
[*Résumé*, 709-710]

2170. Hallett, Garth. *Wittgenstein's Definition of Meaning
as Use*. Bronx (New York): Fordham Univ. Press, 1967. 210p.

2171. Harrison, Frank R. "Wittgenstein and the doctrine
of identical minimal meaning." *Methodos* 14 (1962):61-74.

2172. Hester, Marcus B. *The Meaning as Poetic Metaphor.
An Analysis in the Light of Wittgenstein's Claim that
Meaning is Use*. The Hague: Mouton, 1967, 229p.

2173. Hill, Thomas E. *The Concept of Meaning*. London:
George Allen & Unwin; New York: Humanities Press, 1974.
328p.

2174. Hunter, J. F. M. "Wittgenstein and knowing the
meaning of a word." *American Philosophical Quarterly*
5 (1968):284-304.

2175. Hunter, J. F. M. "Wittgenstein on meaning and use."
In *Essays on Wittgenstein*, E. D. Klemke, ed. Anchor Books,
1966 [see no. 57].

2176. Koehler, Conrad J. "A study in Wittgenstein's theory
of meaning." *Kinesis* 1 (1968):36-42.

2177. Lanfear, Jimmy R. "An Analysis of Wittgenstein's
Locution 'Meaning as Use'." Ph.D. Dissertation, Rice Univ.,
1968, 223p. *Dissertation Abstracts* 29: 1568A.

2178. Linsky, L. "Meaning and use." *Algemeen Nederlands
Tijdschrift voor Wijsbegeerte en Psychologie* 53 (1960):
201-207.

2179. Mathrani, G. N. "A comparative and critical study
of Wittgenstein's and Ayer's theories of meaning."
Philosophical Quarterly (India) 37 (1965):219-226.

2180. Morrison, James C. "Meaning and Truth in Wittgenstein's *Tractatus*." Ph.D. Dissertation, Pennsylvania State
Univ., 1964, 176p. *Dissertation Abstracts* 25: 4752A.

2181. Novielli, Valeria. "La problematica del significato
nell'ultimo Wittgenstein." *Filosofia* (Italy) 23 (1972):389-
410.

2182. O'Brien, George D. "Meaning and Fact: A Study in
the Philosophy of Wittgenstein." Ph.D. Dissertation,
Univ. of Chicago, 1961.

2183. O'Shoughnessy, Edna. "The picture theory of meaning."
Mind 62 (1953):181-201. Reprinted in Copi and Beard [see
no. 14].

2184. Padinjarekutt, John. "Meaning and verification in
Wittgenstein." *Bijdragen* 36 (1975):250-269.

2185. Rao, A. Pampapathy. *A Survey of Wittgenstein's
Theory of Meaning.* Calcutta: Indian Univ. Press, 1965.
96p.

2186. Stripling, Scott. "The Picture Theory of Meaning.
An Interpretation of Wittgenstein's *Tractatus Logico-
Philosophicus*." Ph.D. Dissertation, Pennsylvania State
Univ., 1976. *Dissertation Abstracts* 37 (1976):1032A.

2187. Sullivan, Thomas D. "Between thoughts and things:
The status of meaning." *New Scholasticism* 50 (1976):
85-95.

2188. Tilghman, Benjamin R. "Seeing and meaning."
Southern Journal of Philosophy 14 (1976):523-533.

2189. Todd, William. "The theory of meaning and some
related theories of the learning of language." *Inquiry*
8 (1965):355-374.

2190. Tominaga, Thomas T. "A Wittgensteinian Inquiry into
the Confusion Generated by the Question 'What is the
Meaning of a Word?'" Ph.D. Dissertation, Georgetown Univ.,
1973. *Dissertation Abstracts* 34 (1974):4335A.

2191. Wallace, Kyle L. "Wittgenstein's Theory of Meaning."
Ph.D. Dissertation, Univ. of Miami, 1969, 234p. *Dissertation Abstracts* 30: 3509A.

2192. Weiler, G. "A note on meaning and use." *Mind*
76 (1967):424-427.

2193. Weinberg, Julius R. "Wittgenstein's theory of
meaning." In his *An Examination of Logical Positivism.*
London: Routledge & Kegan Paul, 1936, 31-68.

2194. Wiebenga, William M. "Wittgenstein's Theory of
Meaning." Ph.D. Dissertation, Yale Univ., 1966, 284p.
Dissertation Abstracts 27: 3087A.

Memoirs, Portraits, Recollections

2195. Ambrose, Alice. "Ludwig Wittgenstein: A portrait."
In *Ludwig Wittgenstein. Philosophy and Language*,
A. Ambrose and M. Lazerowitz, eds., 13-25. [See no. 1]

2196. Améry, J. "Ludwig Wittgenstein im Rückblick."
Merkur (Stuttgart) 30 (1976):991-995.

2197. Anonymous. "Obituary. Dr. L. Wittgenstein."
Times (May 2, 1951).

2198. Anonymous. "L. Wittgenstein: Obiter." *Blackfriars*
33 (1952):87. [Correction of Cranston]

2199. Anscombe, G. E. M. "Letter from Wittgenstein's
literary executors." *Mind* 60 (1951):84.

2200. Bartley, William W., III. *Wittgenstein*. Philadelphia: J. B. Lippincott, 1973. 192p.

2201. Britton, Karl. "Portrait of a philosopher."
The Listener 53 (June 10, 1955):1071-1072. Reprinted in
Fann [see no. 23].

2202. Britton, Karl. "Recollections of Ludwig Wittgenstein." *Cambridge Journal* 7 (1954):709-715.

2203. Britton, Karl. "Errinnerungen an Wittgenstein."
Merkur 11 (1957):1066-1072.

2204. Clark, Ronald W. *The Life of Bertrand Russell*.
New York: Knopf, 1976. 766p.

2205. Cranston, Maurice. "L. Wittgenstein." *World Review*
(December 1951):21-24.

2206. Cranston, Maurice. "Vita e morte di Wittgenstein."
Aut Aut (1952):239-245.

2207. Cranston, Maurice. "Bildnis eines Philosophen."
Der Monat 4 (1952):495-497. Reprinted in *Wittgenstein:
Schriften/Beiheft*, 16-20.

2208. Drury, M. O'C. "Some notes on conversations with
Wittgenstein." *Acta Philos. Fenn.* 28 (1976):22-40.

2209. Englemann, Paul. *Ludwig Wittgenstein: A Memoir and
Letters*. Trans. by L. Fürtmuller. Oxford: Basil Blackwell,
1968. [See also nos. 118 and 158]

2210. Falk, B. "Portraits and persons." *Proceedings of
the Aristotelian Society* 75 (1974-75):181-200.

2211. Fann, Kuant T. *Wittgenstein. The Man and his
Philosophy.* An Anthology. New York: Dell, 1967. 415p.
[Includes "A biographical sketch" by von Wright; and
memoirs of Wittgenstein by B. Russell, R. Carnap, G. E.
Moore, J. Wisdom, Gasking and Jackson, and K. Britton.
See no. 23]

2212. Findlay, J. N. "My encounters with Wittgenstein."
The Philosophical Forum (Boston) 3 (1972-73):167-185.

2213. Gasking, D. A. T., and Jackson, A. C. "Ludwig
Wittgenstein." A memorial notice. *Australasian Journal
of Philosophy* 29 (1951):73-80. Reprinted in Fann [see
no 23].

2214. Gass, W. H. "Wittgenstein--A man and a half."
New Republic (June 22, 1968):29-30.

2215. Gass, W. H. "A memory of a master." In *Fiction and
the Figures of Life.* New York: Knopf, 1971, 247-252.

2216. Janik, Allen, and Toulmin, Stephen E. *Wittgenstein's
Vienna.* New York: Simon & Schuster; London: George
Weidenfeld & Nicolson, 1973. 314p.

2217. Kraft, V. "Ludwig Wittgenstein." *Wiener Zeitschrift
für Philosophie, Psychologie, Pädagogik* 3 (1951):161-163.

2218. Lee, H. D. P. "Wittgenstein, 1929-1931." *Philosophy*
54 (1979):211-220.

2219. Lenihan, John. "I taught Wittgenstein." *Books and
Bookmen* 20 (1975):54.

2220. Lowenfels, Walter. "For Ludwig Wittgenstein (1889-
1951) A poem." *ETC* 22 (1965):164.

2221. Malcolm, Norman. *Ludwig Wittgenstein: A Memoir*
(With a biographical sketch by von Wright and a photograph).
London: Oxford Univ. Press, 1958; revised ed., 1966.

2222. Mays, W. "Note on Wittgenstein's Manchester period."
Mind 64 (1955):247-248.

2223. Mays, W. "Recollections of Wittgenstein." In Fann,
79-88 [see no. 23].

2224. Mays, W. "Wittgenstein's Manchester period."
The Guardian (March 24, 1961). Reprinted in Fann [see no.
23].

2225. Mills, John F. "A meeting with Wittgenstein."
Times Literary Supplement (June 12, 1959):353.

2226. Moore, G. E. "An autobiography." In *The Philosophy of G. E. Moore*, Paul A. Schilpp, ed. LaSalle (Illinois): Open Court, 1942. [An excerpt on Wittgenstein reprinted in Fann]

2227. G. N. "Ludwig Wittgenstein (1889-1951)." *Vijsg. Persp. Maatsch. Wet.* 1 (1960-61):246-250.

2228. Pascal, F. "Wittgenstein: A personal memoir." *Encounter* 41 (1973):23-39.

2229. Pascal, Fania. "Wittgenstein: A personal memoir." In *Wittgenstein: Sources and Perspectives*, C. G. Luckhardt, ed. Ithaca (New York): Cornell Univ. Press, 1979, 23-60.

2230. Russell, Bertrand. *The Autobiography*, Vol. 2 (1914-1944). New York: Simon & Schuster. [An account of his friendship with Wittgenstein is contained in 136-140, and his letters to and from G. E. Moore concerning Wittgenstein are included in 294-301.]

2231. Russell, Bertrand. "Ludwig Wittgenstein." *Mind* 60 (1951):297-298. Reprinted in Fann [see no. 23].

2232. Russell, Bertrand. "Philosophers and idiots." *The Listener* (February 10, 1955):248-249. Reprinted in his *Portraits from Memory*. New York: Simon & Schuster, 1951, 23-24. Also reprinted in Fann [see no. 23].

2233. Toulmin, Stephen. "Ludwig Wittgenstein." *Encounter* 32 (1969):58-71.

2234. Tranoy, K. E. "Wittgenstein in Cambridge 1949-1951. Some personal recollections." In *Essays on Wittgenstein in Honour of G. H. von Wright* (Acta Philos. Fenn. 28 (1976)). Amsterdam: North-Holland, 1976, 11-21.

2235. von Wright, G. H. "Ludwig Wittgenstein: A biographical sketch." *Philosophical Review* 64 (1955):527-545. Reprinted in Malcolm's *Memoir*. Also reprinted in Fann [see no. 23]. Finnish version, "Ludwig Wittgenstein. En biografisk skiss." *Ajatus* 18 (1954):4-23.

2236. Wasmuth, E. "Die Tür in Rüken: Hinweis und Lefen und Werk Wittgensteins." *Deutsche Rundschau* 80 (1954): 1018-1023.

Mental Processes and States

2237. Vesey, G. N. A. "Wittgenstein on the myth of mental processes." *Philosophical Review* 77 (1968):350-355.

2238. Weissman, David. "The existence of nonintrospectable mental states." In his *Dispositional Properties*. Carbondale (Illinois): Southern Illinois Univ. Press, 1966, 119-158.

Metaphysics

----- Daly, G. B. [See no. 1700]

2239. Fay, Thomas A. "Wittgenstein's critique of metaphysics in the *Tractatus*." *Philosophical Studies* (Maynooth)
20: 51-61.

2240. Genova, Judith. "An Approach to Wittgenstein's
Metaphysics." Ph.D. Dissertation, Brandeis Univ., 1970,
187p. *Dissertation Abstracts* 31: 2970A.

2241. Hallie, Philip. "Wittgenstein's exclusion of
metaphysical nonsense." *Philosophical Quarterly* 16 (1966):
97-112.

2242. Hamlyn, D. W. "Categories, formal concepts and
metaphysics." *Philosophy* 34 (1959):111-124.

2243. Kluge, Eike-Henner Wendelin. "Functions and Things:
An Essay in the Metaphysics of Frege and Wittgenstein."
Ph.D. Dissertation, Univ. of Michigan, 1968, 380p.
Dissertation Abstracts 39: 2753A.

2244. Miller, Robert G. "Linguistic analysis and metaphysics." *Proceedings of the American Catholic Philosophical Association* 34 (1960):80-109.

2245. Petrie, H. "Science and metaphysics: A Wittgensteinian interpretation." In E. D. Klemke, ed., 138-171
[see no. 57].

2246. Salazar Bondy, Augusto. "Metafísica y antimetafísica
en Wittgenstein." *Diálogos* 6 (1969):75-99.

2247. Schwyzer, H. "Thought and reality: The metaphysics
of Kant and Wittgenstein." *Philosophical Quarterly* 23
(1973):193-206.

2248. Walker, Jeremy. "The tolerability of metaphysics."
International Philosophical Quarterly 13 (1973):5-23.

2249. Walsh, W. H. "Contemporary anti-metaphysics." In
his *Metaphysics*. New York: Harcourt, Brace & World, 1963,
120-130.

Method

2250. Ammerman, R. R. "Wittgenstein's later methods."
[Abstract] *Journal of Philosophy* 58 (1961):707-708.

2251. Goff, Robert A. "The Language of Method in Wittgenstein's *Philosophical Investigations*." Ph.D. Dissertation,
Drew Univ., 1967, 153p. *Dissertation Abstracts* 28: 1847A.

2252. Sanderson, Donald G. "The Philosophical Methods
of Wittgenstein's *Philosophical Investigations*." Master's
Thesis, Florida State Univ., 1969.

2253. Senchuk, Dennis M. "Private objects. A study of
Wittgenstein's method." *Metaphilosophy* 7 (1976):217-240.

Mind (Journal)

2254. Findlay, J. N. "*Mind* under the editorship of David
Hamlyn." *Mind* 85 (1976):57-68.

2255. Lewy, C. "*Mind* under G. E. Moore (1921-1947)."
Mind 85 (1976):37-46.

2256. Warnock, Mary. "Gilbert Ryle's editorship [of *Mind*]."
Mind 85 (1976):47-56.

(Other) Mind

2257. Ameriks, Karlis P. "Cartesianism and Wittgenstein:
The Legacy of Subjectivism in Contemporary Philosophy of
Mind." Ph.D. Dissertation, Yale Univ., 1973. *Dissertation
Abstracts* 34: 2690A.

2258. Ameriks, Karl. "Recent work on Wittgenstein and the
philosophy of mind." *New Scholasticism* 49 (1975):94-118.

2259. Baumli, Francis. "Wittgenstein's theory about the
problem of other minds." *Dianoia* (Spring 1973):1-11.

2260. Buck, R. C. "Non-other minds." In *Analytical
Philosophy*, R. J. Butler, ed. Oxford: Basil Blackwell,
1962, 187-210.

2261. Chihara, Charles S. "Cohen's defense of Cook."
Philosophical Studies (Dordrecht) 29 (1976):353-355.
[See Cohen below, no. 2264]

2262. Chihara, Charles. "Operationalism and ordinary
language revisited." *Philosophical Studies* (Dordrecht)
24 (1973):137-157. [See Cook below, no. 2265]

2263. Cohen, Trevor E. "Criteria and the Problem of Other
Minds in Wittgenstein's Later Philosophy." Ph.D. Disser-
tation, Univ. of New South Wales (Australia), 1975.
Dissertation Abstracts 36 (1976):6143A.

2264. Cohen, Trevor. "Chihara on Cook on other minds."
Philosophical Studies (Dordrecht) 26 (1974):299-300.
[See Chihara above, no. 2262]

2265. Cook, J. W. "Human beings." In *Studies in the
Philosophy of Wittgenstein*, P. Winch, ed. [See Chihara
above, no. 2262]

2266. Kirby, Ronald V. "The Other Mind Quandry." Ph.D.
Dissertation, Univ. of California at Berkeley, 1966.

2267. Lewis, Harry A. "Criteria, Theory and Knowledge of
Other Minds." Ph.D. Dissertation, Stanford Univ., 1967.

2268. Malcolm, Norman. "Wittgenstein on the notion of
mind." In *Studies in the Theory of Knowledge*, Nicholas
Resscher, ed. Oxford: Basil Blackwell, 1970.

2269. Malcolm, Norman. "Knowledge of other minds."
Journal of Philosophy 55 (1958):969-978. Reprinted in
Philosophy of Mind, V. C. Chappell, ed. Englewood Cliffs
(New Jersey): Prentice-Hall, 1962. Also reprinted in
N. Malcolm's *Knowledge and Certainty*, and in Pitcher [see
no. 76].

2270. Malcolm, Norman. "Wittgenstein on the nature of
mind." An Isenberg Lecture.

2271. Malcolm, Norman. *Problems of Mind. Descartes to
Wittgenstein*. London: George Allen & Unwin, 1972, 103p;
New York: Harper & Row, 1971.

2272. Malmgren, Helge. "Immediate knowledge of other
minds." *Theoria* 42 (1976):189-205.

2273. Mellor, W. W. "Three problems about other minds."
Mind 65 (1956):200-217.

2274. Morick, Harold, ed. *Wittgenstein and the Problem
of Other Minds*. New York: McGraw-Hill, 1967, xxiii-231p.

----- Mukherja, S. R. "The problem of other minds."
Philosophical Quarterly (India) 39 (1966):19-25.

2275. Palmer, Anthony. "Understanding and experience.
Recent work in the philosophy of mind." *Philosophy*
50 (1975):333-345.

2276. Pears, D. F. *Questions in the Philosophy of Mind*.
New York: Barnes and Noble; London: Duckworth, 1975.

2277. Reinhardt, L. R. "Wittgenstein and Strawson on
other minds." In *Studies in the Philosophy of Wittgenstein*,
Peter Winch, ed. London: Routledge & Kegan Paul; New York:
Humanities Press, 1969, 152-165.

2278. Sheridan, G. R. "The Privacy of Mind: An Essay on the Logic of Psychological Statements." Ph.D. Dissertation, Univ. of California at Los Angeles, 1966.

2279. Sievert, Donald E. "Austin, Wittgenstein and Strawson on Mind." Ph.D. Dissertation, Univ. of Iowa, 1967, 141p. *Dissertation Abstracts* 28: 3229A.

2280. Van de Vate, Dwight. "Other minds and the uses of language." *American Philosophical Quarterly* 3 (1966): 250-254.

2281. Vesey, Godfrey. "Other minds." In *Understanding Wittgenstein*, Godfrey Vesey, ed. London: Macmillan; New York: St. Martin's Press, 1974, 149-161.

2282. White, J. F. "Cartesian Privacy and the Problem of Other Minds." Ph.D. Dissertation, Univ. of Colorado, 1968.

2283. Wider, Kathleen V. "A Kantian-Wittgensteinian Approach to the Problem of Other Minds." Ph.D. Dissertation, Wayne State Univ., 1978, 314p. *Dissertation Abstracts* 39 (1979):6177A.

Music

2284. Lewis, P. B. "Wittgenstein on words and music." *British Journal of Aesthetics* 17 (1977):111-121.

2285. Norris, Christopher. "Music and pure thought." *British Journal of Aesthetics* 15 (1975):50-58.

Mysticism

2286. Aldrich, V. C. "Linguistic mysticism." *The Monist* 59 (1976):470-492.

2287. Burr, R. "Wittgenstein's later language-philosophy and some issues in philosophy of mysticism." *International Journal of Philosophy of Religion* 7 (1976):261-287.

2288. Ehrlich, Leonard H. "Mysticism or metaphysics? A juxtaposition of Wittgenstein, Aquinas and Jaspers." In *Akten XIV Kongress für Philosophie*, Wien, September 2-9, 1969. Wien: Herder, 651-659.

2289. Ehrlich, Leonard H. "Mystery and mysticism in Wittgenstein, Aquinas, and Jaspers." [Abstract] *Journal of Philosophy* 64 (1967):745-746.

----- Freundlich, R. [See no. 2083]

2290. Harrison, Frank R. "Notes on Wittgenstein's use of 'das Mystiche'." *Southern Journal of Philosophy* 1 (1963):3-9. [See Plochmann below, no. 2294]

2291. Hoffman, Robert. "Logic, meaning and mystical situation." *Philosophical Studies* 11 (1960):65-70.

2292. Irving, J. A. "Mysticism and the limits of communication." In *Mysticism and the Modern World*, A. Stiernotte, ed. New York: Liberal Arts Press, 1959.

2293. McGuinness, Brian F. "The mysticism of the *Tractatus*." *Philosophical Review* 75 (1966):305-328.

2294. Plochmann, G. K. "A note on Harrison's notes on 'das Mystische'." *Southern Journal of Philosophy* 2 (1964): 130-132. [See Harrison above, no. 2290]

2295. Wasmuth, Ewald. "Das Schweigen Ludwig Wittgensteins: Über das Mystische in *Tractatus Logico-Philosophicus*." *Wort und Wahrheit* 7 (1952):815-822.

2296. Wasmuth, Ewald. "Ludwig Wittgensteins tysnad. Om 'det mystika' i *Tractatus Logico-Philosophicus*." *Credo* 36 (1955):118-125.

2297. Xirau, Ramón. "Wittgenstein y 'lo místico'." *Letras* (Lima) (1968):100-108.

2298. Zemach, Eddy. "Wittgenstein's philosophy of the mystical." *Review of Metaphysics* 18 (1964):39-57. Reprinted in Copi and Beard [see no. 14].

Name

2299. Carney, James D. "Wittgenstein's theory of names." *Australasian Journal of Philosophy* 57 (1979):59-68.

2300. Ishiguro, H. "Use and reference of names." In *Studies in the Philosophy of Wittgenstein*, Peter Winch, ed. London: Routledge & Kegan Paul; New York: Humanities Press, 1969, 20-50.

2301. Khatchadourian, H. "Common names and 'family resemblances'." In *Wittgenstein: The* Philosophical Investigations, George Pitcher, ed., 205-230 [see no. 76].

Nihilism

2302. Rosen, Stanley. *Nihilism. A Philosophical Essay.* New Haven: Yale Univ. Press.

Nominalism

2303. Acuto, Italo. "Wittgenstein nominalista deteriore." *Sistematica* (Milano) 1 (1968):33-36.

2304. Centore, F. "A note on Wittgenstein as an unwilling nominalist." *The Thomist* 37 (1973):762-767.

2305. Hodges, Michael. "Nominalism and the private language argument." *Southern Journal of Philosophy* 14 (1976):283-292.

Non-Existent

2306. Deely, John N. "Reference to the non-existent." *The Thomist* 39 (1975):253-308.

2307. Nyiri, J. C. "Beim Sternenlicht der Nichtexistier-enden: Zur ideologiekritischen Interpretation des platon-isierenden Antipsychologismus." *Inquiry* 17 (1974):399-443.

Number

2308. Intisar-ul-Haque. "Wittgenstein on number." *International Philosophical Quarterly* 18 (1978):33-48.

Object

2309. Bambrough, Renford. "Objectivity and objects." *Proceedings of the Aristotelian Society* 72 (1971-72): 65-81.

2310. Burgos, Rafael. "Sobre el concepto de objeto en el *Tractatus*." *Crítica* 2 (1968):71-89. [Summary, 91-94]

2311. Canfield, John V. "*Tractatus* objects." *Philosophia* (Israel) 6 (1976):81-99.

2312. Copi, Irving M. "Objects, properties and relations in the *Tractatus*." [See Copi and Beard, 167-186, no. 14]

2313. Daly, G. B. "Wittgenstein's 'objects'." *Irish Theological Quarterly* 23 (1956):413-414.

2314. Howard, Michael S. "Objects and Social Context in Some Language-games: A Study in Wittgenstein's Later Philosophy." Ph.D. Dissertation, Cornell Univ., 1975. *Dissertation Abstracts* 36 (1976):6750-6751A.

2315. Keyt, David. "Wittgenstein's notion of an object."
Philosophical Quarterly 13 (1963):13-25. Reprinted in
Copi and Beard, 289-304 [see no. 14].

2316. Kluge, Eike-Henner W. "Objects as universals: a
re-appraisal of the *Tractatus*." *Dialogue* 12 (1973):64-77.

2317. Marks, Charles E. "Can one recognize kinds of
private object?" *Canadian Journal of Philosophy*, Suppl.
1 (1974):215-228.

2318. Senchuk, Dennis M. "Private objects: A study of
Wittgenstein's method." *Metaphilosophy* 7 (1976):217-240.

2319. Zemach, Eddy. "*Sachverhalte, Tatsache*, and
properties." *Ratio* 17 (1975):49-51.

Obligation

2320. Slater, B. H. "A grammatical point about obligation."
Philosophical Quarterly 28 (1978):229-233.

Ontology

2321. Bergmann, G. "Ineffability, method, and ontology."
In E. D. Klemke, ed., 3-24 [see no. 57].

2322. Bonessio di Terzet, Ettore. "Ontologia e linguaggio
nel *Tractatus* di Wittgenstein." *Rivista Rosminiana* 69
(1975):344-355.

2323. Cristaldi, Mariano. *Wittgenstein. L'ontologia
Inibita*. Bologna: R. Patron, 1970. 394p.

2324. Daniels, Charles B., and Davison, John. "Ontology
and method in Wittgenstein's *Tractatus*." *Noûs* 7 (1973)
233-247.

2325. Garver, Newton. "Pantheism and ontology in Wittgenstein's early work." *Idealistic Studies* 1 (1971):269-277.

2326. Klemke, E. D. "The ontology of Wittgenstein's
Tractatus." In E. D. Klemke, ed., 104-119 [see Bergmann
above, no. 2321].

2327. Müller, Anselm Winfried. *Ontologie in Wittgensteins
Tractatus*. Bonn: Bouvier, 1967. 250p.

2328. Musciagli, Dario. *Logica e Ontologia in Wittgenstein. Proposta d'analisi su struttura e conoscenza nel
Tractatus*. Lecce: Milella, 1974. 197p.

2329. Narveson, Anne. "The ontology of the *Tractatus*."
Dialogue 3 (1964):273-283.

2330. Pears, D. F. "The ontology of the *Tractatus*."
Teorema, 1972, 49-58.

2331. Suszko, Roman. "Ontology in the *Tractatus*."
Notre Dame Journal of Formal Logic 9 (1968):7-33.

2332. Weissman, David. "Ontology in the *Tractatus*."
Philosophy and Phenomenological Research 27 (1967):475-501.

2333. Wolniewicz, B. "A parallelism between Wittgenstein-
ian and Aristotelian ontologies." In *Boston Studies in the
Philosophy of Science*, Vol. 4: Proceedings of the Boston
Colloquium for the Philosophy of Science, 1966, Robert S.
Cohen and M. W. Wartofsky, eds. Dordrecht-Boston:
D. Reidel, 1969, 218-225.

2334. Wolters, Richard M. "Wittgenstein's Ontology in his
Early Works." Ph.D. Dissertation, Univ. of Massachusetts,
1974. *Dissertation Abstracts* 34 (1974):525A.

Ontological Argument

2335. Feuer, Lewis. "God, guilt and logic: The psychological basis of the ontological argument." *Inquiry* 11 (1968):
268-271.

Operationalism

2336. Chihara, C. S., and Fodor, J. A. "Operationalism
and ordinary language: A critique of Wittgenstein."
American Philosophical Quarterly 2 (1965):281-295.
Reprinted in *Philosophical Essays on Dreaming*, C. E. M.
Dunlop, ed. Ithaca (New York): Cornell Univ. Press, 1977,
174-204. Also reprinted in *Wittgenstein and the Problem
of Other Minds*, Harold Morick, ed., 170-202 [see no. 68],
and in George Pitcher, 384-419 [see no. 76].

2337. Day, W. F. "On certain similarities between the
philosophical investigations of Wittgenstein and the
operationalism of B. F. Skinner." *Journal of Experimental
Analysis of Behavior* 12 (1969):489-506.

Originality (of Ludwig Wittgenstein)

2338. Shibles, Warren. "L'originalité de Wittgenstein."
Etudes Philosophiques 3 (1975):365-372.

Pain

2339. Bertman, Martin A. "Pain." *Philosophical Review* (Taiwan) (1973):73-75.

2340. Grant, Brian E. J. "Wittgenstein on Pain and Privacy." Ph.D. Dissertation, Univ. of California at Irvine, 1968, 137p. *Dissertation Abstracts* 29: 3201A.

2341. Hester, M. B. "Wittgenstein's analysis of 'I know I am in pain'." *Southern Journal of Philosophy* 4 (1966): 274-280.

2342. Long, T. A. "The problem of pain and contextual implication." *Philosophy and Phenomenological Research* 26 (1965):106-111.

2343. Manser, A. "Pain and private language." In *Studies in the Philosophy of Wittgenstein*, Peter Winch, ed. London: Routledge & Kegan Paul; New York: Humanities Press, 1969, 166-183.

2344. Margolis, Joseph. "The problem of criteria of pain." *Dialogue* 4 (1965):62-71.

2345. Montague, Roger. "The always-painfree behaver." *Mind* 84 (1975):47-62.

2346. Radford, Colin. "Pain and pain behavior." *Philosophy* 47 (1972):189-205.

2347. von Morstein, Petra. "Wittgensteins Untersuchungen des Wortes 'Schmerz'. Ein Beitrag zum Verifikationsproblem in Zusammenhang mit der Sprachanalyse." *Archiv für Philosophie* 13 (1964):131-140.

2348. Zemach, Eddy. "Pains and pain-feelings." *Ratio* 13 (1971):150-157.

Pantheism

----- Garver, Newton. [See no. 2325]

Paradoxes

2349. Chihara, Charles S. "Wittgenstein's analysis of the paradoxes in his lectures on the foundations of mathematics." *Philosophical Review* 86 (1977):365-381.

2350. Dumitriu, Anton. "Wittgenstein's solution of the paradoxes." *Journal of the History of Philosophy* 12 (1974): 227-237.

2351. Rovatti, Pier Aldo. "La positività del paradosso in Wittgenstein." *Aut Aut* (1968):79-92.

Past

2352. Anscombe, G. E. M. "The reality of the past." In *Philosophical Analysis*. A collection of essays edited by Max Black. Ithaca (New York): Cornell Univ. Press, 1950.

2353. Butler, Ronald J. "A Wittgensteinian on 'The reality of the past'." *Philosophical Quarterly* 6 (1956):304-314. [See Anscombe above, no. 2352]

Perception

2354. Candlish, Stewart. "The incompatibility of perception: A contemporary orthodoxy." *American Philosophical Quarterly* 13 (1976):663-668.

2355. Goodman, R. B. "An analysis of two perceptual predicates." *Southwestern Journal of Philosophy* 7 (1976): 35-53.

2356. Stawinski, Arthur W. "Wittgenstein and the Perceptual Foundations of Knowledge." Ph.D. Dissertation, Northwestern Univ., 1973. *Dissertation Abstracts* 34 (1974):4345A.

Person

2357. Hurst, Elaine Lancia. "Wittgenstein's Concept of 'person'. A Developmental and Critical Study." Ph.D. Dissertation, Fordham Univ., 1976. *Dissertation Abstracts* 37 (1976):1022A.

2358. Mulligan, R. W. "The nature of person in Wittgenstein." *New Scholasticism* 44 (1970):565-573 [see G. A. Ross below, no. 2359]. [P. F. Strawson, *Persons*. In *Wittgenstein and the Problem of Other Minds*, H. Morick, ed., and *Individuals*]

2359. Ross, Gregory A. "Wittgenstein on Persons." *New Scholasticism* 46 (1972):368-371.

2360. Strawson, P. F. "Persons." In *Wittgenstein and the Problem of Other Minds*, H. Morick, ed. [See no. 68]

2361. Saunders, John T. "Persons, criteria and skepticism." *Metaphilosophy* 4 (1973):95-113.

2362. Teichman, J. "Wittgenstein on persons and human
beings." In *Understanding Wittgenstein*, G. Vesey, ed.
London: Macmillan; New York: St. Martin's Press, 1974,
133-148.

Perspectivism

2363. Wallace, Kyle. "Nietzsche's and Wittgenstein's
perspectivism." *Southwestern Journal of Philosophy* 4
(1973):101-107.

Phenomenalism

2364. Oldenquist, A. "Wittgenstein on phenomenalism,
skepticism and criteria." In E. D. Klemke, 394-424
[see no. 57].

Phenomenology

[See also: Husserl]

2365. Arrington, Robert L. "Can there be a linguistic
phenomenology?" *Philosophical Quarterly* (1975):289-304.

2366. Arrington, Robert L. "Wittgenstein and phenomenology." *Philosophy Today* 22 (1978):287-300.

2367. Colette, J. "Chronique de phenomenologie." *Revue
des Sciences Philosophiques et Théologiques* 59 (1975):
613-644.

2368. Copleston, Frederick C. "Wittgenstein frente a
Husserl." *Revista Portuguesa de Filosofia* 31 (1965):134-
149.

2369. Dufrenne, Mikel. "Wittgenstein et Husserl." In
Jalons. The Hague: Nijhoff, 1966, 188-207.

2370. Erickson, Stephen A. *Language and Being. An
Analytic Phenomenology.* New Haven: Yale Univ. Press, 1970.

2371. Hems, John M. "Husserl and/or Wittgenstein?"
International Philosophical Quarterly 8 (1969):547-578.

2372. Ihde, Don. "Wittgenstein's *Phenomenological
Reduction*." In *Phenomenological Perspectives. Historical
and Systematic in Honor of H. Spiegelberg*, P. H. Bossert,
ed. (Phaenomenologica, 62) The Hague: Nijhoff, 1975,
47-60.

2373. Küng, Guido. "Language analysis and phenomenological analysis." In *Proceedings of the XIV International Congress of Philosophy*, Vol. 2. Vienna: Herder, 1968, 247-253.

2374. Mays, Wolfe, and Brown, C., eds. *Linguistic Analysis and Phenomenology*. Lewisburg (Pennsylvania): Bucknell Univ. Press, 1972.

 book reviews:
 E. Pivcevic, *Mind* 83 (1974):138-140;
 M. Roche, *Inquiry* 17 (1974):126-131.

2375. Munson, T. N. "Wittgenstein's phenomenology." *Philosophy and Phenomenological Research* 23 (1962):37-50.

2376. Paskow, Alan. "A phenomenological view of the beetle in the box." *New Scholasticism* 48 (1974):277-304.

2377. Spiegelberg, Herbert. "The puzzle of Wittgenstein's *Phanomenologie* (1929?)." *American Philosophical Quarterly* 5 (1968):224-256.

2378. Stith, Robert C. "A Phenomenological Interpretation of Wittgenstein." Ph.D. Dissertation, Duquesne Univ., 1972. *Dissertation Abstracts* 33 (1972):2432A.

2379. Van Peursen, Cornelis A. "E. Husserl and L. Wittgenstein." *Philosophy and Phenomenological Research* 20 (1959):181-195.

2380. Weinzweig, Marjorie. "Phenomenology and ordinary philosophy." *Metaphilosophy* 8 (1978):116-146.

2381. Wuchterl, Kurt. "Wittgenstein und die Idee einer operativen Phänomenologie." *Zeitschrift für Philosophische Forschung* 25 (1971):6-24.

Philosophy

2382. Bitar, Byron I. "Wittgenstein's Conception of Philosophy and the Problem of Private Language." Ph.D. Dissertation, Univ. of Virginia, 1978. *Dissertation Abstracts* 39 (1979):4317A.

2383. Bouveresse, Jacques. "Wittgenstein et la philosophie." *Bulletin de la Société Française de Philosophie* 67 (1973): 85-148. Seánce du 23 mars 1973.

2384. Brulisauer, B. "Was mennen wir mit 'philosophisch'?" *Studia Philosophica* 32 (1972):73-84.

2385. Campanale, D. "La filosofia in Wittgenstein." *Rassegna di Scienze Filosofiche* 8 (1955):417-461.

2386. Crittenden, Charles. "Wittgenstein on philosophical therapy and understanding." *International Philosophical Quarterly* 10 (1970):20-43.

2387. Cudahy, B. "Portrait of the analyst as a meta-physician, the ontological status of philosophy in Wittgenstein's *Tractatus*." *Modern Schoolman* 43 (1966):365-373.

2388. Davis, John W. "Is philosophy a sickness or a therapy." *Antioch Review* 23 (1963):5-23.

2389. Dubois, P. "Naturaleza della filosofia segundo as *Investigacões Filosôficas* de Wittgenstein." *Revista Portuguesa di Filosofia* 15 (1959):36-48.

2390. Dufrenne, Mikel. "Wittgenstein et la philosophie." *Etudes Philosophiques* 20 (1965):281-306.

2391. Fann, Kuant Tih. *Wittgenstein's Conception of Philosophy*. Berkeley: Univ. of California Press, 1969, 178p; Oxford: Basil Blackwell & Mott, 1969.

   book review:
   W. G. Lycan, *Metaphilosophy* 3 (1972):301-309.

2392. Farrell, B. A. "An appraisal of therapeutic positivism." *Mind* 55 (1946):25-48; 133-150.

2393. Feyeraband, Paul. "Wittgenstein und die Philosophie." *Wissenschaft und Weltbild* 7 (1954):212-220; 283-292.

2394. Findlay, J. N. "Some reactions to recent Cambridge philosophy." *Australasian Journal of Philosophy* 18 (1940): 193-211; Ibid., 19 (1941):1-13. Reprinted in his *Language, Mind and Value*. London: George Allen & Unwin, 1963, 13-38.

2395. Gargani, A. G. "Filosofia come terapia linguistica e filosofia come visione." *Rivista di Filosofia* 57 (1966): 408-432.

2396. Gill, Jerry H. "Wittgenstein and the function of philosophy." *Metaphilosophy* 2 (1971):137-149.

2397. Goodman, Russell. "Style, dialectic and the aim of philosophy in Wittgenstein and the Taoit." *Journal of Chinese Philosophy* 3 (1976):145-157.

2398. Headlee, Mark B. "Wittgenstein's philosophy: Old and new." *Dialogue* (PST) 15 (1973):39-44.

2399. Hottois, Georges. "Philosophie du sens commun et dissolution de la philosophie." *Logique et Analyse* 17 (1974):253-275.

2400. Kempski, Jurgen von. "Wittgenstein y la filosofia analitica. Trad. de Manfred Kerkhoff." *Diálogos* 5 (1968): 115-129.

2401. Kreisel, G. "Wittgenstein's theory and practice of
Philosophy." *British Journal for the Philosophy of Science*
11 (1960):238-252.

2402. Lazerowitz, Morris. "Wittgenstein on the nature of
philosophy." Part 1 of his joint paper with Ambrose in
British Philosophy in Mid-Century, A. G. Mace, ed., 1966,
155-174. Reprinted in Fann, 131-147.

2403. Lazerowitz, Morris. "Wittgenstein and the notion
of philosophy." In *Philosophy and Illusion*. London:
George Allen & Unwin, 1968, 53-70; New York: Humanities
Press.

2404. Lembridis, Helle. "Erdachtes Gespräch mit Wittgenstein (über die Philosophie)." *Club Voltaire* (Jahrbuch
für Kritisch Aufklarung, München) 1 (1963):257-270, 410.

2405. Levi, Albert W. "Philosophy as literature. The
dialogue." *Philosophy and Rhetoric* 9 (1976):1-20.

2406. Marconi, Diego. "Wittgenstein: Contesto e fondamento." *Filosofia* (Italy) 23 (1972):255-272. [Style of
philosophy]

2407. McMullin, Ernan. "The analytical approach to
philosophy." *Proceedings of the American Catholic
Philosophical Association* 34 (1960):80-109.

2408. Orr, S. S. "Some reflections on the Cambridge
approach to philosophy." *Australasian Journal of Psychology
and Philosophy* 4 (1946):34-76; 120-167.

2409. Moran, John Henry. "Wittgenstein's Philosophical
Therapy." Ph.D. Dissertation, Fordham Univ., 1962, 443p.
Dissertation Abstracts 23: 3420A.

2410. Pole, David. "Wittgenstein et la philosophie."
Archives de Philosophie 24 (1961):450-467.

2411. Roy, D. J. "Is 'philosophy' really possible? A
meditation on Heidegger and Wittgenstein with K.-O. Apel."
Revue de L'Universite Laurentienne (Sudbury) 9 (1977):79-
91.

2412. Saner, Hans. "Von der Zukunft der Philosophie."
Studia Philosophica 30 (1970-71):225-243.

2413. Schulz, Walter. *Wittgenstein: Die Negation der
Philosophie*. Stuttgart: Verlag Gunther Neske Pfullingen,
1967. 113p.

2414. Torretti, Roberto. "Les *Investigaciones* de Wittgenstein y la posibilidad de la filosofia." *Diálogos* 5 (1968):
35-60.

2415.   Winch, Peter.   "The unity of the philosophy of Wittgenstein."   In *Studies in the Philosophy of Wittgenstein*, Peter Winch, ed.   London: Routledge & Kegan Paul, 1969, 1-19.

2416.   Wuchterl, Kurt.   "Wittgenstein's Lehre vom Erde der Philosophie."   *Pädagogische Provinz* (Frankfurt) 20 (1966): 564-570.

Physicalism

2417.   Hopkins, James.   "Wittgenstein and physicalism." *Proceedings of the Aristotelian Society* 7 (1974-75):121-146.

2418.   Lambros, Charles H.   "Carnap's principle of tolerance and physicalism."   *Transactions of the Peirce Society* 10 (1974):17-33.

Picture

[See also: Meaning]

2419.   Aldrich, V. C.   "Pictorial meaning, picture-thinking, and Wittgenstein's theory of aspects."   *Mind* 67 (1958): 70-79.

2420.   Bell, Richard H.   "Names and the picture theory in use."   *Graduate Review of Philosophy* 4 (1962):20-28.

2421.   Buchanan, Rupert.   "Pictures. Imágenes [con original inglese].   Trad. esp. de Luisa C. de Schajowicz." *Diálogos* 5 (1968):130-161.

2422.   Campbell, William E.   "Wittgenstein's Picture Theory of Meaning."   Ph.D. Dissertation, Washington Univ., 1973. *Dissertation Abstracts* 34 (1974):6038A.

2423.   Heil, John.   "*Tractatus* 4.0141."   *Philosophy and Phenomenological Research* 38 (1978):545-548.

2423a.   Lorenz, Kuno.   "Zur Deutung der Abbildtheorie in Wittgensteins *Tractatus*."   *Teorema*, 1972, 67-90.

2424.   McGuinness, Brian F.   "Pictures and forms in Wittgenstein's *Tractatus*."   In *Filosofia e Simbolismo*.   *Archivio di Filosofia* (Roma) (1956):207-228.   [Italian trans., 229-247]

2425.   Pears, D.   "Relation between Wittgenstein's picture theory of proposition and Russell's theories of judgment." *Philosophical Review* 86 (1977):177-196.

2426. Stegmüller, Wolfgang. "Eine Modell theoretische
Prazisiefund der Wittgensteinschen Bildtheorie."
Notre Dame Journal of Formal Logic 7 (1966):181-195.

2427. Yoos, George E. "An Analysis of Three Studies of
Pictorial Representation: M. C. Beardsley, E. H. Gombrich,
and L. Wittgenstein." Ph.D. Dissertation, Univ. of
Missouri-Columbia, 1971, 231p. *Dissertation Abstracts*
32: 3377A.

Platonism

2428. Weissman, David. "Platonism in the *Tractatus*."
Idealistic Studies 2 (1972):51-80.

Poetry

2429. Falck, Colin. "Poetry and Wittgenstein." *Review*
18 (1968):3-16.

2430. Meschonnic, H. "Sur Wittgenstein, philosophie du
langage et poésie." *Les Cahiers du Chemin* (Paris) (1973):
163-182.

Political Philosophy

2431. Danford, John W. *Wittgenstein and Political
Philosophy*. Chicago: Univ. of Chicago Press, 1978, xiv-
265p.

Pragmatism

2432. Rorty, R. "Pragmatism, categories, and language."
Philosophical Review 70 (1961):197-223.

2433. Toland, William G. "The Later Wittgenstein and
Classical Pragmatism: A Critical Appraisal." Ph.D.
Dissertation, Univ. of North Carolina at Chapel Hill, 1967,
262p. *Dissertation Abstracts* 28: 4670A.

Precise Concept

2434. Keyt, David. "Wittgenstein, the Vienna Circle and
precise concepts." In *Akten XIV International Kongress für
Philosophie* (Wien, September 2-9, 1968), Vol. 2. Wien:
Herder, 1968, 237-246.

Principle of Sufficient Reason

2435. Griffiths, A. Phillips. "Wittgenstein and the four-
fold root of the principle of sufficient reason."
Aristotelian Society, Supplement 50 (1976):1-20.

Privacy

2436. Cook, John W. "Wittgenstein on privacy." *Philosophical Review* 74 (1965):281-314. Reprinted in Pitcher,
286-325 [see no. 76]. Also reprinted in E. D. Klemke,
240-272 [see no. 57]. [See Pole below, no. 2440]

2437. Gustafson, D. F. "Privacy." *Southern Journal of
Philosophy* 3 (1965):140-146.

2438. Hill, David K. "Wittgenstein, privacy and sensation."
Journal of West Virginia Philosophical Society (Spring 1975):
12-15.

2439. Kenny, Anthony. "Cartesian privacy." In G. Pitcher
[see no. 76].

2440. Pole, David. "Cook on Wittgenstein's account of
privacy." *Philosophy* 42 (1967):277-279. [See Cook above,
no. 2436]

2441. Solomon, Robert C. "Wittgenstein and Cartesian
privacy." *Philosophy Today* 16 (1972):163-179.

2442. Villanueva, Enrique. "Verificacionismo y clases
naturales en el ataque contra la privacidad." *Crítica*
9 (1977):83-88.

2443. Vohra, Asjok. "Privacy and private language. I &
II." *Indian Philosophical Quarterly* 3 (1976):505-525;
Ibid., 4 (1976):25-40.

Private

[See also: Language]

2444. Morick, Harold. "Logically private ownership and
epistemic privilege--A critique of Wittgenstein." [Abstract]
Journal of Philosophy 43 (1966):583.

Probability

2445. von Wright, G. H. "Wittgenstein's views on
probability." *Revue Internationale de Philosophie* 23
(1969):259-279. [Discussion, 279-283]

2446. Waismann, F. "Logische Analyse der Wahrscheinlich-
keitsbegriffs." *Erkenntnis* 1 (1930-31):228-248.

Propositions

2447. Ayer, A. J. "Atomic propositions." *Analysis*
1 (1933):2-6.

2448. Bertman, Martin A. "Non-extensional propositions
in Wittgenstein." *International Logic Review* 3 (1972):
73-77.

2449. Bickenbach, Jerome. "The status of the propositions
in the *Tractatus*." *Dialogue* 13 (1974):763-772.

2450. Burch, Robert W. "Why elementary propositions
cannot be negative." *Philosophical Studies* 27 (1975):
433-435.

2451. Bywater, William G., Jr. "Wittgenstein's elementary
propositions." *The Personalist* 50 (1969):360-370.

2452. Fogelin, Robert J. "Negative elementary propositions." *Southwestern Journal of Philosophy* 25 (1974):
189-197.

2453. Harward, Donald W. "Wittgenstein and the character
of mathematical propositions." *International Logic Review*
3 (1972):246-251.

2454. Hudson, W. D. "Wittgenstein on fundamental
propositions." *Southwestern Journal of Philosophy* 8
(1977):7-21.

2455. Langford, C. H. "On propositions belonging to
logic." *Mind* 36 (1927):342-346.

2456. McTaggart, J. E. "Propositions applicable to
themselves." *Mind* 32 (1923):462-464.

----- Pears, D. [See no. 2425]

2457. Poulain, Jacques. "La possibilité des propositions
ontologiques dans le *Tractatus Logico-Philosophicus*."
Etudes Philosophiques 4 (1973):529-552.

2458.   Riverso, Emanuele.   "Filosofia ed analisi della
proposizione da Platone a Wittgenstein."   *Giornale Critico
della Filosofia Italiana* 46 (1967):466-483.

2459.   Wholstetter, Albert.   "The structure of the proposition and the fact."   *Philosophy of Science* 3 (1936):
167-184.

Psychoanalysis

2460.   Ambrose, Alice.   "Philosophy, language and illusion."
In *Psychoanalysis and Philosophy*, Charles Hanly and Morris
Lazerowitz, eds.   New York: International Universities
Press, 1970, 14-34.

2461.   Elevitch, Bernard.   "Reasons, motives and psychoanalysis."   *The Philosophical Forum* (Boston) 6 (1974):
143-165.

-----   Frongia, Guido.   [See no. 1530]

2462.   Hanly, Charles.   "Wittgenstein on psychoanalysis."
In *Ludwig Wittgenstein. Philosophy and Language*,
A. Ambrose and M. Lazerowitz, eds.   New York: Humanities
Press, 1972, 73-94.

2463.   Cioffi, F.   "Wittgenstein's Freud."   In *Studies in
the Philosophy of Wittgenstein*, Peter Winch, ed.   New York:
Humanities Press, 1969, 184-209.

2464.   Hottois, Gilbert.   "Esquisse comparative de la
réception de la psychanalyse comme 'art sémantique' dans
la philosophie linguistique thérapeutique de Wittgenstein,
Lazerowitz, et Wisdom."   *Annales de l'Institut de
Philosophie* (1975):177-205.

2465.   Lorenzer, Alfred.   "Wittgensteins Sprachspiel-Konzept
in der Psychoanalyse."   *Psyche H*. 28 (1974):833-852.
[Übersicht, 833; Summary, 851-852]

Psycholinguistics

2466.   Toulmin, Stephen.   "Wittgenstein and psycholinguistics."   Isenberg lecture delivered at Michigan State
Univ., November 22, 1968.

Psychology - Psychologist

2467.   Bogen, James.   "Was Wittgenstein a psychologist?"
Inquiry 7 (1964):374-378.

2468. Hannay, Alastair. "Was Wittgenstein a psychologist?"
Inquiry 7 (1964):379-386.

2469. Osheroff, Steven S. "Wittgenstein: Psychological
disputes and common moves." *Philosophy and Phenomenological
Research* 36 (1976):339-363.

2470. Rorty, Richard. "Wittgensteinian philosophy and
empirical psychology." *Philosophical Studies* (Dordrecht)
31 (1977):151-172.

2471. Waismann, F. "The relevance of psychology to logic."
Proceedings of the Aristotelian Society, Supplement 17
(1938):54-68. Reprinted in *Readings in Philosophical
Analysis*, H. Feigl and W. Sellars, eds. New York:
Appleton-Century-Crofts, 1949, 211-221.

Psychophysical Parallelism

2472. Holborow, L. "The prejudice in favour of psycho-
physical parallelism." In *Understanding Wittgenstein*,
Godfrey Vesey, ed. London: Macmillan; New York: St. Martin's
Press, 1974, 193-207.

Rationality

----- Cavel, Stanley. "The Claim to Rationality." Ph.D.
Dissertation, Harvard Univ., 1961.

Realism

2473. Petri, G. "Realismo ontologico e senso comune."
Revista Critica di Storia della Filosofia 8 (1953):533-544.
[A section on the *Tractatus*]

Reality

2474. Gumpel, Liselotte. "The essence of 'reality' as a
construct of language." *Foundations of Language* 11 (1974):
167-185.

----- Schwyzer, H. [See no. 2247]

2475. Wilson, Fred. "The world and reality in the
Tractatus." *Southern Journal of Philosophy* 5 (1967):253-
260.

Reason, Motive

-----   Elevitch, Bernard.   [See no. 2461]

-----   Engel, S. Morris.   [See no. 1702]

Reference

2475a. Womack, James A.   "Quine and Wittgenstein on
Reference."   Ph.D. Dissertation, New York Univ., 1976,
259p.   *Dissertation Abstracts* 37 (1977):5891A.

Relations

2476.   Allaire, Edwin B.   "Things, relations and identity."
Philosophy of Science 34 (1967):260-272.

2477.   Ambrose, Alice.   "Internal relations."   *Review of
Metaphysics* 21 (1968):256-261.

Religion - Religious

[See also: Fideism, God, Theology]

2478.   Almond, P. C.   "Wittgenstein and religion."   *Sophia*
(Australia) 16 (1977):24-27.

2479.   Antiseri, Dario.   "La 'mistica' di un 'logico':
ovvero la religione in Ludwig Wittgenstein."   *Proteus*
4 (1973):163-170.

2480.   Ard, David J.   "Language, Reality and Religion in
the Philosophy of Ludwig Wittgenstein."   Ph.D. Dissertation,
McMaster Univ., 1978.   *Dissertation Abstracts* 39: 5570A.

2481.   Bejerholm, L.   "Logiken i 'Guds ledning'."   *Svensk
Teologisk Kvartalskift* 41 (1965):25-38.

2482.   Bell, Richard H.   "The fire-festivals: Wittgenstein
and theories of religion."   *Religious Studies* 14 (1978):
113-124.

2483.   Bramann, J. K.   "Religious language in Wittgenstein
and Kafka."   *Diogenes* no. 90 (1975):26-35.

2484.   Bramann, J. K.   "Kafka and Wittgenstein on religious
language."   *Sophia* (Australia) 14 (1975):1-9.

2485. Burhenn, H. "Religious beliefs as pictures."
Journal of the American Academy for Religion 42 (1974):
326-335.

2486. Burr, Ronald. "Wittgenstein's later language-
philosophy and some issues in philosophy of mysticism."
International Journal for the Philosophy of Religion
7 (1976):261-287.

2487. Callopy, Bartholomew J. "Wittgenstein and Religious
Discourse: Some Possibilities for Theological Investigation." Ph.D. Dissertation, Yale Univ., 1972. *Dissertation Abstracts* 33: 2479A.

2488. Campbell, James Ian. *The Language of Religion*.
New York: Bruce Books, 1971.

2488a. Charlesworth, M. T. "Linguistic analysis and
language about God." *International Philosophical Quarterly*
1 (1961):139-157.

2489. Churchill, John H. "Wittgenstein and Philosophy of
Religion." Ph.D. Dissertation, Yale Univ., 1977, 342p.
Dissertation Abstracts 39 (1978):1653-1654A.

2490. Cleobury, F. H. "Wittgenstein and the philosophy
of religion. *Mod. Ch.* n.s. 13 (1970):174-180.

2491. Cox, Charles H., and Cox, Jean W. "Mystical
experience: With an emphasis on Wittgenstein and Zen."
Religious Studies 12 (1976):483-491.

2492. Cruikshank, A. "Wittgenstein and the language of
the Gospels." *Ch. Quarterly* 3 (1970):40-51.

2493. Dilley, Frank B. "The status of religious beliefs."
American Philosophical Quarterly 13 (1976):41-47.

2494. Dilman, Ilham. "Wisdom's philosophy of religion--
Part 1: Religion and reason." *Canadian Journal of
Philosophy* 5 (1975):473-495.

2495. Dilman, Ilham. "Wisdom's philosophy of religion--
Part 2: Metaphysical and religious transcendence."
Canadian Journal of Philosophy 5 (1975):497-521.

2496. Downing, F. Gerald. "Games, families, the public,
and religion." *Philosophy* 47 (1972):38-54.

2497. Evans, D. "Faith and belief." *Religious Studies*
10 (1974):1-19.

2498. Ferrelly, John. "Religious reflection and man's
transcendence." *The Thomist* 37 (1973):1-68.

2499. Fitzpatrick, Joseph. "Philosophy of religion: The
linguistic approach." *The Heythrop Journal* 19 (1978):
285-297.

----- Frongia, G. [See no. 1530]

2500. Garceau, B. "La philosophie analytique de la
religion: Contribution canadienne (1970-1975)."
Philosophiques 2 (1975):301-339.

2501. Gill, Jerry H. "Tacit knowing about religious
belief." *International Journal for the Philosophy of
Religion* 6 (1975):73-88.

2502. Gill, Jerry H. "Wittgenstein and religious language."
Theology Today 21 (1964):59-72.

2503. Grennan, Wayne. "Wittgenstein on religious
utterances." *Sophia* (Australia) 15 (1976):13-18.

2504. High, Dallas M. *Language, Persons, and Belief.
Studies in Wittgenstein's Philosophical Investigations
and Religious Uses of Language.* New York: Oxford Univ.
Press, 1967.

2505. Hudson, W. Donald. "Using a picture and religious
belief." *Sophia* (July 1973):11-17.

2506. Hudson, W. Donald. *Ludwig Wittgenstein. The
Bearing of his Philosophy upon Religious Belief.*
Richmond (Virginia): John Knox Press, 1968; London:
Lutterworth Press, 1968.

2507. Hudson, W. Donald. *Wittgensteinian Fideism.*
New York: Doubleday, Anchor Books, 1970.

2508. Hudson, W. Donald. *Philosophical Approach to
Religion.* London: Macmillan, 1974.

2509. Hudson, W. Donald. *Wittgenstein and Religious
Belief.* New York: St. Martin's Press; London: Macmillan,
1975. 206p.

2510. Hudson, W. Donald. "What makes religious beliefs
religious?" *Religious Studies* 13 (1977):221-242.

2511. Hudson, W. Donald. "Some remarks on Wittgenstein's
account of religious belief." In *Royal Institute of
Philosophy.* Talk of God, 36-51.

2512. Keeling, L. Bryant, and Morelli, Mario F. "Beyond
Wittgensteinian fideism: An examination of John Hick's
analysis of religious faith." *International Journal for
the Philosophy of Religion* 8 (1977):250-262.

2513. Kellenberger, James. "Language-game view of religion and religious certainty." *Canadian Journal of Philosophy* 2 (1972):255-275.

2514. Laura, Roland S. "The positivist poltergeist and some difficulties with Wittgensteinian liberation." *International Journal for the Philosophy of Religion* 2 (1971):183-190.

2515. Laura, Roland S. "Positivism and philosophy of religion." *Sophia* 11 (1972):13-20.

2516. Laura, Roland S. "Epistemic considerations and the religious use of language." *Anglician Theological Review* 52 (1970):142-150.

2516a. Martin, Dean M. "Christian Consciousness: Its Emergence with the Mastery of Concepts within the Christian Community with Special Reference to Wittgenstein." Ph.D. Dissertation, Baylor Univ., 1972. *Dissertation Abstracts* 33 (1973):5279A.

2517. McDermott, R. A. "Religion game; some family resemblances." *Journal of the American Academy of Religion* 38 (1970):390-400.

2518. Muykens, James L. "Religious belief as hope." *International Journal for the Philosophy of Religion* 5 (1974):246-253.

2519. Nielsen, Kai. "The challenge of Wittgenstein. An examination of his picture of religious belief." *Studies in Religion* (Toronto) 3 (1973):29-46. Spanish trans. "El desafío de Wittgenstein. Un examen de su visión de la creencia religiosa." *Folia Humanística* 10 (1972)235-255.

2520. Nielsen, Kai. "Religion and the appeal to forms of life." *Ágora* 3 (1975-76):67-71.

2521. Nielsen, Kai. "Challenge of Wittgenstein: An examination of his picture of religious belief." *Studies in Religion - Sciences Religieuses* 3 (1973):29-46.

2522. Nielsen, Kai. *Contemporary Critique of Religion.* London: Macmillan, 1972.

2523. Poulain, Jacques. *Logique et Religion. L'atomisme logique de L. Wittgenstein et la possibilité des propositions religieuses.* [Suivi de] *Logic and Religion.* A shortened and adapted version (Religion and reason, 7). The Hague-Paris: Mouton, 1973. 228p.

2524. Purtill, Richard L. "Intelligibility of disembodied survival." *Christian Scholar's Review* 5 (1975):3-22.

2525. Raschke, Carl. "Meaning and saying in religion:
Beyond language games." *Harvard Theological Review*
67 (1974):79-116.

2526. Reese, William L. "Religious 'seeing-as'."
Religious Studies 14 (1978):73-87.

2527. Rhees, Rush. *Without Answers*. London: Routledge
& Kegan Paul; New York: Schocken Books, 1969.

2528. Richards, Glyn. "A Wittgensteinian approach to the
philosophy of religion. A critical evaluation of D. Z.
Phillips." *Journal of Religion* 58 (1978):288-302.

2529. Shepherd, W. C. "On the concept of being wrong
religiously." *Journal of the American Academy of Religion*
42 (1974):66-81.

2529a. Sherry, Patrick. *Religion, Truth and Language-games*.
London: Macmillan, 1977. 234p.

2530. Sherry, Patrick. "Is religion a 'form of life'?"
American Philosophical Quarterly 9 (1972):159-167.

2531. Sherry, Patrick. "Truth and the 'religious language-
game." *Philosophy* 47 (1972):18-37.

2532. Spieler, David A. "Disembodied existence and the
private language argument." *The Drew Gateway* 46 (1975-76):
95-105.

2533. Thiselton, A. C. "Meaning of Σάρξ in I Corinthians
5:5; a fresh approach in the light of logical and semantic
factors." *Scottish Journal of Theology* 26 (1973):204-228.

2534. Van Buren, Paul Matthews. *The Edge of Language:
An Essay in the Logic of Religion*. New York: Macmillan,
1972. 178p. [Religious implications of *Philosophical
Investigations*]

Representation

2535. Campanale, D. "La teoria della raffigurazione in
Wittgenstein." *Rassegna di Scienze Filosofiche* 9 (1956):
159-207.

Rule

2536. Ginet, Carl. "Wittgenstein's argument that one
cannot obey a rule privately." *Noûs* 4 (1970):349-365.
[See Marks below, no. 2538]

2537. Goldblatt, David A. "Wittgenstein, Rules and
Logical Necessity." Ph.D. Dissertation, Univ. of Pennsylvania, 1972. *Dissertation Abstracts* 33 (1972):1780A.

2538. Marks, Charles E. "Ginet on Wittgenstein's argument
against private rules." *Philosophical Studies* (Dordrecht)
25 (1974):261-271.

2539. Slovenko, R. "The opinion rule and Wittgenstein's
Tractatus." ETC. *Review of General Semantics* 24 (1967):
289-303.

2540. Winch, Peter. "Rules: Wittgenstein's analysis,"
and "Some misunderstandings of Wittgenstein." In his
The Idea of a Social Science. London: Routledge & Kegan
Paul, 1958, 24-39.

Samkara's Advaita Vedenta

2541. Goldenberg, Daniel S. "A Comparative Analysis of
Wittgenstein's *Tractatus* and Samkara's Advaita Vedanta."
Ph.D. Dissertation, Univ. of Hawaii, 1977, 248p.
Dissertation Abstracts 38 (1977):2845A.

Saying

2542. Sellars, W. "Naming and saying." In *Essays on
Wittgenstein*, E. D. Klemke, ed., 78-103 [see no. 57].

Saying and Showing

2543. Geach, P. T. "Saying and showing in Frege and
Wittgenstein." In *Essays on Wittgenstein in Honour of
G. H. von Wright* (Acta Philos. Fenn. 28 (1976)). Amsterdam:
North Holland, 1976, 54-70.

2544. Harward, Donald W. *Wittgenstein's Saying and Showing
Themes*. Bonn: Bouvier Verlag H. Brundmann, 1976. 71p.

2545. McCormick, Peter, Schaper, Eva, and Heaton, J. M.
"Symposium on saying and showing in Heidegger and Wittgenstein." *Journal of the British Society for Phenomenology*
3 (1972):27-45.

2546. Stampe, D. W. "Tractarian reflections on saying and
showing." In E. D. Klemke, 423-445 [see no. 57].

Science and Scientific

2547. Frommke, Peter. "Die Grammatik der Hypothese. Zur Wissenschaftstheorie des mittleren Wittgenstein." *Zeitschrift für Philosophische Forschung* 26 (1972):426-438.

2548. Gellner, Ernest. "A Wittgensteinian philosophy of [or against] the social sciences." *Philosophy of the Social Sciences* 5 (1975):173-199.

2549. Habermas, Jürgen. "Zur Logik der Sozialwissenschaften." *Philosophische Rundschau* 5 (1967):124ff.

2550. McGuinness, Brian F. "Philosophy of science in the *Tractatus*." *Revue Internationale de Philosophie* 23 (1969): 88-89.

2551. Phillips, Derek L. *Wittgenstein and Scientific Knowledge. A Sociological Perspective*. Totowa (New Jersey): Rowman & Littlefield, 1977. 248p.

2552. Popper, Karl. "The nature of philosophical problems and their roots in science." *British Journal for the Philosophy of Science* 3 (1952):124-156.

2553. Proctor, G. L. "Scientific laws, scientific objects, and the *Tractatus*." *British Journal for the Philosophy of Science* 10 (1959):177-193. Reprinted in Copi and Beard [see no. 14].

2554. Sanchez-Mazas, M. "La ciencia, el lenguaje y el mundo según Wittgenstein." *Cuadernos Hispanoamericanos* 15 (1953):35-44. Also in *Theoria* (Madrid) 2 (1954):127-130.

Seeing

2555. Lewis, P. B. "Wittgenstein on seeing and interpreting." In Royal Institute of Philosophy, *Impressions of Empiricism*, G. Vesey, ed. New York: St. Martin's Press, 1976, 93-108.

2556. Tilghman, B. R. "Seeing and meaning [Wittgenstein]." *Southern Journal of Philosophy* 14 (1976):523-533.

Seeing (As)

2557. Burlingame, Charles E. "On the Logic of 'Seeing As' Locution." Ph.D. Dissertation, Univ. of Virginia, 1965.

2558. Shibles, Warren. "Seeing-as." *ITA-Humanidades*
12 (1976):77-81.

Self

2559. Richards, Glyn. "Conceptions of the self in Wittgenstein, Hume, and Buddhism: An Analysis and Comparison."
The Monist 61 (1978):42-55.

2560. Rosenberg, Jay F. "Intentionality and self in the
Tractatus." *Noûs* 2 (1968):341-358.

2561. Zemach, Eddy M. "The unity and indivisibility of
the self. Three short stories and a Wittgensteinian
commentary." *International Philosophical Quarterly*
10 (1970):542-555.

Self-Description

2562. Harris, Roy. "The semantics of self-description."
Analysis 27 (1967):144. [On *Tractatus* 3.332]

2563. Hope, V. M. "Wittgenstein and self-description."
Inquiry 11 (1968).

Self-Knowledge

2564. Sankowski, Edward. "Wittgenstein on self-knowledge."
Mind 87 (1978):256-261.

Self-Reference and Self-Awareness

2565. Shoemaker, Sydney. "Self-reference and self-aware-
ness." *Journal of Philosophy* 65 (1968):555-568.

Sensation

2566. Anscombe, G. E. M. "The subjectivity of sensation."
Ajatus 36 (1974):3-18.

2567. Buchanan, Rupert. "Wittgenstein's Discussion of
Sensation." Ph.D. Dissertation, Duke Univ., 1966, 260p.
Dissertation Abstracts 27: 3900A.

2568. Donagan, A. "Wittgenstein on sensation." In George
Pitcher [see no. 76]. [See Gustafson below, no. 2570]

2569. Ginet, Carl. "How words mean kinds of sensations."
Philosophical Review 77 (1968):3-24.

2570. Gustafson, Donald. "A note on a misreading of
Wittgenstein." *Analysis* 28 (1967-68):143-144. [See
Gustafson above, no. 2568]

----- Hill, David K. [See no. 2438]

2571. Jones, O. R., ed. *The Private Language Argument.*
London: Macmillan; New York: St. Martin's Press, 1971.
[See H. Hervey, "Private language and private sensations,"
76-95; N. Garver, Ibid., 95-102]

2572. Margolis, Joseph. "The privacy of sensation."
Ratio 6 (1964):147-153.

2573. Melden, A. I. "My kinaesthetic sensations advise
me..." *Analysis* 18 (1957):43-48.

2574. Ruddick, Sara L. "Wittgenstein on Sensation
Statement." Ph.D. Dissertation, Harvard Univ., 1963.

2575. Thomas, George B. "Wittgenstein on sensations."
Philosophical Studies 20 (1969):19-23.

Sense

2576. Diamond, Cora. "Secondary sense." *Proceedings of
the Aristotelian Society* 67 (1966-67):189-208.

Silence

2577. Bindeman, Steven. "The Role of Silence in the
Philosophy of M. Heidegger and L. Wittgenstein." Ph.D.
Dissertation, Duquesne Univ., 1978. *Dissertation Abstracts*
39 (1978):1613A.

2578. Cappeletti, V. "L'imperativo del silenzio. Premessa
a un'interpretazione dell'opera Wittgensteiniana."
Proceedings of the XII International Congress of Philosophy
(Venice) 12 (1958):55-61.

----- Wasmuth, Ewald. [See nos. 2295 and 2296]

2578a. Wisan, R. H. "A note on silence." *Journal of
Philosophy* 53 (1956):448-450.

Simplicity Argument

2579. Mijuskovic, B. "The simplicity argument in Wittgenstein and Russell." *Crítica* 8 (1976):85-99. [Resumen, 100-
103]

Skepticism

2580. Bogen, James. "Wittgenstein and skepticism."
Philosophical Review 83 (1974):364-373.

2581. Nielsen, Kai. *Skepticism*. New York: Macmillan, 1973.

----- Oldenquist, A. [See no. 2364]

2582. Olscamp, Paul J. "Wittgenstein's refutation of
skepticism." *Philosophy and Phenomenological Research*
26 (1965-66):239-247.

2583. Rieman, F. "On linguistic skepticism in Wittgenstein
and Kung-sun Lung." *Philosophy East and West* 27 (1977):
183-193.

2584. Swindler, Jim K. "Some problems in the history of
skepticism." *Auslegung* 1-2 (1973-75):43-59.

2585. Winkler, E. R. "Skepticism and private language."
Mind 81 (1972):1-17.

Social Science

2586. Clammer, John. "Wittgensteinianism and the social
sciences." *Social Analysis and Theory* 6 (1976):241-256.
Also in *Sociological Review* 24 (1976):775-791.
[See J. A. Hughes below, no. 2488]

2587. Gellner, Ernest. "A Wittgensteinian philosophy of
(or against) the social sciences." *Philos. Soc. Sci.*
5 (1975):173-199.

2588. Hugues, J. A. "Wittgenstein and social science.
Some matters of interpretation." *The Sociological Review*
(Keele) 25 (1977):721-741.

Solipsism

2589. Barone, Francesco. "El solipsismo linguistico di
Ludwig Wittgenstein." *Filosofía* (Italy) 2 (1951):543-570.

2590.   Braithwaite, R. B.   "Solipsism and the 'common sense
view of the world'." *Analysis* 1 (1933):13-15. Comments
by M. Cornforth and L. S. Stebbing, 21-28.

2591.   Cook, John W.   "Solipsism and language." In
Ludwig Wittgenstein. Philosophy and Language. New York:
Humanities Press, 1972, 37-72.

2592.   Garcia Suárez, Alfonso.   "Solipsismo y 'experiencia
privada'." *Teorema* 4 (1974):91-106.

2593.   Gutiérrez, Carlos Bernardo.   "El solipsismo en
Wittgenstein. Apreciación crítica desde un punto de vista
fenomenológica, I & II." *Ideas y Valores* (Bogotá) 6
(1964-65):15-35; 103-120.

2594.   Hintikka, J.   "On Wittgenstein's 'solipsism'."
Mind 67 (1958):88-91.

2595.   Pears, D. F.   "Wittgenstein's treatment of solipsism
in the *Tractatus*." *Crítica* 6 (1972):57-80. [Resumen,
81-84]

                              Soul

2596.   Dilman, Ilham.   "Wittgenstein on the soul." In
Understanding Wittgenstein, Godfrey Vesey, ed. London:
Macmillan; New York: St. Martin's Press, 1974, 162-192.

2597.   Fleming, Noël.   "Seeing the soul." *Philosophy*
53 (1978):33-50.

2598.   Hacker, P. M. S.   "Wittgenstein's doctrines of the
soul in the *Tractatus*." *Kantstudien* 62 (1971):162-171.

                             Space

        [See also: Logical Space, nos. 2102, 2103, 2104]

2599.   Schwartz, Elisabeth.   "Remarques sur *L'espace des
choses* de Wittgenstein et ses origines frégéennes."
Dialectica 26 (1972):185-226.

                             Speech

2600.   Young, Iris M.   "From Anonymity to Speech: A
Reading of Wittgenstein's Later Writing." Ph.D. Disserta-
tion, Pennsylvania State Univ., 1974. *Dissertation
Abstracts* 35 (1975):7358A.

Sport

2601. Kretchmar, Scott. "Ontological possibilities: Sport as play." *Journal of the Philosophy of Sport* 11 (1975): 23-30.

Structuralism

2602. Cohen, Sande. "Structuralism and the writing of intellectual history." *History and Theory* 17 (1978):175-206.

2603. Leyvraz, Jean-Pierre. "Wittgenstein orientierter Vortrage zum Strukturalismus." *Studia Philosophica* 30-31 (1970-71):167-195.

2604. Pettit, Philip. "Wittgenstein and the case for structuralism." *Journal of the British Society for Phenomenology* 3 (1972):46-57.

Structure

2605. Moore, Willis. "Structure in sentence and in fact." *Philosophy of Science* 5 (1938):81-88. Reprinted in Copi and Beard [see no. 14].

Subjectivity

2606. Lübbe, Hermann. *Bewusstsein in Geschichten. Studien zur Phänomenologie der Subjektivität. Mach, Husserl, Schapp, Wittgenstein.* Freiburg: Verlag Rombach, 1972. 172p.

Suffering

2607. Kalupahana, David J. "The notion of suffering in early Buddhism compared with some reflections of early Wittgenstein." *Philosophy East and West* 27 (1977):423-431.

Sufficient Reason (principle of)

2608. Griffiths, A. Phillips. "Wittgenstein and the four-fold root of the principle of sufficient reason." *Aristotelian Society, Supplement* 50 (1976):1-20.

Taoist

2609. Goodman, Russell. "Style, dialectic, and the aim of philosophy in Wittgenstein and the taoists." *Journal of Chinese Philosophy* 3 (1975-76):145-157.

Tautology

2610. Lazerowitz, Morris. "Tautologies and the matrix method." *Mind* 46 (1937):191-205.

2611. Moore, G. E. "'Truth possibilities', and Wittgenstein's sense of 'tautology'." In his *Commonplace Books*. London: George Allen & Unwin, 1962, 282-286.

Teaching

2612. McBride, Frank A. "The Later Wittgenstein's Conception of Teaching." Ph.D. Dissertation, Michigan State Univ., 1972. *Dissertation Abstracts* 33 (1972):2428A.

Terms

2613. Brady, Patrick. "Period style terms and concepts. The Wittgenstein perspective." *The Journal of Critical Analysis* 4 (1972):62-70.

2614. Malherbe, Jean-François. "Termes théoriques et référence." *Archives de Philosophie* 38 (1975):201-217.

2615. Plochmann, G. J., and Lawson, J. B. *Terms in Their Propositional Contexts in Wittgenstein's* Tractatus: *An Index.* Carbondale: Southern Illinois Univ. Press, 1962.

Theology

[See also: God, Religion]

2616. Aldwincle, R. F. "Much ado about words; some reflections on language, philosophy, and theology (review article)." *Canadian Journal of Theology* 7 (1961):91-98.

2617. Antiseri, Dario. "Empirismo odierno e teologia nel caso 'Wittgenstein'." In *Filosofia e Teologia Contemporee.* Atti del XXIX Convegno del Centro di Studi Filosofici tra professori universari, Gallarte, 1974. Brescia: Morcelliana, 1975, 109-116.

2618. Bell, Richard H. "Theology as grammar: Is God an object of understanding?" *Religious Studies* 11 (1975): 301-317.

2619. Bell, Richard H. "Wittgenstein and descriptive theology." *Religious Studies* 5 (1969):1-18.

2621. Bell, Richard H. "Kierkegaard and Wittgenstein: Two strategies for understanding theology." *Illif Review* 31 (1974):21-34.

2622. Burke, T. E. "Theological originality." *Religious Studies* 12 (1976):1-20.

2623. Carse, James P. "Wittgenstein's lion and Christology." *Theology Today* 24 (1967-68):148-159.

2624. Clayton, J. P. "Was ist falsch in der Korrelations-theologie?" *Neue Zeitschrift für Systematische Theologie und Religionsphilosophie* 16 (1974):93-111.

2625. Crowe, Charles L. "A New Estimate of the Significance of Wittgenstein's *Tractatus* for the Analysis of Theological Discourse." Ph.D. Dissertation, Columbia Univ.

2626. d'Hert, Ignace. *Wittgenstein's Relevance for Theology*. Bern: Lang - Frankfurt Lang, 1975. 237p.

2627. Ernst, C. "Words, facts and God; problems set by Wittgenstein for metaphysical theology." *Blackfriars* 44 (1963):292-306.

2628. Henry, G. C., Jr. "Mathematics, phenomenology, and language analysis in contemporary theology." *Journal of the American Academy for Religion* 35 (1967):337-349.

2629. Saunders, Lloyd. "Theological consequences of philosophy as immediacy." *American Academy of Religion. Philosophy of Religion and Theology, Proceedings* (1976): 255-264.

                              Thought

2630. Favrholdt, David. "The relation between thought and language in Wittgenstein's *Tractatus*." *Teorema*, 1972, 91-100.

Tie

2631. Martin, Rex. "The problem of the *tie* in von Wright's
schema of practical inference. A Wittgensteinian solution."
In *Essays on Wittgenstein in Honour of G. H. von Wright*
(Acta Philos. Fenn. 28 (1976)). Amsterdam: North-Holland,
1976, 326-363.

Tool

2632. Goff, Robert A. "Wittgenstein's tools and Heidegger's
implements." *Man and World* 1 (1968):447-462.

Transcendental

2632a. Bachmaier, P. *Wittgenstein und Kant. Versuch zum
Begriff d. Transzendentalen*. Frankfurt am Main: P. Lang,
1978, 213p.

Truth

2633. Cohen, Michael. "Truth-tables and truth."
Analysis 35 (1974):1-7.

2634. Gettner, Alan F. "Analytic Truth in the Philosophies
of Quine and the Later Wittgenstein." Ph.D. Dissertation,
Columbia Univ., 1971, 244p. *Dissertation Abstracts* 32:
3209A.

2635. Gill, Jerry H. "Wittgenstein's concept of truth."
International Philosophical Quarterly 6 (1966):71-80.

2636. Hackstaff, L. H. "A note in Wittgenstein's truth-
function generating operation in *Tractatus* 6." *Mind*
75 (1966):255-256.

2637. Hamlyn, D. W. "The correspondence theory of truth."
Philosophical Quarterly 12 (1962):193-205.

2638. Hintikka, Jaakko. "Are logical truths analytic?"
Philosophical Review 74 (1965):178-203.

2639. Hülser, Karlheinz. "Die Unterscheidung 'sagen-
zeigen', das Logische und die 'Warheit' in Wittgensteins
Tractatus." *Kantstudien* 65 (1974):457-475.

2640. Kneale, William. "Truths of logic." *Proceedings
of the Aristotelian Society* 46 (1945-46):207-234.

2641.   Leblanc, Hughes.   "Wittgenstein and the truth-
functionality thesis." *American Philosophical Quarterly*
9 (1972):271-274.

2642.   Lambros, Charles H.   "Four varieties of the logical
positivists' doctrine of necessary truth." *Philosophy
and Phenomenological Research* 35 (1975):512-533.

2643.   Morrison, James C.   "Meaning and Truth in Wittgenstein's *Tractatus*." Ph.D. Dissertation, Pennsylvania
State Univ., 1964, 176p. *Dissertation Abstracts* 25:4752A.

2644.   Plochmann, George K.   "Verdad, tautologia y veri-
ficacion en el *Tractatus* de Wittgenstein." *Dianoia*
(Univ. of México) (1968):122-142.

2645.   Sellars, Wilfrid.   "Truth and correspondence."
Journal of Philosophy 59 (1962):39-56.

2646.   Tonini, V.   "La natura della verità: Una logica
realista." *La Nuova Critica* 7-8 (1958-59):79-180.

Types (theory of)

2647.   Davant, James B.   "Wittgenstein on Russell's theory
of types." *Notre Dame Journal of Formal Logic* 16 (1975):
102-108.

Unconscious

2648.   von Morstein, Petra.   "Zur Funktion des Begriffes
'unbewusst'." *Conceptus* 11 (1977):327-338.

Universals

2649.   Aaron, Richard I.   "Wittgenstein's theory of
universals." *Mind* 74 (1965):249-251.

2650.   Agassi, Joseph, and Sagal, Paul T.   "The problem of
universals." *Philosophical Studies* 28 (1975):289-294.

2651.   Ambrose, Alice.   "Wittgenstein on universals."   In
Wittgenstein. The Man and his Philosophy, K. T. Fann, ed.
New York: Dell, 1967, 336-352.

2652.   Bambrough, J. R.   "Universals and family resemblances."
Proceedings of the Aristotelian Society 61 (1960-61):207-
222.   Reprinted in *Wittgenstein*, G. Pitcher, ed., 186-204.

2653. Fahrnkopf, Robert L. "Wittgenstein on Universals."
Ph.D. Dissertation, Univ. of British Columbia (Canada),
1973. *Dissertation Abstracts* 34 (1974):7820A.

2654. Griffin, Nicholas. "Wittgenstein, universals and
family resemblances." *Canadian Journal of Philosophy*
3 (1973-74):635-651.

2655. Hodges, Michael. "Wittgenstein on universals."
Philosophical Studies (Dordrecht) 24 (1973):22-30.

2656. Kennick, W. E. "Philosophy as grammar and the
reality of universals." In *Ludwig Wittgenstein. Philosophy
and Language*, A. Ambrose and M. Lazerowitz, eds., 140-185
[see no. 1].

2657. McCloskey, A. J. "The philosophy of linguistic
analysis and the problem of universals." *Philosophy and
Phenomenological Research* 24 (1964):329-338.

2658. Nammour, J. "Resemblances and universals." *Mind*
82 (1973):516-524.

----- Schwyzer, Hubert. [See no. 1696]

----- Schwyzer, Hubert. [See no. 1756]

2659. Sullivan, Thomas D. "The Problem of Universals in
the Later Wittgenstein." Ph.D. Dissertation, St. John's
Univ., 1969. *Dissertation Abstracts* 31: 804A.

2660. Teichmann, Jenny. "Universals and common properties."
Analysis (1969):162-165.

----- Thorp, J. W. [See no. 1759]

Use

[See also: Meaning]

2661. Ferrater Mora, José. "Del uso." *Diálogos* 5 (1968):
61-78.

----- Lanfear, Jimmy R. [See no. 2177]

----- Linsky, L. [See no. 2178]

----- Weiler, G. [See no. 2192]

Utilitarianism

2662. Cummins, Robert. "Better total consequences:
Utilitarianism and extrinsic value." *Metaphilosophy* 7
(1976):286-306.

Verifiability

2663. Ambrose, Alice. "Metamorphoses of the principle of
verifiability." In *Current Philosophical Issues*, F. C.
Dommeyer, ed. Springfield (Illinois): Charles C. Thomas,
1966.

2664. Park, Young S. "Wittgenstein's Version of Verifiability in the *Tractatus*." Ph.D. Dissertation, Emory
Univ., 1975. *Dissertation Abstracts* 36 (1976):4564A.

Verification

2665. Clegg, J. S. "Wittgenstein on verification and
private language." In *New Essays on the Philosophy of
Mind*, John King-Farlow and Roger A. Shiner, eds. Edmonton:
Univ. of Alberta (Canada), 1976.

----- Plochmann, George K. [See no. 2644]

Verificationism

2666. Black, Max. "Verificationism and Wittgenstein's
reflections on mathematics." *Revue Internationale de
Philosophie* 23 (1969).

2667. Brunton, J. A. "Logical wedges and the turning of
spades. Some comments on Wittgenstein, philosophers he
has influenced and verificationism." *Second Order*. An
African Journal of Philosophy (Ile Ife) 3 (1974):3-28.

(Basic) Views

2668. Schmucker, Larry A. "Wittgenstein's Remarks on
Basic Views." Ph.D. Dissertation, Univ. of Texas at
Austin, 1970, 263p. *Dissertation Abstracts* 32: 4066A.

Volition

[See also: Will]

2669. Benjamin, M. "Vesey on volition. The *second
mistake*." *Michigan Academian*. Michigan Academy of
Science, Art and Letters 6 (1974):377-387.

2670. McCann, Hugh. "Volition and basic action."
Philosophical Review 83 (1974):451-473.

Weltanschaaung

2671. Kolenda, K. "Wittgenstein's *Weltanschaaung*."
Rice University Studies 50 (1961):23-37. [Papers in
philosophy]

2672. Miller, J. "Wittgenstein's *Weltanschaaung*."
Philosophical Studies (Maynooth) 13 (1964):127-140.

Will

2673. Walker, Jeremy. "Wittgenstein's early theory of the
will: An analysis." *Idealistic Studies* 3 (1973):179-205.

2674. Winch, Peter. "Wittgenstein's treatment of the
will." *Ratio* 10 (1968):38-53. Reprinted in his *Ethics
and Action*. London: Routledge & Kegan Paul, 1972.

Word

2675. Tominaga, Thomas T. "A Wittgensteinian Inquiry into
the Confusions Generated by the Question 'What is the
Meaning of a Word?'" Ph.D. Dissertation, Georgetown Univ.,
1973. *Dissertation Abstracts* 34 (1974):4335A.

2676. Wright, E. L. "Words and intentions." *Philosophy*
52 (1977):45-62.

World

2677. Campanale, D. "Il mondo in Wittgenstein."
Rassegna di Scienze Filosofiche 9 (1956):38-76.

2678. Fay, Thomas A. "Early Heidegger and Wittgenstein on
world." *Philosophical Studies* (Maynooth) 21 (1973):161-
171.

2679. Puligandla, R. "Can philosophers avoid the world?"
Pakistan Philosophical Journal 13 (1974):51-62.

2680. Sefler, G. F. *Language and the World.* A *Methodo-
logical-structural Synthesis within the Writings of Heidegger
and Wittgenstein.* Atlantic Highlands (New Jersey):
Humanities Press, 1974, xxxiii-228p.

    <u>book review:</u>
    K. Harries, *The Philosophical Review* 85 (1976):422-426.

<u>Zen</u>

[See also: Buddhism]

2681. Canfield, John V. "Wittgenstein and Zen."
Philosophy 50 (1975):383-408. [See Gudmunsen and Phillips
below, nos. 2683 and 2686]

2682. Cox, C. H., and Cox, J. W. "Mystical experience:
with an emphasis on Wittgenstein and Zen." *Religious
Studies* 12 (1976):483-491.

2683. Gudmunsen, Chris. "The 'empty mind' of Professor
Canfield." *Philosophy* 52 (1977):482-485. [See Canfield
above, no. 2681]

2684. Hardwick, Charles S. "Doing philosophy and doing
Zen." *Philosophy East and West* 13 (1963):227-234.

2685. Hudson, H. "Wittgenstein and Zen Buddhism."
Philosophy East and West 23 (1973):471-481.

2686. Phillips, D. Z. "On wanting to compare Wittgenstein
and Zen." *Philosophy* 52 (1977):338-343. [See Canfield
above, no. 2681]

2687. Wienpahl, P. D. "Zen and the work of Wittgenstein."
Chicago Review 12 (1958):67-72.

Addendum

BOOKS

Baker, Gordon P., and Baker, P. M. S. *Wittgenstein: Understanding and Meaning.* [Volume I of an analytical commentary on the *Philosophical Investigations*]

Leinfellner, Elisabeth, et al., eds. *Wittgenstein and his Impact on Contemporary Thought.* Proceedings of the II International Wittgenstein Symposium, August 29–September 4, 1977, Kirchberg/Wechsel (Austria). Vienna: Hölder-Pichler-Tempsky, 1978.

Grabner-Haider, A.   "Wissenschaft und Religion:
  Gedanken im Anschluss an L. Wittgenstein."   529;
15. Ästhetik/Aesthetics
Conroy, G. P.   "The view atop the ladder: Wittgen-
  stein's early aesthetics."   535;
Zimmermann, J.   "Zur ästhetischen Relevanz der
  Philosophie Wittgensteins."   539;
Birnbacher, D.   "Wittgenstein und die Musik."   542;
Liste der Vortragenden und Vorsitzenden/List of
  speakers and chairpersons, 545.

ARTICLES AND DISSERTATIONS

Aeniskänslin, M.   "La structure cyclique du *Tractatus* de
Wittgenstein."   In *Systèmes Symboliques. Science et
Philosophie*.   Travaux du Séminaire d'Epistémologie
comparative d'Aix-en-Provence.   Paris: Editions du
C.N.R.S., 1978, 243-258.

Arnhart, Larry.   "Language and nature in Wittgenstein's
Philosophical Investigations."   *Journal of Thought* 10
(1975):194-199.

Barrett, William.   "Wittgenstein the pilgrim."   *Commentary*
66 (1978):40-52.

Bouveresse, Jacques.   "L'animal ceremonial. Wittgenstein
et l'anthropologie."   *Actes de la Recherche en Sciences
Sociales* 16 (1977):43-54.

Dickie, George.   "The institutional concept of art."   In
*Language and Aesthetics. Contributions to the Philosophy
of Art*.   Benjamin R. Tilghman, ed.   Lawrence (Kansas):
The Univ. Press of Kansas, 1973, 7-20.   [First part of
the chapter discusses Morris Weitz, "Wittgenstein's
Aesthetics."]

Ellis, Anthony.   "Review of Garth Hallett, A *Companion to
Wittgenstein's* Philosophical Investigations."   *Mind* 88
(1979):452-454.

Fleming, Richard. *Auslegung* 6 (1978):65-69. [Review of Barrett's book, see no. 4]

Greenwood, E. B. "Tolstoy, Wittgenstein, Schopenhauer: Some connections." *Encounter* 36 (1971):60-72.

Hacker, Peter. "Nets of language. Between sense and nonsense." *Encounter* 36 (1971):84-89. [Review of books on Wittgenstein]

Hayek, Friedrich A. "My cousin, Ludwig Wittgenstein." *Encounter* 49 (1977):20-22.

Hoffman, Robert L. "Kakania und Kultur. Review of *Wittgenstein's Vienna*, by Allan Janik and Stephen Toulmin." *Dissent* 22 (1975):203-205.

Kreisel, Georg. "The motto of *Philosophical Investigations* and the philosophy of proofs and rules." *Grazer Philosophische Studien* 6 (1978).

Lazerowitz, Morris, and Ambrose, Alice. *Philosophical Thories*. Paris-The Hague: Mouton, 1976.

Lycan, William G., and Machamer, Peter K. "A theory of critical reasons." In *Language and Aesthetics*. Contributions to the Philosophy of Art. B. R. Tilghman, ed. Lawrence (Kansas): The Univ. Press of Kansas, 1973, 87-112.

Morawski, Stefan. *Inquiries into the Fundamentals of Aesthetics*. Cambridge (Massachusetts)-London: The MIT Press, 1974, 15-16, 30-33, 118-119 et passim.

Moreno, A. R. "Le système de numérotation du *Tractatus*." In *Systèmes Symboliques. Science et Philosophie*. Travaux du Séminaire d'Epistémologie comparative d'Aix-en-Provence. Paris: Editions du C.N.R.S., 1978, 259-282.

Osborne, Harold. "Reasons and description in criticism."
The Monist 50 (1966):204-212.

Paetzold, Heinz. "Philosophie im Zeichen der Sprache.
Wittgenstein und die Idee einer kritischer Transzendental-
philosophie." *Neue Rundschau* 88 (1977):76-90.

Power, William L. "Musings on the mystery of God."
International Journal for the Philosophy of Religion
7 (1976):300-310.

Raschke, Carl A. "Revelation and conversion: A semantic
appraisal." *Anglican Theological Review* 60 (1978):420-
436.

Rochester, Judith Ann. "Philosophy as Therapy: An
Examination of Wittgenstein's Philosophical Method."
Ph.D. Dissertation, Univ. of Toronto, 1978. *Dissertation
Abstracts* 40 (1979):905A.

Saunders, Lloyd. "Theological consequences of philosophy
as immediacy." *American Academy of Religion. Philosophy
of Religion and Theology, Proceedings* (1976):255-264.

Schwartz, E. "Remarques sur le 'sujet' selon Wittgenstein."
In *Systèmes Symboliques. Science et Philosophie.* Travaux
du Séminaire d'Epistémologie comparative d'Aix-en-Provence.
Paris: Editions du C.N.R.S., 1978, 283-303.

Stock, Guy. *Mind* 87 (1978):291-293. [Review of no. 104]

Toulmin, Stephen. "Ludwig Wittgenstein." *Encounter* 32
(1969):58-71. [See no. 1183, General Discussion]

Toulmin, Stephen. "Review essay: A sociologist looks at
Wittgenstein." *American Journal of Sociology* 84 (1979):
996-999. [On Derek Phillips, *Wittgenstein and Scientific
Knowledge.* See no. 74]

Whittaker, John H. "Wittgenstein and religion: Some
later views of his later work." *Religious Studies Review*
4 (1978):188-193.

Wollheim, Richard. "The art of lession." In his *On Art
and the Mind*. Cambridge (Massachusetts): Harvard Univ.
Press, 1974, 130-150. (Originally published in *Studio
International* 181 (1971):278-283.) [On language]

Index

[Numbers followed by an "r" refer to book reviews]